Nutshell Series

of

WEST PUBLISHING COMPANY

P.O. Box 64526

St. Paul, Minnesota 55164–0526

Accounting—Law and, 1984, 377 pages, by E. McGruder Faris, Late Professor of Law, Stetson University.

Administrative Law and Process, 2nd Ed., 1981, 445 pages, by Ernest Gellhorn, Former Dean and Professor of Law, Case Western Reserve University, and Barry B. Boyer, Professor of Law, SUNY, Buffalo.

Admiralty, 2nd Ed., 1988, 379 pages, by Frank L. Maraist, Professor of Law, Louisiana State University.

Agency-Partnership, 1977, 364 pages, by Roscoe T. Steffen, Late Professor of Law, University of Chicago.

American Indian Law, 2nd Ed., 1988, about 319 pages, by William C. Canby, Jr., Adjunct Professor of Law, Arizona State University.

Antitrust Law and Economics, 3rd Ed., 1986, 472 pages, by Ernest Gellhorn, Former Dean and Professor of Law, Case Western Reserve University.

Appellate Advocacy, 1984, 325 pages, by Alan D. Hornstein, Professor of Law, University of Maryland.

Art Law, 1984, 335 pages, by Leonard D. DuBoff, Professor of Law, Lewis and Clark College, Northwestern School of Law.

Banking and Financial Institutions, 2nd Ed., 1988, about 455 pages, by William A. Lovett, Professor of Law, Tulane University.

Church-State Relations—Law of, 1981, 305 pages, by Leonard F. Manning, Late Professor of Law, Fordham University.

Civil Procedure, 2nd Ed., 1986, 306 pages, by Mary Kay Kane, Professor of Law, University of California, Hastings College of the Law.

Civil Rights, 1978, 279 pages, by Norman Vieira, Professor of Law, Southern Illinois University.

Commercial Paper, 3rd Ed., 1982, 404 pages, by Charles M. Weber, Former Professor of Business Law, The Wharton School of Finance and Commerce, University of Pennsylvania and Richard E. Speidel, Professor of Law, Northwestern University.

Community Property, 2nd Ed., 1988, 432 pages, by Robert L. Mennell, Former Professor of Law, Hamline University, and Thomas M. Boykoff.

Comparative Legal Traditions, 1982, 402 pages, by Mary Ann Glendon, Professor of Law, Harvard University, Michael Wallace Gordon, Professor of Law, University of Florida, and Christopher Osakwe, Professor of Law, Tulane University.

Conflicts, 1982, 470 pages, by David D. Siegel, Professor of Law, St. John's University.

Constitutional Analysis, 1979, 388 pages, by Jerre S. Williams, Professor of Law Emeritus, University of Texas.

Constitutional Federalism, 2nd Ed., 1987, 411 pages, by David E. Engdahl, Professor of Law, University of Puget Sound.

Constitutional Law, 1986, 389 pages, by Jerome A. Barron, Professor of Law, George Washington University, and C. Thomas Dienes, Professor of Law, George Washington University.

Consumer Law, 2nd Ed., 1981, 418 pages, by David G. Epstein, Dean and Professor of Law, Emory University, and Steve H. Nickles, Professor of Law, University of Minnesota.

Contract Remedies, 1981, 323 pages, by Jane M. Friedman, Professor of Law, Wayne State University.

Contracts, 2nd Ed., 1984, 425 pages, by Gordon D. Schaber, Dean and Professor of Law, McGeorge School of Law, and Claude D. Rohwer, Professor of Law, McGeorge School of Law.

NUTSHELL SERIES

Corporations—Law of, 2nd Ed., 1987, 515 pages, by Robert W. Hamilton, Professor of Law, University of Texas.

Corrections and Prisoners' Rights—Law of, 2nd Ed., 1983, 386 pages, by Sheldon Krantz, Professor of Law, University of San Diego.

Criminal Law, 2nd Ed., 1987, 321 pages, by Arnold H. Loewy, Professor of Law, University of North Carolina.

Criminal Procedure—Constitutional Limitations, 4th Ed., 1988, 461 pages, by Jerold H. Israel, Professor of Law, University of Michigan, and Wayne R. LaFave, Professor of Law, University of Illinois.

Debtor-Creditor Law, 3rd Ed., 1986, 383 pages, by David G. Epstein, Dean and Professor of Law, Emory University.

Employment Discrimination—Federal Law of, 2nd Ed., 1981, 402 pages, by Mack A. Player, Professor of Law, Florida State University.

Energy Law, 1981, 338 pages, by Joseph P. Tomain, Professor of Law, University of Cincinnatti.

Environmental Law, 2nd Ed., 1988, about 348 pages by Roger W. Findley, Professor of Law, University of Illinois, and Daniel A. Farber, Professor of Law, University of Minnesota.

Estate and Gift Taxation, Federal, 3rd Ed., 1983, 509 pages, by John K. McNulty, Professor of Law, University of California, Berkeley.

Estate Planning—Introduction to, 3rd Ed., 1983, 370 pages, by Robert J. Lynn, Professor of Law, Ohio State University.

Evidence, Federal Rules of, 2nd Ed., 1987, 473 pages, by Michael H. Graham, Professor of Law, University of Miami.

Evidence, State and Federal Rules, 2nd Ed., 1981, 514 pages, by Paul F. Rothstein, Professor of Law, Georgetown University.

Family Law, 2nd Ed., 1986, 444 pages, by Harry D. Krause, Professor of Law, University of Illinois.

Federal Jurisdiction, 2nd Ed., 1981, 258 pages, by David P. Currie, Professor of Law, University of Chicago.

Future Interests, 1981, 361 pages, by Lawrence W. Waggoner, Professor of Law, University of Michigan.

NUTSHELL SERIES

Government Contracts, 1979, 423 pages, by W. Noel Keyes, Professor of Law Emeritus, Pepperdine University.

Historical Introduction to Anglo-American Law, 2nd Ed., 1973, 280 pages, by Frederick G. Kempin, Jr., Professor of Business Law, Wharton School of Finance and Commerce, University of Pennsylvania.

Immigration Law and Procedure, 1984, 345 pages, by David Weissbrodt, Professor of Law, University of Minnesota.

Injunctions, 1974, 264 pages, by John F. Dobbyn, Professor of Law, Villanova University.

Insurance Law, 1981, 281 pages, by John F. Dobbyn, Professor of Law, Villanova University.

Intellectual Property—Patents, Trademarks and Copyright, 1983, 428 pages, by Arthur R. Miller, Professor of Law, Harvard University, and Michael H. Davis, Professor of Law, Cleveland State University, Cleveland-Marshall College of Law.

International Business Transactions, 3rd Ed., 1988, about 484 pages, by Ralph H. Folsom, Professor of Law, University of San Diego, Michael Wallace Gordon, Professor of Law, University of Florida, and John A. Spanogle, Jr., Professor of Law, State University of New York, Buffalo.

International Human Rights, 1988, about 275 pages, by Thomas Buergenthal, Professor of Law, Emory University.

International Law (Public), 1985, 262 pages, by Thomas Buergenthal, Professor of Law, Emory University, and Harold G. Maier, Professor of Law, Vanderbilt University.

Introduction to the Study and Practice of Law, 1983, 418 pages, by Kenney F. Hegland, Professor of Law, University of Arizona.

Judicial Process, 1980, 292 pages, by William L. Reynolds, Professor of Law, University of Maryland.

Jurisdiction, 4th Ed., 1980, 232 pages, by Albert A. Ehrenzweig, Late Professor of Law, University of California, Berkeley, David W. Louisell, Late Professor of Law, University of

California, Berkeley, and Geoffrey C. Hazard, Jr., Professor of Law, Yale Law School.

Juvenile Courts, 3rd Ed., 1984, 291 pages, by Sanford J. Fox, Professor of Law, Boston College.

Labor Arbitration Law and Practice, 1979, 358 pages, by Dennis R. Nolan, Professor of Law, University of South Carolina.

Labor Law, 2nd Ed., 1986, 397 pages, by Douglas L. Leslie, Professor of Law, University of Virginia.

Land Use, 2nd Ed., 1985, 356 pages, by Robert R. Wright, Professor of Law, University of Arkansas, Little Rock, and Susan Webber Wright, Professor of Law, University of Arkansas, Little Rock.

Landlord and Tenant Law, 2nd Ed., 1986, 311 pages, by David S. Hill, Professor of Law, University of Colorado.

Law Study and Law Examinations—Introduction to, 1971, 389 pages, by Stanley V. Kinyon, Late Professor of Law, University of Minnesota.

Legal Interviewing and Counseling, 2nd Ed., 1987, 487 pages, by Thomas L. Shaffer, Professor of Law, University of Notre Dame, and James R. Elkins, Professor of Law, West Virginia University.

Legal Research, 4th Ed., 1985, 452 pages, by Morris L. Cohen, Professor of Law and Law Librarian, Yale University.

Legal Writing, 1982, 294 pages, by Lynn B. Squires and Marjorie Dick Rombauer, Professor of Law, University of Washington.

Legislative Law and Process, 2nd Ed., 1986, 346 pages, by Jack Davies, Professor of Law, William Mitchell College of Law.

Local Government Law, 2nd Ed., 1983, 404 pages, by David J. McCarthy, Jr., Professor of Law, Georgetown University.

Mass Communications Law, 3rd Ed., 1988, 538 pages, by Harvey L. Zuckman, Professor of Law, Catholic University, Martin J. Gaynes, Lecturer in Law, Temple University, T. Barton Carter, Professor of Public Communications, Boston University, and Juliet Lushbough Dee, Professor of Communications, University of Delaware.

Medical Malpractice—The Law of, 2nd Ed., 1986, 342 pages, by Joseph H. King, Professor of Law, University of Tennessee.

Military Law, 1980, 378 pages, by Charles A. Shanor, Professor of Law, Emory University, and Timothy P. Terrell, Professor of Law, Emory University.

Oil and Gas Law, 2nd Ed., 1988, about 402 pages, by John S. Lowe, Professor of Law, Southern Methodist University.

Personal Property, 1983, 322 pages, by Barlow Burke, Jr., Professor of Law, American University.

Post-Conviction Remedies, 1978, 360 pages, by Robert Popper, Dean and Professor of Law, University of Missouri, Kansas City.

Presidential Power, 1977, 328 pages, by Arthur Selwyn Miller, Professor of Law Emeritus, George Washington University.

Products Liability, 3rd Ed., 1988, 307 pages, by Jerry J. Phillips, Professor of Law, University of Tennessee.

Professional Responsibility, 1980, 399 pages, by Robert H. Aronson, Professor of Law, University of Washington, and Donald T. Weckstein, Professor of Law, University of San Diego.

Real Estate Finance, 2nd Ed., 1985, 262 pages, by Jon W. Bruce, Professor of Law, Vanderbilt University.

Real Property, 2nd Ed., 1981, 448 pages, by Roger H. Bernhardt, Professor of Law, Golden Gate University.

Regulated Industries, 2nd Ed., 1987, 389 pages, by Ernest Gellhorn, Former Dean and Professor of Law, Case Western Reserve University, and Richard J. Pierce, Professor of Law, Southern Methodist University.

Remedies, 2nd Ed., 1985, 320 pages, by John F. O'Connell, Dean and Professor of Law, Southern California College of Law.

Res Judicata, 1976, 310 pages, by Robert C. Casad, Professor of Law, University of Kansas.

Sales, 2nd Ed., 1981, 370 pages, by John M. Stockton, Professor of Business Law, Wharton School of Finance and Commerce, University of Pennsylvania.

Schools, Students and Teachers—Law of, 1984, 409 pages, by Kern Alexander, President, Western Kentucky University and M. David Alexander, Professor, Virginia Tech University.

Sea—Law of, 1984, 264 pages, by Louis B. Sohn, Professor of Law, University of Georgia, and Kristen Gustafson.

Secured Transactions, 3rd Ed., 1988, about 390 pages, by Henry J. Bailey, Professor of Law Emeritus, Willamette University, and Richard B. Hagedorn, Professor of Law, Willamette University.

Securities Regulation, 3rd Ed., 1988, 316 pages, by David L. Ratner, Dean and Professor of Law, University of San Francisco.

Sex Discrimination, 1982, 399 pages, by Claire Sherman Thomas, Lecturer, University of Washington, Women's Studies Department.

State Constitutional Law, 1988, about 300 pages, by Thomas C. Marks, Jr., Professor of Law, Stetson University, and John F. Cooper, Professor of Law, Stetson University.

Taxation and Finance, State and Local, 1986, 309 pages, by M. David Gelfand, Professor of Law, Tulane University, and Peter W. Salsich, Professor of Law, St. Louis University.

Taxation of Individuals, Federal Income, 4th Ed., 1988, about 500 pages, by John K. McNulty, Professor of Law, University of California, Berkeley.

Torts—Injuries to Persons and Property, 1977, 434 pages, by Edward J. Kionka, Professor of Law, Southern Illinois University.

Torts—Injuries to Family, Social and Trade Relations, 1979, 358 pages, by Wex S. Malone, Professor of Law Emeritus, Louisiana State University.

Trial Advocacy, 1979, 402 pages, by Paul B. Bergman, Adjunct Professor of Law, University of California, Los Angeles.

Trial and Practice Skills, 1978, 346 pages, by Kenney F. Hegland, Professor of Law, University of Arizona.

NUTSHELL SERIES

Trial, The First—Where Do I Sit? What Do I Say?, 1982, 396 pages, by Steven H. Goldberg, Professor of Law, University of Minnesota.

Unfair Trade Practices, 2nd Ed., 1988, about 430 pages, by Charles R. McManis, Professor of Law, Washington University.

Uniform Commercial Code, 2nd Ed., 1984, 516 pages, by Bradford Stone, Professor of Law, Stetson University.

Uniform Probate Code, 2nd Ed., 1987, 454 pages, by Lawrence H. Averill, Jr., Dean and Professor of Law, University of Arkansas, Little Rock.

Water Law, 1984, 439 pages, by David H. Getches, Professor of Law, University of Colorado.

Welfare Law—Structure and Entitlement, 1979, 455 pages, by Arthur B. LaFrance, Professor of Law, Lewis and Clark College, Northwestern School of Law.

Wills and Trusts, 1979, 392 pages, by Robert L. Mennell, Former Professor of Law, Hamline University.

Workers' Compensation and Employee Protection Laws, 1984, 274 pages, by Jack B. Hood, Former Professor of Law, Cumberland School of Law, Samford University and Benjamin A. Hardy, Former Professor of Law, Cumberland School of Law, Samford University.

Hornbook Series

and

Basic Legal Texts

of

WEST PUBLISHING COMPANY

P.O. Box 64526

St. Paul, Minnesota 55164–0526

Admiralty and Maritime Law, Schoenbaum's Hornbook on, 1987, 692 pages, by Thomas J. Schoenbaum, Professor of Law, University of Georgia.

Agency and Partnership, Reuschlein & Gregory's Hornbook on the Law of, 1979 with 1981 Pocket Part, 625 pages, by Harold Gill Reuschlein, Professor of Law Emeritus, Villanova University, and William A. Gregory, Professor of Law, Georgia State University.

Antitrust, Sullivan's Hornbook on the Law of, 1977, 886 pages, by Lawrence A. Sullivan, Professor of Law, University of California, Berkeley.

Civil Procedure, Friedenthal, Kane and Miller's Hornbook on, 1985, 876 pages, by Jack H. Friedental, Dean and Professor of Law, George Washington University, Mary Kay Kane, Professor of Law, University of California, Hastings College of the Law, and Arthur R. Miller, Professor of Law, Harvard University.

Common Law Pleading, Koffler and Reppy's Hornbook on, 1969, 663 pages, by Joseph H. Koffler, Professor of Law, New York Law School, and Alison Reppy, Late Dean and Professor of Law, New York Law School.

Conflict of Laws, Scoles and Hay's Hornbook on, 1982, with 1986 Pocket Part, 1085 pages, by Eugene F. Scoles, Professor of Law, University of Illinois, and Peter Hay, Dean and Professor of Law, University of Illinois.

HORNBOOKS & BASIC TEXTS

Constitutional Law, Nowak, Rotunda and Young's Hornbook on, 3rd Ed., 1986, with 1988 Pocket Part, 1191 pages, by John E. Nowak, Professor of Law, University of Illinois, Ronald D. Rotunda, Professor of Law, University of Illinois, and J. Nelson Young, Late Professor of Law, University of North Carolina.

Contracts, Calamari and Perillo's Hornbook on, 3rd Ed., 1987, 1049 pages, by John D. Calamari, Professor of Law, Fordham University, and Joseph M. Perillo, Professor of Law, Fordham University.

Contracts, Corbin's One Volume Student Ed., 1952, 1224 pages, by Arthur L. Corbin, Late Professor of Law, Yale University.

Corporations, Henn and Alexander's Hornbook on, 3rd Ed., 1983, with 1986 Pocket Part, 1371 pages, by Harry G. Henn, Professor of Law Emeritus, Cornell University, and John R. Alexander.

Criminal Law, LaFave and Scott's Hornbook on, 2nd Ed., 1986, 918 pages, by Wayne R. LaFave, Professor of Law, University of Illinois, and Austin Scott, Jr., Late Professor of Law, University of Colorado.

Criminal Procedure, LaFave and Israel's Hornbook on, 1985 with 1986 pocket part, 1142 pages, by Wayne R. LaFave, Professor of Law, University of Illinois, and Jerold H. Israel, Professor of Law University of Michigan.

Damages, McCormick's Hornbook on, 1935, 811 pages, by Charles T. McCormick, Late Dean and Professor of Law, University of Texas.

Domestic Relations, Clark's Hornbook on, 2nd Ed., 1988, 1050 pages, by Homer H. Clark, Jr., Professor of Law, University of Colorado.

Economics and Federal Antitrust Law, Hovenkamp's Hornbook on, 1985, 414 pages, by Herbert Hovenkamp, Professor of Law, University of Iowa.

Employment Discrimination Law, Player's Hornbook on, 708 pages, 1988, by Mack A. Player, Professor of Law, Florida State University.

HORNBOOKS & BASIC TEXTS

Environmental Law, Rodgers' Hornbook on, 1977 with 1984 Pocket Part, 956 pages, by William H. Rodgers, Jr., Professor of Law, University of Washington.

Evidence, Lilly's Introduction to, 2nd Ed., 1987, 585 pages, by Graham C. Lilly, Professor of Law, University of Virginia.

Evidence, McCormick's Hornbook on, 3rd Ed., 1984 with 1987 Pocket Part, 1156 pages, General Editor, Edward W. Cleary, Professor of Law Emeritus, Arizona State University.

Federal Courts, Wright's Hornbook on, 4th Ed., 1983, 870 pages, by Charles Alan Wright, Professor of Law, University of Texas.

Federal Income Taxation, Rose and Chommie's Hornbook on, 3rd Ed., 1988, 923 pages, by Michael D. Rose, Professor of Law, Ohio State University, and John C. Chommie, Late Professor of Law, University of Miami.

Federal Income Taxation of Individuals, Posin's Hornbook on, 1983 with 1987 Pocket Part, 491 pages, by Daniel Q. Posin, Jr., Professor of Law, Catholic University.

Future Interest, Simes' Hornbook on, 2nd Ed., 1966, 355 pages, by Lewis M. Simes, Late Professor of Law, University of Michigan.

Insurance, Keeton and Widiss on, 1988, about 1050 pages, by Robert E. Keeton, Professor of Law Emeritus, Harvard University, and Alan I. Widiss, Professor of Law, University of Iowa.

Labor Law, Gorman's Basic Text on, 1976, 914 pages, by Robert A. Gorman, Professor of Law, University of Pennsylvania.

Law Problems, Ballentine's, 5th Ed., 1975, 767 pages, General Editor, William E. Burby, Late Professor of Law, University of Southern California.

Legal Ethics, Wolfram's Hornbook on, 1986, 1120 pages, by Charles W. Wolfram, Professor of Law, Cornell University.

Legal Writing Style, Weihofen's, 2nd Ed., 1980, 332 pages, by Henry Weihofen, Professor of Law Emeritus, University of New Mexico.

HORNBOOKS & BASIC TEXTS

Local Government Law, Reynolds' Hornbook on, 1982 with 1987 Pocket Part, 860 pages, by Osborne M. Reynolds, Professor of Law, University of Oklahoma.

New York Estate Administration, Turano and Radigan's Hornbook on, 1986, 676 pages, by Margaret V. Turano, Professor of Law, St. John's University, and Raymond Radigan.

New York Practice, Siegel's Hornbook on, 1978 with 1987 Pocket Part, 1011 pages, by David D. Siegel, Professor of Law, St. John's University.

Oil and Gas Law, Hemingway's Hornbook on, 2nd Ed., 1983, with 1986 Pocket Part, 543 pages, by Richard W. Hemingway, Professor of Law, University of Oklahoma.

Property, Boyer's Survey of, 3rd Ed., 1981, 766 pages, by Ralph E. Boyer, Professor of Law Emeritus, University of Miami.

Property, Law of, Cunningham, Whitman and Stoebuck's Hornbook on, 1984 with 1987 Pocket Part, 916 pages, by Roger A. Cunningham, Professor of Law, University of Michigan, Dale A. Whitman, Professor of Law, University of Missouri, Columbia, and William B. Stoebuck, Professor of Law, University of Washington.

Real Estate Finance Law, Nelson and Whitman's Hornbook on, 2nd Ed., 1985, 941 pages, by Grant S. Nelson, Professor of Law, University of Missouri, Columbia, and Dale A. Whitman, Professor of Law, University of Missouri, Columbia.

Real Property, Moynihan's Introduction to, 2nd Ed., 1988, 239 pages, by Cornelius J. Moynihan, Late Professor of Law, Suffolk University.

Remedies, Dobbs' Hornbook on, 1973, 1067 pages, by Dan B. Dobbs, Professor of Law, University of Arizona.

Secured Transactions under the U.C.C., Henson's Hornbook on, 2nd Ed., 1979 with 1979 Pocket Part, 504 pages, by Ray D. Henson, Professor of Law, University of California, Hastings College of the Law.

Securities Regulation, Hazen's Hornbook on the Law of, 1985 with 1988 Pocket Part, 739 pages, by Thomas Lee Hazen, Professor of Law, University of North Carolina.

Sports Law, Schubert, Smith and Trentadue's, 1986, 395 pages, by George W. Schubert, Dean of University College, University of North Dakota, Rodney K. Smith, Professor of Law, Delaware Law School, Widener University, and Jesse C. Trentadue, Former Professor of Law, University of North Dakota.

Torts, Prosser and Keeton's Hornbook on, 5th Ed., 1984 with 1988 Pocket Part, 1286 pages, by William L. Prosser, Late Dean and Professor of Law, University of California, Berkeley, Page Keeton, Professor of Law Emeritus, University of Texas, Dan B. Dobbs, Professor of Law, University of Arizona, Robert E. Keeton, Professor of Law Emeritus, Harvard University, and David G. Owen, Professor of Law, University of South Carolina.

Trial Advocacy, Jeans' Handbook on, Soft cover, 1975, 473 pages, by James W. Jeans, Professor of Law, University of Missouri, Kansas City.

Trusts, Bogert's Hornbook on, 6th Ed., 1987, 794 pages, by George T. Bogert.

Uniform Commercial Code, White and Summers' Hornbook on, 3rd Ed., 1988, about 1200 pages, by James J. White, Professor of Law, University of Michigan, and Robert S. Summers, Professor of Law, Cornell University.

Urban Planning and Land Development Control Law, Hagman and Juergensmeyer's Hornbook on, 2nd Ed., 1986, 680 pages, by Donald G. Hagman, Late Professor of Law, University of California, Los Angeles, and Julian C. Juergensmeyer, Professor of Law, University of Florida.

Wills, Atkinson's Hornbook on, 2nd Ed., 1953, 975 pages, by Thomas E. Atkinson, Late Professor of Law, New York University.

Wills, Trusts and Estates Including Taxation and Future Interests, McGovern, Rein and Kurtz' Hornbook on, 1988, about 924 pages by William M. McGovern, Professor of Law, University of California, Los Angeles, Jan Ellen Rein, Professor of Law, Gonzaga University, and Sheldon F. Kurtz, Professor of Law, University of Iowa.

Advisory Board

LANDLORD
AND
TENANT LAW

IN A NUTSHELL

By

DAVID S. HILL
Associate Professor of Law,
University of Colorado

ST. PAUL, MINN.
WEST PUBLISHING CO.
1986

Library of Congress Cataloging in Publication Data

Hill, David S.   1940–
   Landlord and tenant law in a nutshell.

   (Nutshell series)
   Includes index.
   1. Landlord and tenant—United States. I. Title.
II. Series.
KF590.Z9H45   1986   346.7304'34   85–26461
                347.306434

ISBN 0–314–97189–0

     Hill, Landlord and Tenant, 2nd Ed., NS
     1st Reprint—1988

TO JANE

*

PREFACE

Since 1979, when the first edition of this book was published, the movement of landlord-tenant law toward a greater emphasis on the contractual aspects of a lease has continued relatively unabated. The most notable development in this trend continues to be the implied warranty of habitability, and the accompanying idea of dependence of covenants. The trend is also reflected in the doctrines of mitigation, illegality, and in other areas of landlord-tenant law. Particular attention has been given to these areas; and a section on retaliatory eviction has been added to this edition. And, of course, I have tried to make all the subjects covered by this book as current as possible.

The coverage and organization of this book remains essentially the same as that of the first edition. With respect to the purpose of the book, perhaps the preface to the first edition bears repeating:

"It has been said, and it is probably true, that no first year law school course is as rule-laden and complex as Real Property. A substantial portion of the law of Real Property concerns the relationship of landlord and tenant. This book is intended as a succinct presentation of landlord-tenant law, designed primarily to aid first year law students. It contains an exposition of most of the rules that govern the legal relations of landlords and tenants, and the exceptions thereto, and also encompasses some exploration of the underlying reasons for the rules. The policy-oriented discussions are included in the hope that they will help the student to better understand the rules and to begin to examine them from a more critical perspective. . . ."

Because of the limitations of the Nutshell format, I believe that this book should be merely the beginning of a student's study of landlord-tenant law. Within these limitations, I hope that I have provided a tool that students will find useful in their study of the law of landlord and tenant.

DAVID S. HILL

Boulder, Colorado
December, 1985

OUTLINE

	Page
PREFACE	XIX
TABLE OF CASES	XXXVI

CHAPTER I. INTRODUCTION

I. **Historical Background**	1
A. Classification of the Lease as a Non-freehold Estate	1
B. Remedies Granted Tenants to Protect their Possessory Rights	2
II. **The Landlord and Tenant Relationship**	4
III. **Requisites of the Lease**	4
IV. **The Lease Distinguished From Licenses, Easements and Profits**	6
V. **The Lease, a Conveyance or a Contract**	8

CHAPTER II. CREATION, DURATION AND TERMINATION OF THE SEVERAL TENANCIES

I. **Introduction**	11
II. **Term for Years**	12

		Page
A.	Creation	12
B.	Duration	12
C.	Termination	13
III.	**The Periodic Tenancy**	13
A.	Creation	13
	1. Entry Under a Void Lease—Determination of the Period	14
B.	Duration	15
C.	Termination	15
D.	Distinguishing the Term for Years and Periodic Tenancy	17
IV.	**Tenancy at Will**	17
A.	Creation	17
B.	Duration	18
C.	Termination	18
V.	**Tenancy at Sufferance**	18
A.	Creation	18
B.	Duration	19
C.	Termination	19
VI.	**Statutory Modification of the Several Tenancies**	19

CHAPTER III. TERMINATION OF THE LEASE OTHER THAN BY EXPIRATION OF ITS TERMS

I. Grounds for Termination 20

OUTLINE

		Page
A.	Special Limitations	20
B.	Breach of Condition by Tenant	21
	1. Statutory Modification	21
	2. Reserved Power of Termination	22
	3. Restatement View	22
	4. Waiver by the Landlord	23
	5. Other Equitable Relief	24
C.	Breach of Condition by Landlord—Covenant of Quiet Enjoyment	25
	1. Actual Eviction	25
	2. Constructive Eviction	26
	3. Eviction Under Paramount Title	29
	a. Breach of the Covenant of Power to Demise	30
	b. Termination of Landlord's Supporting Estate	30
D.	Illegality and Frustration of Purpose	32
	1. Intended Use Illegal at Time of Letting	32
	a. Leases for Illegal and Immoral Purposes	32
	b. Lease for a Purpose Requiring a Permit, License or Zoning Variance	33
	(i) Duty to Obtain the Permit, License or Variance	35
	(ii) Mistake of Law	35
	(iii) Landlord's Warranty of Use	36
	c. Multiple Uses—One Use Prohibited	37
	d. Right to Possession of the Premises	37

D. Illegality and Frustration of Purpose—
Continued   **Page**

    e. Leases Which Violate Housing
        Codes 38

        (i) Landlord's Right to Posses-
            sion 38

        (ii) Landlord's Right to Rent 41

  2. Supervening Illegality 42

E. Destruction of the Premises 43

F. Surrender and Abandonment 45

  1. Surrender 45

  2. Abandonment 46

  3. The Landlord's Options After Aban-
    donment by the Tenant 47

    a. Mitigation 47

      (i) No Duty to Mitigate 47

        (a) Recovery of Future
           Rent 47

        (b) Rent Acceleration
           Clauses 48

      (ii) The Landlord's Affirmative
        Duty to Mitigate 49

    b. Voluntary Reletting for the Bene-
      fit of the Tenant 50

    c. Landlord's Election to Terminate
      the Lease 51

G. Expiration of the Landlord's Estate 52

II. **Method of Termination** 52

A. Self-help 53

  1. Use of Reasonable Force 54

  2. Peaceful Repossession 54

A. Self-help—Continued   **Page**
    3. Lease Provision Allowing Reentry
           Without Judicial Process _____ 55
    4. Remedies of the Tenant for Landlord's
           Wrongful Reentry _____ 56
B. Summary Process Statutes_____ 56

III. The Holdover Problem _____ 58
A. Necessity for Termination of the Lease__ 59
B. Nature of the Tenancy Created _____ 61
C. Modification of the Holdover Doctrine____ 62
D. Election to Treat the Holdover as Wrong-
     ful—Remedies of the Landlord_____ 63

CHAPTER IV. POSSESSION AND USE OF THE DEMISED PREMISES

I. The Landlord's Duty to Put the Tenant
     in Possession _____ 64
A. American Rule_____ 64
B. English Rule_____ 65

II. Fitness for Use _____ 67
A. Change in Condition of Premises Between
     the Time of Leasing and the Time of
     Possession _____ 68
B. "Public Use" Exception _____ 68
C. Buildings Under Construction _____ 69
D. Latent Defects _____ 70

                                                          Page
E. "Furnished House" Exception 72
F. Implied Warranty of Habitability in Resi-
      dential Leases 73
G. Illegal Use 74

III. **Interference With the Tenant's Pos-
        session and Use of the Premises** ... 75
A. Interference by the Landlord 75
B. Interference by Third Parties 75
    1. Acts of Another Tenant 76
    2. Criminal Acts of Third Parties 77

IV. **The Effect of Eminent Domain (Con-
        demnation) Proceedings** 79
A. Condemnation of the Entire Leasehold ... 79
B. Partial Condemnation 81

V. **Duty of the Tenant to Occupy the
      Premises** 82

CHAPTER V. REPAIRS AND IMPROVEMENTS

I. **Introduction** 84
II. **The Duty to Repair in the Absence of
        an Express Covenant to Repair** 85
A. Duty of the Landlord to Repair the Com-
      mon Areas 88
    1. Common Areas Defined 89
    2. Landlord's Notice of Defect 91
    3. Conduct of the Landlord After Notice
        of the Dangerous Condition 93
    4. Tenant's Notice of Defect 93

OUTLINE

A. Duty of the Landlord to Repair the Common Areas—Continued   **Page**
    5. Assumption of Risk—Contributory Negligence 93
B. Areas Retained Under the Landlord's Exclusive Control But Necessary to the Use of the Leased Premises 94
    1. Landlord's Notice of Defect 95
    2. Conduct of the Landlord After Notice of the Dangerous Condition 96
    3. Assumption of Risk—Contributory Negligence 96
C. Repairs, Alterations and Improvements Required by Government Regulations .. 96
D. Statutory Duty to Repair 99
    1. Criminal Sanctions 100
    2. Civil Sanctions 101
    3. Statutory Civil Sanctions Enforced by the Tenant 102
    4. Tort Liability Arising Out of the Statutory Duty to Repair 103
        a. Criminal Statutes 103
        b. Civil Statutes 107
E. Implied Warranty of Habitability 108
    1. History and Development 108
    2. Procedure for Raising Implied Warranty of Habitability 115
    3. Scope of the Implied Warranty of Habitability 116
        a. Leases in Which the Warranty of Habitability Will Be Implied ... 117

E. Implied Warranty of Habitability—Continued   **Page**

    b. Standard of Habitability—Breach of Warranty 118

        (i) "Goods and Services" Covered by the Implied Warranty 121

        (ii) Substantial or Material Defects Constituting a Breach of the Implied Warranty 121

    c. Landlord's Notice of Defect 123

  4. Remedies of the Tenant 126

    a. Termination and Rescission 127

    b. Repair and Deduct 128

    c. Specific Performance 130

    d. Rent Abatement and Withholding 131

        (i)   Rent Withholding Statutes.. 136

        (ii) Protective Orders 137

        (iii) Turnover Orders 138

    e. Damages 140

  5. Landlord's Defenses to the Implied Warranty of Habitability 141

  6. Tort Liability for Breach of the Implied Warranty of Habitability 142

F. Retaliatory Eviction 144

  1. Conduct of Landlord and Tenant 146

  2. Burden of Proof 147

  3. Remedies 149

Page

G. Defenses of the Landlord to Tort Liability 149
   1. Express Assumption of Risk 149
   2. Implied Assumption of Risk and Con-
      tributory Negligence 153
     a. Implied Assumption of Risk 155
     b. Contributory Negligence 157

III. **Express Covenant to Repair** 158
A. Covenants Made by the Tenant 158
   1. Destruction of the Premises 160
B. Covenants Made by the Landlord 162
   1. Remedies of the Tenant 164
   2. Liability of the Landlord for Personal
      Injury and Property Damage........... 165
   3. Notice of the Defect 167

IV. **Negligent Repairs** 168
A. Massachusetts Rule 169
B. Knowledge of the Tenant 170
C. Landlord's Use of an Independent Con-
   tractor 171
D. Effect of Transfer of the Parties' Interest 172

V. **Liability for Injury to Persons and
  Property Outside the Leased Property** 172
A. Dangerous Conditions Antedating Transfer of Possession to the Tenant 175
   1. Covenant by the Tenant to Eliminate
      the Dangerous Condition 176
   2. Sublease 177

Page

B. Effect of the Landlord's Covenant to Repair _____ 177

C. Landlord Under a Statutory Duty to Repair _____ 179

D. Activities Conducted on the Leased Premises After Transfer of Possession _____ 181

VI. Changes in the Condition of the Demised Premises—Rights and Duties of the Tenant _____ 182

A. Physical Changes Due to Acts of a Stranger or Acts of God_____ 182

B. Ordinary Wear and Tear and Voluntary Alterations to the Leased Property Made by the Tenant _____ 184

   1. Alterations by the Tenant_____ 184

   2. Ordinary Wear and Tear _____ 186

C. Waste _____ 187

   1. Conduct of the Tenant Constituting Waste _____ 189

      a. Cutting Timber _____ 189

      b. Removal of Valuable Minerals by the Tenant _____ 191

      c. Permissive Waste_____ 192

      d. Equitable Waste_____ 192

   2. Effect of a Covenant to Repair_____ 193

   3. Effect of an Assignment or Sublease 194

   4. Statute of Limitations_____ 195

   5. Remedies of the Landlord _____ 195

		Page
D.	Fixtures	198
	1. Tenant's Right to Remove Tenant Fixtures	199
	a. Trade Fixtures	200
	b. Agricultural Fixtures	202
	c. Domestic Fixtures	202
	d. Limitations on the Tenant's Right of Removal	203
	(i) Character of the Annexation	203
	(ii) Time Limitations	203

CHAPTER VI. TRANSFERS BY THE LANDLORD AND TENANT

I.	Introduction	206
II.	Transfers by the Tenant	207
A.	Assignment and Sublease Distinguished	208
B.	Covenants Against Transfer of the Tenant's Interest	211
	1. Breach of Covenant	213
	a. Reassignment to the Original Tenant	214
	b. Cotenancy, Partnership and Corporate Tenants	214
	c. Leasehold Mortgages	215
	d. Involuntary Assignments	216
	2. The Rule in Dumpor's Case	217
	3. Landlord's Consent Unreasonably Withheld	218
	4. Waiver	220
	5. Remedies of the Landlord	221

OUTLINE

Page

III. Transfers by the Landlord 221

A. Restraints on Alienation 222

B. Lease in Reversion 223

C. Concurrent Leases 223

D. Mortgage of the Reversion 224

IV. Effect of Transfers by the Landlord or the Tenant—Covenants Running With the Land 225

A. Assignments by the Tenant 225

B. Sublease by the Tenant 227

C. Transfer of the Landlord's Reversion 228

D. Covenants Running With the Land 229

   1. Writing 230

   2. Intent That the Covenant Run 231

   3. Touch and Concern 232

   4. Privity of Estate 234

   5. Transfer of the Covenantee's Entire Estate 235

   6. Transfer of the Covenantor's Entire Estate 235

   7. Partial Transfers 237

   8. Duration and Waiver 239

     a. Express Covenants 239

     b. Implied Obligations 240

   9. Covenants Not to Compete 240

     a. Running of Covenants Made by the Tenant 242

     b. Running of Covenants Made by the Landlord 243

CHAPTER VII. EXTENSIONS, RENEWALS, AND OPTIONS TO PURCHASE

Page

I.   Introduction _____ 245

II. Extensions and Renewals Distinguished _____ 246

III. Construction and Operation of Renewal and Extension Provisions ____ 248

IV. Options to Purchase _____ 250

A. Right of First Refusal Distinguished _____ 252

B. Duration of the Option _____ 253

C. Effect of Exercise of the Option to Purchase _____ 255

CHAPTER VIII. RENT AND SECURITY

I.   Rent Defined _____ 257

II. Duty to Pay Rent _____ 258

III. Rent Reserved in the Lease _____ 260

A. Stepup Leases _____ 260

B. Consumer Price Index Leases _____ 261

C. Appraisal Leases _____ 261

D. Percentage Leases _____ 262

IV. Agreements to Modify Rent _____ 264

V.   Payment of Rent _____ 265

Page

A. Time of Payment 265

   1. Effect of Termination of the Lease—
     Apportionment 267

   2. Waiver of the Right to Prompt Payment 269

B. Place and Manner of Payment 269

C. Agreements to Pay Rent After Termination of the Lease 270

VI. Assignment of the Landlord's Right to Rent 272

VII. Remedies of the Landlord for Nonpayment of Rent 273

VIII. Security Deposits 275

IX. Landlord's Lien 279

A. Contractual Liens 279

   1. Property to Which the Lien Attaches 280

   2. Priority of the Landlord's Lien 281

   3. Effect of Transfer of the Reversion .. 281

B. Statutory Liens 281

   1. Property to Which the Lien Attaches 282

   2. Priority of the Landlord's Lien 282

   3. Enforcement of the Lien 283

X. Distress for Rent 284

A. Property Subject to Distraint 286

   1. Chattels of the Tenant Exempt from Distraint 287

   2. Chattels of Third Parties 287

		Page
B.	Effect of Assignment	288
C.	Waiver	289
D.	Statutory Modifications	290

XI. Estoppel to Deny the Landlord's Title 290

CHAPTER IX. INSURANCE AND TAXES

I.	**Insurance**	292
II.	**Taxes**	294
A.	Covenants by the Tenant	296
	1. Scope of the Covenant	296
	2. Remedies of the Landlord	297
B.	Covenants by the Landlord	298
	1. Scope of the Covenant	298
	2. Remedies of the Tenant	298
C.	Transferee Liability	299

Index 301

TABLE OF CASES

References are to Pages

Academy Spires, Inc. v. Brown, 123
Altz v. Leiberson, 104, 106
Anderson v. Ferguson, 161

Barfield v. Damon, 65
Bedwick v. Mecham, 228
Bell v. Tsintolas Realty Co., 137
Benjamin v. Kimble, 106, 107
Blackwell v. Del Bosco, 110
Brown v. Southall Realty Co., 38
Burt, Inc., Charles E. v. Seven Grand Corp., 29

Capital Amusement Co. v. Anheuser-Busch, 70
Chambers v. North River Line, 161
Chess v. Muhammad, 125
Continental Oil Co. v. McNair Realty Co., 267
Cooks v. Fowler, 139
Corbett v. Derman Shoe Co., 160

Dameron v. Capitol House Associates Ltd. Partnership, 139
Davis, Inc., William J. v. Slade, 41, 42
DeBaca v. Fidel, 212
Dickhut v. Norton, 146, 147
Didriksen v. Havens, 247

Economy v. S.B. & L. Bldg. Corp., 34
Edwards v. Habib, 145

TABLE OF CASES

First National Bank v. Omaha National Bank, 266
Fuentes v. Shevin, 284, 290

Gaddis v. Consolidated Freightways, Inc., 97
Gately v. Campbell, 107
Granucci v. Claasen, 175
Greenfield & Co., Albert M. v. Kolea, 44

Hannan v. Dusch, 64
Harden v. Drost, 48
Harry's Village, Inc. v. Egg Harbor Township, 17, 60
Hendrickson v. Freericks, 213
Herter v. Mullen, 63
Heyman v. Linwood Park, Inc., 276

Jaber v. Miller, 210
Javins v. First National Realty Corp., 111, 141
Jordan v. Nickell, 48

Kline v. 1500 Mass. Ave. Apartment Corp., 77, 78
Knight v. Hallsthammar, 125

Lawson v. Taylor Hotels, Inc., 43
Liebowitz v. Christo, 247
Lindsay v. Normet, 57
Lochner v. Martin, 276
Lommori v. Milner Hotels, Inc., 177

McCutcheon v. United Homes Corporation, 151, 152
Macy & Co., R.H. v. Fall River, 228
Maguire v. Haddad, 17, 60
Marini v. Ireland, 129
Markoe v. Naiditch & Sons, 47
Martin, Inc., J.E. v. Interstate 8th Street, 226
Mease v. Fox, 122, 132
Miller v. A & R Joint Venture, 151
Moretti v. C.S. Realty Co., 179

National Bank of Commerce v. Dunn, 259
National Bank of Detroit v. Estate of Voight, 160
NEBACO, Inc. v. Riverview Realty Co., 35
Nicklis v. Nakano, 249

Otto v. Hongsermeier Farms, Inc., 59

Parkin v. Fitzgerald, 148
Pennsylvania State Shopping Plaza, Inc. v. Olive, 35
Peters Motors v. Poyner, 91
Posnanski v. Hood, 110
Primus v. Bellevue Apartments, 88, 90

Reste Realty Corp. v. Cooper, 26, 28
Robinson v. Diamond Housing Corporation, 147, 148

Sargent v. Ross, 143
Scirpo v. McMillan, 249
Segre v. Ring, 211
Sheppard v. Nienow, 165
Sherman v. Concourse Realty Corp., 78
Smith v. Green, 71
Sniadach v. Family Finance Corp., 283, 290
Spencer's Case, 231
Sprecher v. Adamson Companies, 175

Teaff v. Hewitt, 198

Vernon Fire & Casualty Company v. Graham, 152

Walker v. Southern Trucking Corp., 35
Warshawsky v. American Automotive Products Co., 37
Weigand v. Afton View Apartments, 146
Wilson v. Savon Stations, Inc., 276

Youngset, Inc. v. Five City Plaza, Inc., 168

LANDLORD
AND
TENANT LAW

IN A NUTSHELL

*

CHAPTER I

INTRODUCTION

I. HISTORICAL BACKGROUND

A. Classification of the Lease as a Non-freehold Estate

One of several ways which interests in land are classified is the division of such interests into freehold and nonfreehold estates. The freeholder is seized of the land and his interest descends to his heirs as real property. At common law, the free-holder's possessory interest was protected by use of the assize of novel disseisin, a writ which permitted a dispossessed freeholder to move against the wrongdoing disseisor. The nonfreeholder is not seized; his interest is personal property, a chattel real. A lease is classified as a nonfreehold estate.

The probable reason for the classification of leasehold interests as personal property lay in the origin of the term for years. By the end of the 12th century, when leasehold interests first began to appear in significant numbers, leases were entered into as a means of evading the ecclesiastical rules against usury and as security for the repayment of money loaned to the landlord by the tenant. As was to be expected, one who invested

1

money in a premium lease or took a lease as security for a loan would want some power of a testamentary disposition over his interest. Prior to enactment of the Statute of Wills in 1540, real property interests could not be devised by will. This prohibition did not extend to personal property. Thus, from an early date lawyers claimed leasehold interests to be personal property. The courts concurred and leaseholds were so classified. While a leasehold was an estate in real property, it was *not real property* for purposes of determining a leaseholder's property rights. The leasehold became a hybrid known as a chattel real.

B.   Remedies Granted Tenants to Protect their Possessory Rights

Since the leasehold interest of the tenant was characterized as personal rather than real property, the assize of novel disseisin and other forms of real actions were not available to him and adequate protection of his interest had to await the further development of the English common law. At the end of the 12th century the remedy of the tenant for a wrongful dispossession by the landlord was an action of covenant in which a prevailing tenant was permitted to recover possession of land. The tenant also had the right to use physical force to resist an attempted wrongful ouster by the landlord.

As against the world at large, including purchasers from the landlord, the tenant had no direct cause of action and was fearfully unprotected.

However, in almost all cases a landlord was deemed to warrant the tenant's enjoyment of the land. This warranty extended to cases of dispossession of the tenant by third parties. Thus, where the tenant was wrongfully evicted by a third party the tenant's remedy was an action against the landlord, and the landlord's remedy was against the third party.

In 1235, tenants were given a new form of action which permitted them to recover possession from one who purchased from the landlord. By the middle of the 13th century the action of trespass had become common and a tenant was permitted to sue in trespass for damages against those who wrongfully disturbed his possession of the land. A special writ of trespass *de ejectione firmae* was developed to meet the tenant's particular needs. By the 16th century this action of ejectment had evolved to an action in which the tenant could recover, not only damages, but also possession of the land—in effect, the modern action of ejectment. After ejectment evolved into a possessory action, the tenant for years was in a better position, vis-a-vis ejectors, than the owners of estates in fee; so superior, in fact, that fee owners, through the use of fictional leases, began to use the action of ejectment to try title to land.

Today the fact that a tenant is not seized has relatively few practical consequences with regard to the tenant's possession, use and enjoyment of the premises. However, the lease has not completely outlived its historical classification as personal property. The fact that this interest may be classified as personal property has significant practical consequences in those jurisdictions which have different schemes of intestate succession or taxation for real and personal property.

II. THE LANDLORD AND TENANT RELATIONSHIP

The landlord and tenant relationship arises by reason of an agreement, express or implied, between the landlord and the tenant. A tenancy is created when an owner of an estate in land grants to another the right to exclusive possession of the land. Without such an agreement, there can be no landlord and tenant relationship. The agreement is called a lease, and the relationship may be referred to as lessor-lessee or landlord-tenant. Similarly, the parties may be referred to as lessor and lessee, or as landlord and tenant. The possession of the tenant must be in subordination to the interest of the landlord, as the owner of the supporting estate, and with the landlord's consent.

III. REQUISITES OF THE LEASE

No formal agreement is necessary to the creation of a tenancy, nor is any particular form of words necessary to create a tenancy. Whether a tenancy is created depends on the intention of the parties. The intent of the parties may be determined by the language they have used or, in the absence of a clearly expressed intent, may be implied in fact from their conduct and surrounding circumstances.

The validity of oral leases has been limited by American versions of the English Statute of Frauds (1677) which provided, in effect, that leases for more than three years must be in writing to be enforceable. Most American jurisdictions follow this statutory pattern but reduce the term of valid oral leases to leases for a term not exceeding one year. Where the parties attempt to create an oral lease for a term longer than that permitted by the applicable Statute of Frauds, the agreement as to the duration of the lease is void. A tenancy at will is created which will become a periodic tenancy upon periodic payment of rent. The other terms and conditions of the oral lease will be enforceable.

One particularly troublesome question involving the Statute of Frauds is the validity of an oral lease for the term of a year, which term is to commence on a date subsequent to the making of the lease. The narrow, but majority, view is that if the end of the term is more than one year after the making of the lease, the lease must be in writing. A substantial minority of jurisdictions follows the English view holding that the Statute of Frauds requires a writing only when the term of the lease exceeds one year.

Where a writing is required, the lease must contain (i) the names of the parties, (ii) an adequate description of the property, (iii) the term of the lease, and (iv) the rent reserved. By the better view the lease need only be signed by the party to be charged in a suit thereunder. There is substantial authority for the view that the lease need only be signed by the party creating it, i.e., the landlord. Under the latter view the tenant is bound by his acceptance of the leasehold.

IV. THE LEASE DISTINGUISHED FROM LICENSES, EASEMENTS AND PROFITS

The right to exclusive possession is the primary feature of a tenancy and is the feature which distinguishes a tenant's interest from a license, easement or profit. The term possession is a variable term which has been defined to mean many different things for many different purposes, but it is generally agreed that to constitute possession there must be some minimal amount of physical control over the premises and an intent to possess to the exclusion of others. A license merely permits a person to enter and go upon the land in possession of another for a specific purpose, or to do an act or series of acts. For example, a landowner may permit a third party to hunt on his land or to use his land as a shortcut to get from one place to another. The license is nonexclusive; i.e., the landlord is entitled to concurrent use of the land and may grant additional licenses to others. Whether a license or tenancy exists is a matter of fact. The test is whether the owner of the proper-

ty has retained control of and access to the premises. The provision of utilities, furnishings, and
cleaning service; the owner's retention of access to
the premises; and the owner's repair and maintenance of the premises are all factors indicating
that the owner has retained control, and that the
occupant has only received a license. As might be
expected, there are areas in which the ideas of
license and tenancy become blurred. For example,
guests in hotels and rooming house occupants are
usually considered to be licensees, not tenants. In
contrast, there is substantial authority for the view
that occupants of so-called "apartment hotels" are
tenants, not licensees; and this is true even where
the occupant is provided some of the services normally found in a hotel—e.g., cleaning services.
The license is also generally deemed to be revoca-
ble at the will of the licensor.

An easement may be fairly defined as the
right of one person to go onto land in possession of
another and to make a limited use of the land (e.g.,
the right to string telephone wires across the owner's land); a profit is the right to take some part of
the land itself or some product of the land (e.g., the
right to cut timber or mine coal). Although the
easement (profit), like the tenant's interest in his
leasehold, is irrevocable, the easement (profit) holder's rights are not exclusive. The grantor may use
the property encumbered by the easement (profit)
in any manner he wishes so long as such use does
not interfere with that of the easement (profit)

holder. In contrast, in the absence of an agreement to the contrary, the tenant's right to possession is exclusive and the tenant may use the premises for any lawful purpose, subject, of course, to the common law prohibition against the commission of waste. (See "The Duty to Repair in the Absence of an Express Covenant to Repair", page 85.)

V. THE LEASE, A CONVEYANCE OR A CONTRACT

Although the authorities are not in complete agreement, a lease of real property may be fairly characterized as a blend of property and contract doctrines. Under the more traditional view a lease is treated as a conveyance of an interest in land to which the covenants are incidentally attached. Thus, a lease is generally considered to be a conveyance for purposes of execution and delivery. Leases also fall within the purview of the recording acts. With the exception of short-term leases, leases are usually required to be recorded to protect the tenant against a subsequent conveyance by the landlord. Generally, a subsequent purchaser from the landlord takes the property free and clear of all outstanding interests of which he has no notice. The tenant's possession of the leased property ordinarily gives a subsequent purchaser the requisite notice. In the absence of such possession, recordation of the lease serves as constructive notice of the tenant's leasehold interest to all subsequent purchasers, and they take the land subject to the prior rights of the tenant.

Under the traditional view the covenants in the lease are usually considered to be independent of the parties' respective "property" interests unless expressly or impliedly made dependent. Thus, breach of a substantial covenant by one party will not justify nonperformance by the other unless the lease so specifies. An exception to this latter rule exists where the covenant is so important as to go to the whole of the consideration for the lease; for example, performance of a covenant not to compete has been held to be essential to the beneficial enjoyment of the leasehold by the tenant. The landlord's breach of such a covenant is deemed to deprive the tenant of the beneficial enjoyment of the demised premises, causing a constructive eviction of the tenant which entitles him to terminate the lease.

The transition from a predominantly rural, agrarian society to a predominantly urban, industrial society during the past 150 years has altered substantially the true subject matter of most modern day leases. In the majority of modern leases, the land is of minimal importance and the primary subject of the lease is the structure (or portion thereof) located on the land and the services which are to be provided to the tenant by the landlord. The myriad problems arising under this new landlord-tenant relationship are commonly handled by the insertion of specific clauses into the lease, thus reinforcing the contractual aspects of the lease. At present, following what many believe to be the better view, there is a substantial and growing judicial and legislative trend toward implying mutual dependency to the important covenants of a lease. This trend has evolved primarily in the area of residential leases.

Although the trend toward emphasizing the contractual aspects of the lease has been accelerated by legislation in many jurisdictions, judicial modification of the common law is a time-consuming process and new concepts may not necessarily meet with universal acceptance. Thus, the results in many cases will vary depending upon whether the court emphasizes the more traditional view of the lease as a conveyance of an interest in land, or follows the trend and places its emphasis on the contractual aspects of a lease.

CHAPTER II

CREATION, DURATION AND TERMINATION OF THE SEVERAL TENANCIES

I. INTRODUCTION

Leasehold interests have been traditionally separated into four categories: (i) the term for years, (ii) the periodic tenancy, (iii) the tenancy at will, and (iv) the tenancy at sufferance. These tenancies are most readily differentiated by their respective durations and the manner of termination. The term for years is a lease for a definite term which automatically terminates upon expiration of the term. The periodic tenancy is a transfer of a possessory interest for a recurring term (e.g., month-to-month). The duration of the periodic tenancy is indefinite and continues until terminated by one party giving proper notice of termination to the other. A tenancy at will is an estate of indefinite duration where the tenant has no obligation to pay rent on a regular basis. The estate is terminable at the will of the landlord or tenant. The tenancy at sufferance arises when the tenant originally takes possession rightfully, but wrongfully remains in possession after the termination of his interest. The tenant remains at the sufferance

of the landlord and may be ejected at the landlord's pleasure.

II.　TERM FOR YEARS

A.　Creation

The term for years is created by express agreement, written or oral, subject to the requirements
and limitations of the applicable statute of frauds.
To qualify as a term for years, the lease must be
for a fixed or computable period of time. A fixed
period of time means the term has specific beginning and ending calendar dates. When the lease
sets forth a formula for determining the beginning
and ending dates, the lease is deemed to be for a
computable period of time. The interest of the
landlord is described as a reversion, and the interest of the tenant is described as a term for years.

B.　Duration

The duration of a term for years is a fixed or
computable period of time in units of one year, or
multiples or divisions thereof. The term may be
one month, six months, one year, five years, or
longer. A number of states have enacted statutes
which place a limitation on the duration of leases.
The statutes vary with some applying to all leases
and some applying only to leases of particular
kinds of real property (e.g., agricultural land, urban lots, etc.). In the absence of such statutes,
there is no limitation on the duration of the term
for years.

Classification as a term for years is not negated by the fact that the leasehold interest may be terminated upon the happening of some contingency. Thus, the term for years may be subject to a right of entry, an executory limitation, or a possibility of reverter.

C. Termination

The term for years is terminated by expiration of the specified period of time set forth in the lease. Since the lease itself sets forth a termination date, no further notice is required to be given by the parties. The term for years may also be terminated by the happening of a specified contingency, surrender of the unexpired term, by release, and under certain other circumstances discussed below under "Termination of the Lease Other than by Expiration of its Term", page 20.

III. THE PERIODIC TENANCY

A. Creation

The periodic tenancy is most commonly created by express agreement, written or oral. A periodic tenancy also arises when: (i) a landlord gives possession to a tenant for an unspecified period of time coupled with an agreement that rent will be paid periodically, i.e., weekly, monthly, or annually; (ii) a tenant remains in possession with the consent of the landlord after termination of a prior tenancy and makes periodic payments of rent; or

(iii) a tenant takes possession under a void lease and makes periodic rent payments.

By the majority view each successive period is treated as a continuation of the original lease rather than the creation of the new tenancy at the beginning of each period. However, there is authority for the view that each period constitutes a new and separate demise.

1. *Entry Under a Void Lease—Determination of the Period*

When a tenant enters into possession under a lease which is invalid for failure to comply with the Statute of Frauds or some other reason (e.g., no acknowledgement where one is required), a tenancy at will arises which is converted into a periodic tenancy upon payment of rent.

There are several views as to how the "period" should be determined. Most courts hold that the period, in no event to exceed one year, is determined by the manner in which the rent is reserved in the lease.

Example: an invalid five year lease providing for an annual rent of $1200 will be held to be a year-to-year lease.

A distinction should be made between the "rent reserved" and the manner of payment. Thus, if in the above example the lease should also provide that the $1200 annual rent is payable in installments of $100 per month, the period should still be one year (the manner in which the rent is reserved), and the lease a year-to-year periodic tenancy. On the other hand, some courts hold that the period is determined by how the rent is actually paid. A few courts hold that a year-to-year lease is created regardless of how the rent is reserved. Finally, a few decisions have held that mere entry under a void lease gives rise to a year-to-year tenancy, even though the tenant has paid no rent.

B. Duration

The periodic tenancy is an indefinite tenancy which continues for successive like periods until it is terminated by proper notice given by either the landlord or the tenant. The period may be a week, a month, or a year, or any portion thereof; for example, a month-to-month or a year-to-year tenancy.

C. Termination

Absent a "notice to terminate" provision in a lease, the notice required to be given to terminate a periodic tenancy is determined by the period itself. Where the tenancy is year-to-year, the common law rule required notice be given six months prior to the end of the period. Most states have enacted statutes which modify the notice required to be given to terminate the year-to-year tenancy. The statutory notice requirements vary from thirty days to three months.

Where the period is less than one year, the required notice is one full period; for example, a one month notice is required to terminate a month-

to-month tenancy. In addition to giving notice of
at least one full period, the termination date must
coincide with the beginning of a new period. Giving proper notice can prove to be troublesome if
the tenant is careless.

Example: T entered into a month-to-month
tenancy on May 10, 1977, with L. On August
15, 1977, T gave L notice of his election to
terminate the lease as of September 15, 1977.
The notice is ineffective because the termination date does not coincide with the beginning
of the new period.

Realizing his mistake, on October 10, 1977, T
wrote and mailed to L a notice of his election
to terminate the lease as of 12:01 a.m., Novem-
ber 10, 1977. Since L probably did not receive
the mailed notice until after October 10, 1977,
one full period of notice was not given and the
notice is ineffective.

Some states have statutes which impose notice
requirements which may exceed the periodic rent
payment term; for example, a statute may require
a minimum of 30 days notice to terminate a periodic tenancy, a notice which would be required even
though the rent is paid weekly.

Landlords often give tenants a written "notice
of termination" coupled with a demand for increased rent if the tenant "elects" to remain in
possession. The courts are divided on the effectiveness of such notice to terminate the lease. A
probable majority of jurisdictions hold that the

notice is equivocal, and therefore, ineffective as a
notice of termination.   Maguire v. Haddad, 325
Mass. 590, 91 N.E.2d 769 (1950).   A substantial
minority hold that the landlord has given an effective notice of termination; and, if the tenant elects
to remain in possession, he must pay the higher
rent specified in the notice.   Harry's Village, Inc.
v. Egg Harbor Township, 89 N.J. 576, 446 A.2d 862
(1982).

D. Distinguishing the Term for Years and Pe-
    riodic Tenancy

The primary distinction between the term for
years and the periodic tenancy is that the term for
years will terminate automatically upon the expiration of the term set forth in the lease, while the
periodic tenancy continues indefinitely or until terminated by proper notice.   Except for the method
of termination, the characteristics and incidents of
the term for years and the periodic tenancy are the
same.

IV. TENANCY AT WILL

A. Creation

A tenancy at will is a landlord-tenant relationship which is terminable at the will of either the
landlord or the tenant.   The tenancy may be created by express agreement or may be implied from
the surrounding circumstances.   Where a tenant
takes possession with the consent of the landlord
and there is no stated duration for the possession

and no reservation of payment of periodic rent, a tenancy at will is created. A tenancy at will is also created where a tenant takes possession under a void lease; however, the tenancy is converted into a periodic tenancy upon the making of periodic rental payments.

B. Duration

The tenancy continues so long as neither the landlord nor the tenant takes any action inconsistent with its continuation.

C. Termination

The tenancy may be terminated by either party giving notice to the other of his intent that the tenancy come to an end. The termination is effective upon receipt of notice unless another date is specified. The tenancy is also terminated by a conveyance of the reversion by the landlord, the death of either the landlord or the tenant, or an attempted assignment by the tenant of his possessory interest. Such acts or occurrences terminate the mutual desire for the tenancy which is necessary for its continuance.

V. TENANCY AT SUFFERANCE

A. Creation

When one originally enters into possession rightfully and after the end of the tenancy retains possession wrongfully, a tenancy at sufferance is created. The tenancy at sufferance is not a true tenancy, but rather an estate created by the courts to distinguish the holdover tenant from a rank trespasser.

B. Duration

The tenancy continues until the landlord makes demand for possession or elects to treat the tenancy as a new consensual tenancy—periodic, at will, or for a term.

C. Termination

There is no true leasehold; and therefore, there is no tenancy to terminate. The continued possession may not be defended against any reasonable action by the owner in fee to remove the wrongful holdover tenant. As an alternative to dispossession, the landlord may elect to consider the holdover tenant as holding under a new tenancy for an additional period of time and may charge a higher rent.

VI. STATUTORY MODIFICATION OF THE SEVERAL TENANCIES

Many states have statutes which provide a different classification of the several tenancies developed in the common law. The majority of the statutes simply provide new definitions of old common law labels, and the change in substance is considerably less than what would appear from the new definitions. One must, however, become familiar with the terminology used in the statutes of the state in which he or she is particularly interested.

CHAPTER III

TERMINATION OF THE LEASE OTHER THAN BY EXPIRATION OF ITS TERM

I. GROUNDS FOR TERMINATION

A. Special Limitations

A leasehold interest may be created subject to a special limitation, the limitation being some stated event the occurrence or non-occurrence of which will automatically terminate the leasehold. Such special limitations must be distinguished from conditions subsequent. The distinction is generally a matter of the intent of the parties, which intent is determined from the terms of the instrument and the surrounding circumstances. The words "while", "as long as," "until," and "during" are generally construed to create an interest subject to a special limitation.

The importance of the distinction is that a lease subject to a special limitation will terminate automatically upon the occurrence or non-occurrence of the stated event; whereas, a lease subject to a condition subsequent will continue after breach of the condition until such time as the landlord takes affirmative action to exercise his power of termination. For example, if the lease is for three years "so long as" liquor is not sold on the premises, the sale of liquor by the tenant on the leased property will cause an automatic termination of the lease, and the tenant for years becomes a tenant at sufferance. On the other hand, if the lease provides "but if liquor is sold on the premises the landlord is entitled to immediately terminate the lease and re-enter and retake possession of the premises," the lease provision is usually construed as a condition subsequent and the lease continues until the landlord takes steps to terminate it.

B. Breach of Condition by Tenant

At common law, covenants in leases were deemed to be independent unless expressly made dependent. As a result, nonperformance by one of the parties to the lease did not excuse performance by the other. The remedy of the landlord was to enforce the particular covenant involved. If the tenant refused to pay the rent, the remedy of the landlord would be to bring suit to recover the rent, but the landlord could not terminate the lease and remove the tenant from the premises. This common law rule is generally considered to be valid today with several caveats.

1. *Statutory Modification*

The most commonly breached covenant in a lease is the covenant to pay rent. Today, most states have statutes that permit the landlord to terminate a lease upon the failure of the tenant to pay the reserved rent, and the power of termination is granted even where no such right is reserved in the lease. Generally, this statutory right of termination does not extend to the breach of other lease covenants. In addition to statutes permitting termination for non-payment of rent, statutes in some jurisdictions permit a landlord to terminate the lease where the premises are used for an illegal purpose, where the tenant assigns without the written consent of the landlord, or for the tenant's commission of waste.

2. Reserved Power of Termination

Almost all leases reserve unto the landlord the power to terminate the lease (often called a right of entry) in the event the tenant defaults in the performance of any of the lease covenants. A tenant may reserve similar rights unto himself with respect to the landlord's breach of his covenants, but this is not a common practice, at least not in residential leases. The doctrine of independence of covenants is effectively negated to the extent that the continuance of a leasehold is expressly conditioned upon the performance of the covenants in the lease.

3. Restatement View

In the Restatement, Second, Property (Landlord and Tenant) § 13.1, the American Law Institute has suggested that a landlord be given the option to terminate a lease whenever the tenant

fails to perform a valid covenant contained in the
lease which requires the tenant to do, or refrain
from doing, something on the leased property or
elsewhere. In support of its position the Institute
states:

> "The promises made by the tenant to the
> landlord . . . are usually a part of the in-
> ducement to the landlord to make the lease.
> When a tenant's promise is such a significant
> inducement, the failure on the part of the
> tenant to perform that promise justifies the
> landlord, . . . to step clear of his obligations
> under the lease by terminating it." Restate-
> ment, Second, Property (Landlord and Tenant)
> § 13.1, Comment a.*

This position is consistent with the present judicial
trend toward emphasis of the contractual rather
than the property aspects of a lease. However,
this trend has been limited primarily to cases
involving residential leases.

4. Waiver by the Landlord

A landlord may waive his power to terminate
the lease for breach of condition. The waiver may
be express, or implied from the landlord's conduct.
Any act by the landlord which acknowledges the
continuing existence of the lease after a breach of
condition will generally be held to constitute a
waiver of his right to terminate the lease. The

* Copyright 1977 by The American Law Institute. Reprinted
with the permission of The American Law Institute.

acceptance of rent accruing after the breach, with knowledge of the breach, is the most common act of the landlord giving rise to the implied waiver. The acceptance of rent which accrued prior to the breach generally does not constitute a waiver. Where the landlord has acted to effectively terminate the lease, his subsequent acceptance of post breach rent will not be construed as a waiver.

Where the tenant's default is of a continuing nature or is a recurring breach of condition, waiver by the landlord as to one breach does not prevent the landlord from terminating the lease for later breaches.

5. *Other Equitable Relief*

When the default by the tenant is failure to pay a sum certain, equity will normally intervene and relieve the tenant from forfeiture of the lease upon payment or tender of the sum due. A forfeiture clause is, in part, inserted as security for the payment of rent and if payment of the sum due puts the landlord in essentially the same position he would have been in had there been no default, in equity there is no good reason to permit the forfeiture. Of course, the tenant must come into court with clean hands, and where the tenant has acted in bad faith (e.g., given bad checks to the landlord) equity will not intervene on behalf of the tenant.

C. Breach of Condition by Landlord—Covenant of Quiet Enjoyment

The landlord's promise that the tenant shall have the right to quietly enjoy the demised premises is the landlord's single most important promise contained in the lease. The covenant of quiet enjoyment is often found in the express language of the lease, but where there is no express covenant, the great weight of authority is to the effect that a covenant of quiet enjoyment will be implied. Contrary to the general rule that the covenants in a lease are independent, the landlord's covenant of quiet enjoyment is a dependent covenant. Breach of the covenant justifies the tenant's nonperformance, and permits termination of the lease by the tenant. The landlord's breach of covenant may take the form of an actual eviction, a constructive eviction, or an eviction by a third party holding paramount title.

1. *Actual Eviction*

To constitute an actual eviction there must be a wrongful physical expulsion or exclusion of the tenant from the leased premises by the landlord. For example, where a landlord physically bars a tenant from entering the premises, or changes the locks on the door to the premises, or padlocks the entrances to the premises, there has been an actual eviction. The eviction may be full or partial. In the event of an actual eviction the tenant's

Hill 2nd Ed., NS—3

liability for all rent is suspended. Even where the tenant is only partially evicted and remains in possession of the balance of the premises, there is a suspension of the entire rent because the courts will not permit the landlord to apportion his own wrong. For example, suppose the landlord leases a parcel of land with a house and garage on it to the tenant and subsequently the landlord uses the garage to store old furniture to the exclusion of the tenant. Under such circumstances the tenant is completely relieved of his duty to pay rent even though he retains possession of the house.

If the lease is terminated by actual eviction, the tenant may bring an action for damages. The measure of damages is the difference between the rent reserved in the lease and the fair rental value of the premises for the balance of the term (reduced to present value). Courts also permit the recovery of special damages: e.g., the costs of relocation are recoverable; and a few courts have included lost profits in the damage award. Where the tenant prefers to retain possession of the premises, an action to recover possession may be commenced; and some courts have granted injunctive relief prohibiting the landlord from further engaging in the conduct giving rise to the eviction.

2. *Constructive Eviction*

The doctrine of constructive eviction is set forth with great clarity in Reste Realty Corp. v.

Cooper, 53 N.J. 444, 251 A.2d 268 (1969). There the court stated that

". . . any act or omission of the landlord or anyone who acts under authority or legal right from the landlord, . . . which renders the premises substantially unsuitable for the purpose for which they are leased, or which seriously interferes with the beneficial enjoyment of the premises, is a breach of the covenant of quiet enjoyment and constitutes a constructive eviction of the tenant." 251 A.2d at 274.

In order to have a valid constructive eviction, the interference must be substantial. The most common incidents of constructive eviction involve breach of a covenant to repair or to furnish heat or other services. Usually, such covenants are regarded as independent, but where the breach by the landlord renders the premises substantially unsuitable, or substantially interferes with the beneficial enjoyment of the premises, the tenant is deemed to be constructively evicted and is entitled to terminate the lease.

A second requirement for a valid claim of constructive eviction is that the tenant abandon the premises within a reasonable time after the interference by the landlord. An undue delay in the abandonment of the premises may be deemed a waiver on the part of the tenant. What constitutes a reasonable period of time will be determined by the facts of each particular case. Comparatively long periods of time have been found to constitute no waiver where the delay in abandonment has been induced by the promises or assurances of the landlord. In the Reste case, the tenant rented office space in a basement which was flooded by water seeping through the basement walls whenever heavy rains occurred. The original landlord promised and unsuccessfully attempted to correct the problem, but promptly removed all water when flooding occurred. The landlord's successor in interest ignored the tenant's repeated complaints of flooding. Nine months after the landlord's successor in interest took title the tenant vacated the premises. The court held that under the circumstances remaining in possession for nine months was reasonable, and the subsequent vacation and termination of the lease was valid.

Where the interference is a breach of covenant by the landlord, such as a covenant to repair, the landlord must be given notice of the breach and an opportunity to perform before the tenant will be entitled to terminate the lease.

The major disadvantage of constructive eviction from the tenant's perspective is that the tenant must, at his own expense, remove himself from the premises and find other tenantable premises (presumably another lease) with no assurance that a court will find that the landlord's interference was in fact substantial. If the tenant's claim of constructive eviction is later held to be unfounded, then the tenant has merely abandoned the premises and is subject to all of the liability that an abandoning tenant normally incurs. (See "Surrender and Abandonment", page 45.)

There is some authority for the view that abandonment of the leased premises is not essential in order for the tenant to receive equitable relief. In Charles E. Burt, Inc. v. Seven Grand Corp., 340 Mass. 124, 163 N.E.2d 4 (1959), the court held that even in the absence of an abandonment by the tenant there was no reason why equitable relief should not be given by way of a judicial declaration that the wrongful acts of the landlord justified the tenant treating those acts as a constructive eviction. Such relief is much more satisfactory than requiring the tenant to vacate the premises at his own peril.

The remedies of a tenant for constructive eviction are essentially the same as those for one actually evicted. (See page 26, supra.) However, a number of courts have held that the tenant may not recover damages for breach of the covenant of quiet enjoyment unless the tenant has vacated the premises. Where permitted, the measure of damages is the diminution in rental value caused by the landlord's interference.

3. *Eviction under Paramount Title*

Eviction under paramount title usually arises because of breach of the landlord's covenant of power to demise, or because of termination of the landlord's estate.

a. Breach of the Covenant of Power to Demise. The weight of authority is that in the absence of an express covenant of power to demise, a covenant of power to demise will be implied in a lease. Some courts hold that the covenant is implied from use of the words "grant" or "demise" or similar language in the lease. Others have implied such a covenant without reference to the technical language of the lease. On the other hand, a small number of jurisdictions have refused to imply a covenant in the absence of such technical words. Where the covenant of power to demise exists, express or implied, and the landlord has no such power, the landlord is liable to the tenant for damages for breach of covenant.

If the tenant acquires possession his damages are nominal unless he is subsequently evicted. Where the tenant is evicted, the covenant breached by the landlord is actually the covenant of quiet enjoyment. The measure of damages is the difference between the fair rental value of the premises for the balance of the term and the contract rent (which sum is reduced to present value), plus any special damages suffered by the tenant. If possession is not acquired by the tenant, he is entitled to terminate the lease and recover the damages set forth above.

b. Termination of the Landlord's Supporting Estate. There are two common situations in which termination of the landlord's supporting estate occur. The first is where an owner of a life estate executes a term for years lease with a tenant who is aware of the landlord's limited ownership, and the landlord dies prior to the expiration of the term. There is authority for the view that the landlord-tenant relationship ceases with the death of the landlord; therefore, there can be no breach of the implied covenant of quiet enjoyment founded upon that relationship. This result is probably in accord with the intent of the parties, at least where the tenant is aware of the landlord's limited estate. In contrast, some courts take the view that any extinguishment of the landlord's supporting estate which results in the termination of the lease by one holding paramount title constitutes a breach of the landlord's implied covenant of quiet enjoyment for which the landlord, or his estate, will be liable for damages. If the lease contains an express covenant of quiet enjoyment, the landlord's estate will be liable.

A more common situation is where, prior to the execution of the lease, the landlord's estate is subject to a condition (or a prior mortgage or other lien) and the estate is subsequently extinguished for breach of condition. If the tenant is ousted by the new owner, the landlord will be liable for breach of the covenant of quiet enjoyment. A similar result occurs when a sublease is terminated because of termination of the supporting prime lease and the subtenant is ousted by the owner of the fee. In such cases, the subtenant may sue the prime tenant for breach of the implied covenant of quiet enjoyment.

The measure of damages is the same as that set forth in "Breach of the Covenant of Power to Demise", above.

D. Illegality and Frustration of Purpose

A lease may be illegal because the intended use violates some law existing at the inception of the lease, or it may become illegal after commencement of the term because of a change of law. The latter situation is referred to as a supervening illegality.

1. *Intended Use Illegal at Time of Letting*

a. Leases for Illegal and Immoral Purposes. It may generally be said that if premises are leased for a purpose prohibited by law, the lease is unenforceable by either the landlord or the tenant. To permit enforcement by either party would be to have the courts assist the party in his or her unlawful activities. Most cases involve leases for prostitution, gambling or the illegal sale of liquor, although the rule is applied to leases for other illegal uses.

Where the lease is silent as to the use to be made of the premises by the tenant, the authorities are split as to when a lease will be deemed to have been made for an illegal purpose. The majority of courts holds that the landlord's knowledge of the tenant's proposed illegal use at the time the lease is executed is sufficient to make the lease one for an illegal purpose. The minority view requires some degree of culpability on the part of the landlord and holds that knowledge alone is not enough; the landlord must intend, or in some way participate in, the illegal use of the demised premises.

Some courts look at the seriousness of the illegal conduct in determining which rule to apply. Where the use is deemed to be *mala in se* (e.g., prostitution) the majority rule is followed; whereas, when the use is merely *mala prohibita* (e.g., illegal sale of liquor) the court will look to the landlord's intent that the premises be used for the illegal purpose.

If the landlord is not implicated in the tenant's illegal conduct, the landlord may enforce the lease against the tenant. The landlord may also enjoin continuation of the illegal use, and recover damages arising out of the tenant's illegal use of the premises.

b. Lease for a Purpose Requiring a Permit, License or Zoning Variance. A lease often contains language regarding the use to be made of the premises. Such language will be construed as permissive, or descriptive of the use contemplated by the parties, unless the language clearly restricts the tenant's use of the premises. Where the language is deemed to be permissive or descriptive, the "illegality" of a *contemplated use* will not be grounds for terminating the lease. The reasoning is that the tenant suffers no harm because the premises may still be used for any lawful purpose.

Where the provisions of the lease limit the use of the premises to a single purpose and the contemplated use is conclusively prohibited by law, the lease is usually deemed to be illegal and unenforceable. Many cases with similar facts and results can be found whose decisions are based on theories of "failure of consideration," "mistake of law," or "commercial frustration." The fundamental similarities between all of these cases are: there is a lease for a specific purpose, the purpose is conclusively prohibited by law, and as a result the premises are totally unusable to the tenant. See Economy v. S.B. & L. Bldg. Corp., 138 Misc. 296, 245 N.Y.S. 352 (1930).

Uses illegal under certain circumstances may be permissible if a permit, license or zoning variance is obtained. Ordinarily, a lease for a purpose regulated by government is not deemed to be a lease for an illegal purpose even though the tenant fails to obtain the necessary permit, license or variance prior to the inception of the lease. Normally the parties contemplate that the necessary license, permit or variance will be obtained, and there is no intent to act unlawfully. However, if both parties enter into the lease with no intent to attempt to obtain the necessary permit, license or variance, then the lease is one for an illegal purpose and is unenforceable; the intent to violate the law is clear.

Where a permit, license or variance is necessary to use the premises for the purposes set forth in the lease, the courts have generally refused to imply an agreement that the tenant's liability under the lease is conditioned upon his ability to obtain the permit, license or variance. The risk of denial is assumed by the tenant. The lease remains valid although the required governmental consent has been denied. NEBACO, Inc., v. Riverview Realty Co., Inc., 87 Nev. 55, 482 P.2d 305 (1971). The rationale is that the tenant bargained for and received an estate in land, an estate he still owns although it may be unusable to him.

On the theory that to burden a tenant with a lease of unusable property is too great a penalty, a few jurisdictions relieve the tenant of liability if the necessary governmental consent cannot be obtained after a good faith effort. Walker v. Southern Trucking Corp., 283 Ala. 551, 219 So.2d 379 (1969).

(i) Duty to Obtain the Permit, License or Variance. One who seeks to have a lease declared void and unenforceable because the intended use is prohibited by a licensing or zoning law must first make a diligent, good-faith effort to obtain the necessary permit, license or variance which would allow the contemplated use. Pennsylvania State Shopping Plaza, Inc., v. Olive, 202 Va. 862, 120 S.E.2d 372 (1961).

(ii) Mistake of Law. Recent cases are split as to the effect of the parties' lack of actual knowledge of the existence, nature or application of the restrictive statute or regulation. Some jurisdic-

tions have held that the parties are presumed to
know the applicable law, including the nature and
effect of the law, and that ignorance of the particular statute or regulation will not affect the rights
of the parties. Other courts have held that a
mutual mistake of law will relieve the parties of
their liability under the lease, rejecting the aforementioned presumption of knowledge of the law,
apparently on the theory that the actual or implied
intent of the parties is not to do an illegal act.
Where such leases are voidable for mistake of law,
the tenant is still required to make a good-faith
effort to obtain the necessary governmental consent to allow the premises to be used as contemplated, if such consent is possible.

(iii) Landlord's Warranty of Use. Where the
landlord expressly warrants that the restricted use
set forth in the lease does not violate existing law,
and the use in fact is prohibited, the tenant is
entitled to damages for breach of warranty. The
warranty is enforced even though the lease is otherwise unenforceable and even though enforcement of the warranty is inconsistent with the
general view that the illegality of a major provision in a lease renders the entire lease illegal and
unenforceable. It appears that recovery is permitted on the ground that the lease and the warranty
are two separate agreements; and therefore, the
illegality of the lease does not invalidate the warranty. A similar result has been reached under a
fraud theory. When recovery by the tenant is

under a fraud theory, the recovery is based on tort grounds rather than the contractual relations of the parties; and therefore, the allowance of damages is not inconsistent with a finding that the lease is void.

c. Multiple Uses—One Use Prohibited. Often a tenant's interest will be restricted to several permissible uses, or will contemplate certain uses which are incidental to the primary purpose of the lease. If one of the purposes is illegal but the property may be feasibly used for the remaining legal purposes, the lease remains valid and enforceable. See Warshawsky v. American Automotive Products Co., 12 Ill.App.2d 178, 138 N.E.2d 816 (1956). However, if the primary purpose of the lease is illegal, the entire lease agreement will be unenforceable.

d. Right to Possession of the Premises. Although an illegal lease is generally unenforceable, the landlord may maintain a suit to cancel the lease and regain possession of the premises. The reason for allowing the landlord this action is not to give the landlord relief, but rather to prevent the continuance of the tenant's illegal use. This would seem to be the better view with respect to commercial leases, although there are a few cases to the contrary.

A number of the more recent residential landlord-tenant cases involving illegal leases have held that the fact that the lease is void and unenforceable does not result in a rescission of the lease agreement which requires the tenant to return possession of the premises to the landlord. For the reasoning in such cases, see "Leases Which Violate Housing Codes" below.

e. Leases Which Violate Housing Codes. The doctrine of illegality has recently been extended and applied to urban residential leases which substantially violate municipal housing codes. This application has its origins in Brown v. Southall Realty Co., 237 A.2d 834 (D.C.App.1968), where the court quoted the following with approval: " '(t)he general rule is that an illegal contract, made in violation of the statutory prohibition designed for police or regulatory purposes, is void and confers no right upon the wrongdoer.' " 237 A.2d at 837. To justify a finding of illegality, the code violation must be substantial and must go to the habitability of the premises. The violation must also have existed prior to and at the time the lease was executed.

(i) Landlord's Right to Possession. In traditional illegality cases, the landlord is generally entitled to recover possession of the premises. This view can be justified in general on the ground that recovery of possession by the landlord is necessary in order to prevent the continuing wrongful use by the tenant. A more theoretical approach to the problem yields the same result, i.e., since the illegality voids the lease, the tenant is a mere tenant at will and any manifestation by the land-

lord of his intent to terminate the tenancy will result in its termination.

In the area of residential leases however, there is authority for the position that the landlord may not recover possession on the basis of the illegal use where the tenant has previously reported housing code violations to public authorities, or successfully defended a summary possession action on grounds of illegality or breach of the implied warranty of habitability. As noted above, theoretically, a tenant's entry under a void lease creates a tenancy at will at common law. The tenant's interest then becomes subject to termination at the will of the landlord or as otherwise provided by statute. However, this right of termination is subject to any recognized defenses the tenant may have to such termination. Retaliatory eviction is often a valid defense for a tenant who has reported housing code violations to a code enforcement agency, or successfully defended a summary possession action on grounds of illegality or breach of the implied warranty of habitability. See, "Retaliatory Eviction", page 144.

Although to allow the tenant to remain in possession is to allow a continuing residency in violation of statute, the result seems to be a proper one. The reason most often set forth by the courts is that because of existing housing shortages in urban areas and the absence of economic parity between the landlord and tenant, the residential tenant has little, if any, bargaining power to nego-

tiate for premises free from code violations. The
tenant, in effect, is forced by circumstances into
the tenancy, and therefore, the tenant is not *in
pari delicto* with the landlord. Under such circumstances, there is no good reason why the courts
should effect a repossession of the premises on
behalf of the landlord, particularly if the tenant is
required to make *quantum meruit* payment to the
landlord. (See, "Landlord's Right to Rent", below.)
Further, in a summary action for possession, to
give the landlord possession totally negates the
defense of illegality and gives the landlord precise-
ly the relief prayed for despite the landlord's culpability; an incongruous result at best.

Most jurisdictions which have addressed the
illegality problem in residential leases have also
had occasion to address the question of implied
warranty of habitability. The latter theory imposes an affirmative duty to repair on the landlord
on the ground of an implied contractual undertak-
ing. Since the duty is founded in contract, the
remedies available for the landlord's breach are
numerous, and give the courts more flexibility in
tailoring the remedies in a particular case to fit
the needs of the parties. (See, "Implied Warranty
of Habitability—Remedies of the Tenant", page
126.) In jurisdictions which have adopted the implied warranty of habitability doctrine, most litigation is taking place under that doctrine and as a
consequence it is unlikely that the illegality theory
will be used extensively in those jurisdictions in
the future.

(ii) Landlord's Right to Rent. If the illegal lease is treated as void *ab initio* the landlord is not entitled to receive any rent and the tenant should be able to recover any rent paid to the landlord under the provisions of the void lease. Some courts have adopted this view. Others have granted relief more favorable to the landlord. In William J. Davis, Inc. v. Slade, 271 A.2d 412 (D.C.App. 1970), the court held that the tenant was entitled to recover the rent it had paid to the landlord under a void lease, but that the landlord was entitled to offset the reasonable value of the premises in their defective condition. This result was based in part upon the court's findings that since the lease was void *ab initio,* the tenant was a tenant at sufferance under the District of Columbia statutes (a tenancy similar to the common law tenancy at will) and therefore, the rule allowing quasi-contractual relief would be followed.

Other courts have elected to leave the landlords and tenants as they find them and denied recovery of payments voluntarily made under the provisions of the illegal lease on the ground that if the tenant is going to deny the validity of the lease, he must do so at the outset. The reasoning seems to be that if the tenant is allowed to recover all rent paid, the following scenario will take place: the tenant will knowingly go into possession of the defective premises, pay rent for a substantial period of time, reap the benefits of the tenancy, and then recover all of the rent previously paid in an action based upon the illegality of the lease. The inequities of such an action are clear, but do not call for denial of all relief to the tenant. Under such circumstances, the *quantum meruit* approach taken in Davis v. Slade, supra, would be more equitable. Further, denying relief to the tenant encourages the letting of substandard housing, a result directly counter to the public policy of assuring habitable dwellings—a policy evidenced by state and local housing codes, and the growing number of decisions granting the tenant relief on the theories of illegality and implied warranty of habitability.

Although the trend is to extend the illegality doctrine to apply to residential leases, the recent decisions are not unanimous. Further, when the violation arises after the inception of the lease, the defense of illegality does not apply.

2. *Supervening Illegality*

Often a lease will restrict the tenant to one particular use of the premises, which use is subsequently prohibited by law. Under such circumstances, the majority of jurisdictions holds that the tenant's liability for rent terminates and that the landlord is entitled to recover possession of the premises. The theories adopted by the courts in granting relief vary, but include impossibility of performance, a finding that the lease became illegal, and the finding of an implied agreement by the landlord and tenant not to do an illegal act. Perhaps a more accurate term, although also imprecise, is "frustration of purpose." However, in the interest of accuracy it must be noted that it is usually the tenant's purpose which is frustrated, not the landlord's.

In order for the rule to operate there must be an almost complete frustration. Thus, it must be the main use to which the tenant is restricted that is subsequently prohibited. Where the tenant is restricted to several uses, only one of which is prohibited, the lease continues unabated.

A minority of jurisdictions views the lease as primarily a conveyance of an interest in land. Since the impact of the law on the tenant's use of the land does not alter the fact that the tenant still retains an interest in the land, a subsequent prohibition of the tenant's use does not terminate the leasehold interest. The tenant bears the risk of any change in the law.

E. Destruction of the Premises

The majority rule is that the tenant may terminate the lease upon the destruction of the subject matter of the lease. However, the subject matter of the lease is presumed to be the land, not the structures situated thereon. Thus, where the structures on the premises are destroyed without fault on the part of the landlord, as, for example, by fire, flood, wind or the public enemy, the lease continues unabated. Lawson v. Taylor Hotels, Inc., 242 Ark. 6, 411 S.W.2d 669 (1967).

To this harsh common law rule there are several exceptions. First, where the lease expressly provides that only the structure is being leased, the structure is the subject matter of the lease and its destruction will terminate the leasehold. Second, where the tenant leases only a portion of a building he is presumed not to have leased the land. Again, destruction of the premises will allow the tenant to terminate the lease.

In addition, a small minority of courts holds that destruction of the main structure on the leased premises entitles the tenant to terminate the lease. Albert M. Greenfield & Co. v. Kolea, 475 Pa. 351, 380 A.2d 758 (1977). This rule has been adopted by statutes in several jurisdictions and has been adopted by the American Law Institute as § 5.4 of the Restatement, Second, Property (Landlord and Tenant). In order for the tenant to be entitled to the relief of termination, the destruction of the premises must be almost total.

In a modern industrial and urban society the structure is the subject matter of most leases, rather than the land on which it sits; therefore, in most instances it is not reasonable to assume that a lease is primarily a lease of the land. This modern reality lends support to the minority position and it is thought by many to be the better view. However, if the primary subject matter of the lease is in fact the land (e.g., an agricultural lease, or a ground lease), destruction of the buildings thereon does not entitle the tenant to terminate the lease.

F. Surrender and Abandonment

1. *Surrender*

A lease may be terminated by surrender. Surrender is the return of the leasehold interest by the tenant to the holder of the reversion (the landlord) prior to the time the lease would normally come to an end. To have a valid surrender, there must be mutual agreement between the landlord and the tenant, i.e., an acceptance by the landlord of the tenant's offer of surrender. An effective surrender extinguishes the lease and tenant's liability thereunder.

A surrender ordinarily will not affect any interest acquired by third parties in the leasehold; for example, where a tenant has sublet the premises, a surrender by the tenant will not terminate the sublease. The tenant is deemed to have merely yielded up his interest as tenant-sublandlord to the original landlord.

Generally, since a surrender is in essence a reconveyance of the balance of the leasehold, it must be in writing and comply with the Statute of Frauds to be valid. In some jurisdictions surrenders of short terms are excepted from the writing requirement, either expressly by statute or on the theory that no greater formality is required for surrender than is required to create a leasehold estate for a like term. Where oral surrenders of short terms are permitted, it is the balance of the term, not the length of the original term, which determines whether there can be a valid oral surrender.

A valid surrender may also arise out of the conduct of the parties. Thus, where the landlord and tenant execute a new lease of the premises prior to the expiration of the old lease, the execution of the second lease is evidence of the parties' mutual intent to surrender the first. Also, a landlord who reenters and takes possession or relets the premises on his own behalf (a matter of fact) after the wrongful abandonment by the original tenant may be deemed to have consented to the tenant's abandonment, thus effecting a valid surrender by operation of law. The landlord is in effect estopped from denying the surrender. Since the surrender is by operation of law, the Statute of Frauds is not applicable.

2. *Abandonment*

Abandonment may be fairly described as the unjustified vacation of the leased premises by the tenant with no present intent to return, coupled with a default in the payment of rent. Abandonment is in effect an offer of surrender. The test in determining whether a landlord has accepted the tenant's offer is whether the acts of the landlord, with respect to the abandoned property, are inconsistent with the rights of the tenant. In each case,

acceptance or nonacceptance of the offer of surrender is a matter of fact.

3. The Landlord's Options After Abandonment by the Tenant

There is a considerable conflict among the
jurisdictions with regard to the landlord's options
after the tenant has abandoned the leased premises. This conflict is particularly acute with regard to whether the landlord must make a reasonable attempt to relet the property to mitigate the
tenant's damages or may stand idly by and sue for
the rent as it comes due.

a. Mitigation.

(i) No Duty to Mitigate. Under the majority
view, a landlord is not required to relet the premises to mitigate the damages of the tenant. The
underlying reason for the rule is that a lease
creates an interest in land and the landlord need
not concern himself with a tenant's abandonment
of his own property. Markoe v. Naiditch & Sons,
303 Minn. 6, 226 N.W.2d 289 (1975). In these
jurisdictions, one option of the landlord is to stand
idly by and sue for the rent due.

(a) Recovery of Future Rent. If the landlord
elects to simply sue for rent, the question arises as
to whether he can sue for future rent or must wait
and sue for rent as it accrues. The traditional
view has been that future rent cannot be recovered. The tenant's obligation to pay rent is simply

a promise to pay money at certain specified intervals. Analogizing to the debtor's obligation to make installment payments under a promissory note, most courts hold that in the absence of a rent acceleration clause there can be no acceleration of rent which has not accrued under the terms of the lease. Jordan v. Nickell, 253 S.W. 237, (Ky.App. 1952). The landlord must wait and sue for the rent as it accrues.

A recent trend toward the application of contract principles to leases has resulted in a growing body of decisions which recognizes that anticipatory breach of contract doctrines should be applied to leases. Ordinarily, failure to pay an installment of rent is not sufficient cause to invoke the doctrine; there must be an unequivocal repudiation of the entire lease by the tenant. Where future rent is recoverable, it is treated as damages and the sum recoverable is the difference between the reserved rent and the fair rental value of the premises for the balance of the term, reduced to present value. Harden v. Drost, 156 Ga.App. 363, 274 S.E.2d 748 (1980). If the landlord elects this remedy, the lease terminates and the landlord is entitled to possession of the leased property.

(b) Rent Acceleration Clauses. It is common for leases to contain a provision stating that upon the tenant's default in the payment of rent (or upon the happening of some other event, e.g., bankruptcy of the tenant), the entire rent for the balance of the term shall immediately become due and payable. Most decisions on the subject hold that such clauses are valid on the theory that an agreement to pay the rent in advance is valid and an acceleration clause is no more than an agreement to pay the rent in advance upon the happening of a specified event. A few courts hold such clauses void as a penalty, or limit the recovery by the landlord to rent due for a reasonable period of time.

Where the rent is accelerated and the tenant compelled to pay, the landlord is usually not entitled to possession. However, there is a split of authority on the validity of a lease provision which expressly provides that upon default in payment of rent the landlord may terminate the lease and hold the tenant liable for the full amount of the unaccrued rent. Most courts hold that the agreement is unconscionable and unenforceable, particularly where the amount of the accelerated rent bears no reasonable relation to the true potential damages to the landlord. A few courts uphold such clauses if the language is sufficiently explicit, apparently on the basis of the parties' freedom to contract as they see fit, including contractually establishing the liquidated damages to be paid in the event of default. Absent such an agreement, if the landlord elects to terminate the lease, he may recover rent only up to the date of termination.

(ii) The Landlord's Affirmative Duty to Mitigate. A substantial number of jurisdictions have held that the landlord is under a duty to accept or

acquire a new tenant in mitigation of the original tenant's damages. Most courts adopting this view emphasize the contractual aspects of a lease and apply the well-settled contract rule that a promisee cannot recover damages for breach of contract where those damages could have been avoided by him through the exercise of reasonable diligence. Where the duty to mitigate is imposed upon the landlord, the landlord is required to make a diligent effort to procure a new tenant. The decisions are almost evenly split as to whether the landlord or the tenant has the burden of proof with respect to showing the requisite exercise of due diligence (or lack thereof) on the part of the landlord in reletting the premises.

b. Voluntary Reletting for the Benefit of the Tenant. In jurisdictions where the landlord is under no duty to mitigate the tenant's damages, the landlord may relet the premises without releasing the tenant's liability under the lease. The landlord is deemed to have the option to relet on behalf of the tenant, acting as the tenant's "agent". In such cases, the lease continues and the tenant remains liable thereon, but his liability for rent is limited to the difference between the rent reserved in the lease and the rent paid by the new tenant. Since the landlord is merely acting as the agent of the original tenant, the new tenant is treated as an assignee of the original tenant. Since the lease is deemed to be continuing, theoretically, the tenant should be entitled to the benefit of any relet at a rent in excess of the rent reserved in the original lease. The limited authority on the issue is to the contrary, however.

In the absence of an express provision on the subject, perhaps the primary issue arising out of a reletting by the landlord is whether such reletting is on behalf of the tenant, or conduct which constitutes an acceptance of the tenant's abandonment. Some courts hold that any relet by the landlord constitutes an acceptance of the tenant's offer of surrender. Other courts hold that any attempt to relet for the benefit of the tenant without prior notification of the tenant is an act inconsistent with the tenant's rights under the lease. Such acts are deemed to constitute consent by the landlord to the tenant's abandonment. Still other courts hold that prior notice to the tenant of such a reletting is not essential in order to prevent a surrender by operation of law.

c. Landlord's Election to Terminate the Lease. Upon the tenant's wrongful abandonment of the premises, the landlord may elect to accept the "offer of surrender" and terminate the lease. Unless otherwise agreed, termination of the lease ends all of the tenant's obligations thereunder as of the date of termination. The tenant remains liable for unpaid rent and other unperformed obligations which accrued prior to the date of termination.

Leases often contain provisions which require the tenant to pay "rent" after termination of the

lease. By the majority view, such provisions are
deemed to be penalties and are unenforceable. In
jurisdictions enforcing such agreements, the intent
of the parties to reach this result must be clear.
Where there is ambiguity, such provisions are
strictly construed against the landlord. Where the
landlord relets the premises, the landlord's recovery under the "continuing rent" clause is limited
to the difference between the "continuing rent"
and the rent received under the new lease. The
recovery under such clauses may be more accurately described as damages rather than as rent.

G. Expiration of the Landlord's Estate

It is fundamental that a grantor cannot convey
an estate which is greater or longer than his own.
Thus, where a landlord has a life estate or an
estate otherwise limited and makes a lease for a
term which has not come to an end at the expiration of the landlord's estate, the tenant's estate
nevertheless terminates with that of his landlord.
Similarly, where the landlord's estate is subject to
a mortgage or other lien made prior to the lease,
the tenant's estate is subject to the rights of the
mortgagee or lienholder and his leasehold will be
terminated by a sale of the landlord's estate pursuant to a foreclosure.

II. METHOD OF TERMINATION

Ordinarily, a landlord is entitled to recover
possession of the premises only when the lease has
come to an end. Except as noted above, the lease

is usually terminated (i) by expiration of the term, (ii) by giving proper notice when the tenancy is one of indefinite duration, or (iii) by the exercise of a right of entry (power of termination) expressly reserved in the lease. The traditional interpretation of leases is that the promises of the parties are independent and in the absence of a reserved right of entry, breach of a covenant by the tenant, including the covenant to pay rent, does not confer on a landlord the right to terminate the lease or evict the tenant. Where the landlord is entitled to possession of the premises and the tenant wrongfully holds over, the question becomes: what steps may the landlord take to remove the tenant from the premises.

Summary possession statutes (often included as part of a Forcible Entry and Detainer Statute) exist in every state and provide landlords with a relatively quick judicial procedure for the recovery of possession of the leased premises. The rights arising under such statutes are usually independent of any right of entry (power of termination) reserved in the lease by the landlord. The grounds reserved for application of the remedy vary, but usually include default in the payment of rent. In addition to the judicial remedies, many jurisdictions permit the landlord to use self-help in the recovery of the premises.

A. Self-help

Although every state has a summary process statute for the recovery of possession of real property, a substantial number of jurisdictions continue to permit the landlord to use some degree of self-help in the recovery of his property. The degree of permissible self-help varies from the use of "reasonable force" to those jurisdictions which permit only "peaceful reentries".

1. *Use of Reasonable Force*

A substantial number of American jurisdictions follow the so-called English rule which holds that a landlord may, without legal process, use such force as may be reasonably necessary to remove the tenant from the leased premises. Most courts frown on the use of self-help and will closely scrutinize the actions of the landlord to see if they are "reasonable". If the landlord uses more force than is necessary to effect the removal of the tenant and his possessions, the landlord will be liable to the tenant in damages and the tenant may be entitled to recover possession of the premises.

2. *Peaceful Repossession*

Today, in most jurisdictions there exists legislation which prohibits the use of force in the eviction of a tenant wrongfully holding over after the termination of the lease. However, in such jurisdictions the majority view is that the landlord may, where possible, regain possession peaceably. The conduct which will be construed as "peaceable" repossession varies from jurisdiction to jurisdiction. In some jurisdictions the unlocking or removal of a door in order to gain reentry will be deemed peaceable; while in others such actions will constitute force which contravenes the applicable forcible entry and detainer statute. Still other courts have held that entry by trick or deception, or any entry without the consent of the tenant, is wrongful.

Where the landlord has peaceably regained possession, he may maintain it and lawfully resist any attempt on the part of the tenant to oust him. Such resistance has been held to include the right to use reasonable force. A few courts have held that possession obtained by peaceful reentry but required to be held by a show of force constitutes a violation of the forcible entry and detainer statute. The trend established by recent decisions is to require the landlord to resort to the remedy provided by the summary process statutes to obtain possession of real property from a tenant wrongfully holding over.

3. *Lease Provision Allowing Reentry Without Judicial Process*

A probable majority of jurisdictions holds that a provision in a lease giving the landlord the right to reenter without judicial process, using reasonable force where necessary, is valid. However, the more recent cases indicate a trend toward holding such provisions void as violative of the public policy against the use of force to settle private disputes, and holding the landlord liable for damages when reentry is made without legal process. In jurisdictions where the landlord is required to use the judicial process to remove a wrongfully holding over tenant, a lease provision waiving the tenant's right to appeal to the courts for redress of wrongs is void and of no effect.

4. *Remedies of the Tenant for Landlord's Wrongful Reentry*

In some jurisdictions, where the landlord has used force to reenter and such force is prohibited, or where the landlord has used excessive force where reasonable force is permitted, the tenant is entitled to recover possession of the leased premises. In addition, if the tenant or the tenant's property is injured by such conduct, the landlord will be liable for damages.

B. Summary Process Statutes

The restrictions on self-help have made landlords increasingly dependent upon judicial proceedings to recover possession of leased property. One possible remedy is an action for ejectment. However, ejectment is a slow and expensive proceeding, and accordingly is seldom used in the landlord-tenant situation. Eviction by summary process is the remedy usually sought by the landlord.

As the label "summary possession statute" indicates, these statutes were enacted to provide a simple, expeditious remedy for the recovery of possession of real property. In conformity with this purpose these statutes expressly, or by construction, often prohibit the introduction of affirmative or equitable defenses during the summary proceeding. This means that a tenant may not plead breach of covenant by the landlord as justification for the tenant's default. This is also consistent with the traditional doctrine of independence of covenants in a lease.

The doctrine of independence of covenants in leases and the procedural limitations of the summary possession statutes are now under attack in the courts. In large part the attack has been successful. A substantial number of courts have recently held that affirmative defenses are admissible, and extended the contract principle of mutuality of covenants to include the landlord's duty to repair.

Those advocating the introduction of affirmative defenses suffered a substantial setback in Lindsey v. Normet, 405 U.S. 56, 92 S.Ct. 862, 31 L.Ed.2d 36 (1972), where the U.S. Supreme Court held that it was constitutionally *permissible* for the state to limit actions under its forcible entry and detainer statute to the determination of a single issue, and preclude the introduction of affirmative or equitable defenses by the tenant when the tenant's claims can be litigated in a separate proceeding. However, Lindsey did not address the question of whether affirmative defenses must be entertained when such defenses directly relate to the basis of the landlord's claim to possession. E.g., many jurisdictions now impose an implied warranty of habitability on a landlord (see, "Implied Warranty of Habitability", page 108), and permit the tenant to withhold rent when the landlord has breached this implied warranty (see, "Rent Abatement and Withholding", page 131). In such jurisdictions, where the landlord sues for possession on the basis of nonpayment of rent, due process would seem to require that the tenant be afforded an opportunity to raise the defense of breach of the implied warranty of habitability. If the warranty has been breached, no rent is "due"; and therefore, the landlord should not be entitled to recover possession for "nonpayment of rent".

In most states, the remedy of summary eviction is available only in statutorily specified types of cases. The fact that the landlord has a right to terminate under the terms of the lease and has elected to do so does not necessarily mean he can avail himself of the summary process statute. The grounds stated for application of the remedy vary, but all include nonpayment of rent due under a lease; and, of course, recovery of possession when the term of the tenancy has expired.

III. THE HOLDOVER PROBLEM

A tenant who originally entered into possession rightfully but wrongfully continues in possession after the termination of his lease acquires the status of a tenant at sufferance (see "Tenancy at

Sufferance", page 18), and is commonly referred to as a "holdover". The landlord may elect to treat the holdover as a trespasser and evict him and recover damages; or, alternatively, the landlord may elect to treat the holdover as a tenant. Otto v. Hongsermeier Farms, Inc., 217 Neb. 45, 348 N.W.2d 422 (1984). Not only may the landlord treat the holdover as a tenant, the landlord may, by proper notice, charge the tenant rent in an amount which is substantially higher than the rent reserved in the original lease. A few cases limit the landlord's recovery to reasonable compensation for use and occupancy of the premises by the tenant.

Where the landlord elects to treat the holdover as a tenant, the tenancy is deemed to be a new tenancy rather than an extension of the original lease. In some jurisdictions, liability is founded on the theory that the tenant's continuing possession constitutes an offer which the landlord may accept, thus raising an implied agreement. By the majority view, liability is imposed upon the tenant by law regardless of his intent, express or implied. The resulting liability, at least theoretically, is noncontractual. In such cases, it may be that liability is imposed to provide the landlord with a sanction to induce tenants to move promptly at the end of the term.

A. Necessity for Termination of the Lease

In order for one who has acquired possession rightfully under a lease to be treated as a holdover, the lease must first be terminated. With respect to a term for years, the termination is automatic upon expiration of the term. The termination of other tenancies depends upon the conduct of the parties and, more particularly, the validity of the notice of termination. Generally, the notice must be in writing, timely (e.g., one month's notice must be given to terminate a month-to-month periodic tenancy), and unequivocal.

As noted earlier (See "The Periodic Tenancy— Termination," page 15), landlords frequently give tenants a written "notice of termination" coupled with a demand for increased rent if the tenant elects to remain in possession. There is a split of authority on the effectiveness of such a notice to terminate a periodic tenancy. A probable majority of jurisdictions holds that the notice is equivocal, and therefore, ineffective as notice of termination of the lease. Maguire v. Haddad, 325 Mass. 590, 91 N.E.2d 769 (1950). The lease is not terminated, and since there is no mutual consent to the rent increase the periodic rent remains unchanged. Id.

A substantial minority of jurisdictions has held that a timely notice from the landlord to the tenant that the landlord intends to terminate the lease or continue the lease at a higher rent is effective as a notice of termination, and results in the continuation of the tenancy at the higher rent if the tenant holds over beyond the specified termination date. Harry's Village, Inc. v. Egg Harbor Township, 89 N.J. 576, 446 A.2d 862 (1982). It should be noted, however, that at least one court has held that the tenant's silence, i.e., the mere retention of possession without more, cannot be construed as consent; and that no agreement for increased rent can be made without the consent of both parties.

B. Nature of the Tenancy Created

The holdover tenancy is treated as a new tenancy rather than an extension of the first lease. However, the rights and obligations of the parties under the new tenancy are governed by the terms and conditions of the first lease, except as those terms are modified by the parties (e.g., an increase in rent charged by the landlord), and except the duration of the new lease.

Most jurisdictions hold that proper notice must be given to terminate the new holdover tenancy and therefore, the tenancy may be fairly classified as a periodic tenancy. The minority holds that the new tenancy is a term for years which ends without notice upon expiration of the term.

The authorities are divided as to the basis for determining the length of the period or term. Some courts look to the term or period reserved in the original lease to determine the term or period of the new lease, provided however, in no event will the term or period of the new lease exceed one year. Therefore, if the first lease was for a year or more, the holdover tenancy is from year to year or for a term of one year.

A second method is to determine the period or term of the new lease based upon the manner in which the rent is reserved in the first lease. Where the first lease reserves an annual rent, or an annual rent payable in installments, the new tenancy is from year to year or for the term of the year. Where the rent is reserved on a monthly basis, the new tenancy is from month-to-month or a term for one month.

C. Modification of the Holdover Doctrine

The harsh consequences of the holdover doctrine (e.g., unilaterally raising the rent and holding the tenant for an additional term against his will) have been alleviated in some jurisdictions by statutes which reduce the length of the term for which the tenant becomes bound. Although generally approving the rule, the courts have also acted to relieve its harshness. Some courts exhibit a tendency to interpret the facts in such a manner that they do not amount to a retention of possession beyond the termination date; for example, retention of keys to the premises and leaving a few items of personal property on the premises have been held not to constitute a retention of possession.

Most courts also recognize an exception (an "impossibility of performance" type claim) when the tenant's failure to vacate the premises is due to circumstances beyond his control; usually an inevitable accident or act of God. In the leading case of

Herter v. Mullen, 159 N.Y. 28, 53 N.E. 700 (1899), the court held that the tenant could not be held to have "agreed" to a new one year term where the failure to vacate was due to the serious illness of a member of the family. Under such circumstances it is inequitable to imply, as a matter of law, that the tenant has agreed to a new tenancy.

D. Election to Treat the Holdover as Wrongful—Remedies of the Landlord

The landlord may elect to treat the holdover tenant as a trespasser and evict him. Eviction is usually pursuant to a summary process statute. There is a split of authority as to whether the landlord may use self-help to remove the tenant, and the form that self-help may take where permitted. (See "METHOD OF TERMINATION—Self-help," page 53.)

In addition to recovery of the premises, the landlord is also entitled to recover damages from the tenant. The damages are held to include the fair rental value of the property during the period of the wrongful holdover and any special damages, including costs incurred by the landlord in securing possession of the premises from the holdover tenant.

CHAPTER IV

POSSESSION AND USE OF THE DEMISED PREMISES

I. THE LANDLORD'S DUTY TO PUT THE TENANT IN POSSESSION

A landlord impliedly covenants that the tenant will have the legal right to possession of the premises at the beginning of the term. The authorities are divided with regard to the landlord's obligation to put the tenant in actual possession in the absence of an express covenant obligating the landlord to do so. The issue usually arises where a prior tenant holds over beyond the termination of his tenancy.

A. American Rule

The American rule provides that the landlord has no duty to put the tenant into actual possession of the premises. The landlord's duty is merely to give the tenant the superior legal right to possession; it is up to the tenant to assert his own legal rights. Hannan v. Dusch, 154 Va. 356, 153 S.E. 824 (1930). The rationale underlying the rule is that the landlord has not agreed to protect the tenant from the wrongful acts of third parties and, in the absence of an express agreement, one should not be held responsible for the wrongful acts of third parties. Once the tenant is given the legal right to possession, the landlord is deemed to have done all that he is required to do under the terms of an ordinary lease.

B. English Rule

Under the English rule, in the absence of a covenant to the contrary, there is an implied covenant on the part of the landlord that the premises will be open to entry by the tenant at the commencement of the term. Barfield v. Damon, 56 N.M. 515, 245 P.2d 1032 (1952). Several reasons are given for the rule. One is that the tenant would not enter into the lease if he thought he could not obtain possession on the appointed day, but rather would be compelled to institute a lawsuit. Thus, the rule more accurately reflects the probable intent of the parties. Futher, as between the landlord and the tenant, the landlord is generally regarded as in a better position to discover, at an earlier stage, facts which would indicate that the existing tenant is likely to wrongfully hold over against the interest of the incoming tenant, and thus, is both able to and induced to commence proceedings expeditiously against the wrongful holdover. Finally, the landlord is also better able to avoid or reduce the probability of such holdovers at the outset; for example, by requiring the prior tenant to deposit security for the performance of his duty to vacate the premises at the end of the term, or by specifying liquidated damages to be paid by the prior tenant in the event he holds over.

Some courts have stated that the duty arises as a part of the implied covenant of quiet enjoyment; but, since a landlord is usually not held liable for the independent acts of third parties under the covenant of quiet enjoyment, the better view is that the implied covenant to deliver possession is a separate implied covenant.

Although, as between the landlord and the incoming tenant, the burden of removing the prior tenant is imposed on the landlord, the holdover constitutes a wrong to the incoming tenant, and in some jurisdictions he may elect to proceed directly against the wrongful holdover.

In jurisdictions which imply a covenant to deliver possession, the duty to deliver possession does not extend beyond the day on which the tenant's term commences. If after that day a stranger wrongfully obtains and withholds possession from the tenant, the tenant's remedy is against the stranger and not against the landlord.

Under both the English and the American rules where the acts of the landlord prevent the tenant from taking possession, the landlord will be liable.

Where the landlord has a duty to put the tenant in possession and fails to do so, the tenant may bring an action for possession and/or damages. On occasion, a mandatory injunction against the landlord has been granted, although they are denied in most cases. Alternatively, the tenant may rescind the lease agreement. If the tenant's suit is for damages, the measure of damages is usually the excess of the market rental value of the leased property for the term over the rent reserved in the lease, plus any special damages incurred by the tenant. Special damages include prepaid rent, losses from the depreciation or resale of goods and supplies, business and family moving and storage expenses, lost profits (where reasonably ascertainable), and similar losses and expenditures.

II. FITNESS FOR USE

In general, the landlord does not impliedly covenant or warrant that the leased premises are tenantable, or that they are suitable for the purposes for which the premises are leased. The reason usually given is that the lease constitutes a conveyance of an estate in land subject to the doctrine of *caveat emptor*. Under the old agrarian economy where the doctrine of *caveat emptor* evolved the rule was reasonable. The land was the primary subject matter of the lease. Any dwellings included on the leased premises were incidental, and any defects in the structures were readily detectable and fairly easily repaired. The rule has been modified by statute in a substantial number of jurisdictions, and there are several notable judicial exceptions to the rule which are discussed below.

A. Change in Condition of Premises between the Time of Leasing and the Time of Possession

A tenant has the right to receive the leased premises in substantially the same condition they were in when the lease was executed. The landlord bears the risk of damage to the premises during the period between the date of execution of the lease and the day the tenant is entitled to possession. The principal reason for this exception is that prior to the date the tenant is entitled to possession, he is not in a position to prevent or correct any change in the condition of the premises. No matter what the cause of the change in condition, if the landlord fails to correct the defect the tenant may terminate the lease. Where the changed condition is the fault of the landlord, the tenant may also recover damages.

The allocation of risk rule in the landlord-tenant situation is contrary to the majority rule in ordinary vendor-purchaser situations. In the latter situations, the risk of loss arising from damage to the premises occurring between the execution of the purchase agreement and the transfer of title is placed on the purchaser on the theory that upon execution of the purchase agreement the purchaser becomes the equitable owner of the land.

B. "Public Use" Exception

When a landlord knowingly leases property for a purpose which involves the admission of the public, the weight of authority is that he will be liable to members of the public who suffer harm because of defects existing on the premises at the commencement of the lease. The theory of liability is negligence, and the landlord is liable only for defective conditions of which he has actual knowledge or could have discovered by the exercise of reasonable care. The duty extends beyond discovery and disclosure of the defect; it requires that the landlord correct the defective condition.

This enlargement of the landlord's duties is based in part upon the idea that the landlord, as well as the tenant, invited the public to come onto the premises. A better reason is grounded in the public policy that where the safety of the public is involved the landlord should not be allowed to shift complete responsibility to the tenant.

The landlord's liability is limited to members of the public who enter the premises for a reason related to the purpose for which the public was invited and suffer harm on that part of the premises open to the public. The landlord's liability usually does not extend to the tenant or his employees. Under the "public use" exception the landlord is not liable for defects arising after the beginning of the term, apparently on the theory that the landlord is not in control of the premises at the time these later defects arise.

C. Buildings Under Construction

If a tenant leases a building while it remains under construction and the tenant's use of the premises is restricted by the lease, there arises an implied covenant by the landlord that the building will be suitable for the restricted use. The reason for this exception is that since the building is under construction at the direction of the landlord, the tenant has no opportunity to inspect the building to determine or assure its suitability for the intended use. For example, if the tenant's intended use is the operation of a restaurant, there is an implied covenant that the building will comply with fire and building code provisions applicable to such uses.

D. Latent Defects

The landlord is under a duty to disclose to the tenant all latent defects existing on the property at the time of the leasing. Capitol Amusement Co. v. Anheuser-Busch, 94 Colo. 372, 30 P.2d 264 (1934). A latent defect is one existing at the time of the lease of which the landlord has knowledge, *and* of which the tenant has no knowledge and could not be expected to discover in the course of a reasonable inspection of the premises. Id. Some jurisdictions hold that the landlord must have actual knowledge; while others impose liability if the landlord knows of facts which would cause an ordinary reasonable man to suspect the existence of the defective condition. A few courts impose liability on the landlord for failure to disclose hidden defects if he "knew or should have known" of the defective condition. Implicit in the latter view is the obligation of the landlord to take reasonable steps to discover any hidden defects. Liability is imposed on the theory of negligence; or, alternatively, on the theory that nondisclosure of a defective condition of which the landlord has knowledge constitutes fraud.

One would assume that, ordinarily, defects discoverable by the landlord would also be discoverable by a reasonable inspection by the tenant, and therefore, the landlord would not be liable. However, the landlord's past experience with the property may give him knowledge of a defect which a reasonable inspection by the tenant would not disclose. For example, a prior tenant of the landlord may have told him of a roof leak which would not be apparent to one making an ordinary inspection of the premises.

The landlord's failure to disclose the hidden defects entitles the tenant to terminate the lease. Whether or not such an election is made, the tenant is entitled to recover damages arising from the landlord's failure to disclose. The landlord's failure to disclose also imposes tort liability upon him for injuries resulting from the defective condition of the premises. Smith v. Green, 358 Mass. 76, 260 N.E.2d 656 (1970). His liability extends to the tenant and all persons on the premises with the consent of the tenant. Since the landlord is under no duty to repair, mere disclosure of the defect to the tenant prior to injury relieves the landlord of tort liability to the tenant and to others on the premises with the consent of the tenant.

E. "Furnished House" Exception

A number of jurisdictions which ordinarily follow the rule of *caveat emptor* have held by way of exception that there is an implied warranty of habitability by the landlord in the case of a short-term lease of a furnished dwelling. The underlying reason for this exception is said to be that the parties to such a lease usually intend an immediate possession by the tenant without time for the tenant to inspect the premises to determine their suitability. A breach of the warranty entitles the tenant to rescind the agreement, to recover damages, and is a valid defense to an action for rent by the landlord.

The courts are divided on the question of whether the landlord is liable for personal injury and property damage arising from a breach of this implied warranty of habitability. The difference of opinion appears to be a result of the fact that the concept of warranty is a hybrid of tort and contract law, originally sounding in tort and later evolving primarily to contract theory. If the warranty is treated as contractual in nature, the landlord's liability is ordinarily limited to parties in privity of contract with him, i.e., the tenant. In such jurisdictions, the tenant's recovery of damages for personal injury or property damage appears to be grounded in the contract concept of consequential damages. Accordingly, the liability of the landlord is limited to damages which were foreseeable or within the contemplation of the parties at the time the lease was executed. As a further limitation, liability is usually imposed only for defects existing at the commencement of the lease of which the landlord had knowledge, or which could have been discovered by a reasonable inspection of the premises. If the "furnished house" exception is applicable, strict liability is imposed on the landlord.

Under contract law persons not party to the lease are not in privity of contract with the landlord and therefore, he is not liable to such third parties for breach of warranty. However, as a possessor of land, the tenant will be liable to third parties for injuries resulting from defects on the premises. If the damages paid by the tenant to the third party are foreseeable, that is, are within the ambit of consequential damages suffered by the tenant and recoverable from the landlord, then the landlord is indirectly liable to third parties for injuries to the person and property.

Although there is authority to the contrary, a few cases hold that injuries resulting from the landlord's breach of warranty give rise to a cause of action in tort. Although the rationale for this view is not clearly articulated, the decisions suggest that the implied warranty imposes a tort duty on the landlord, and that the duty extends to third parties rightfully on the demised premises.

F. Implied Warranty of Habitability in Residential Leases

A substantial number of recent cases have abandoned the doctrine of *caveat emptor* with respect to residential leases and adopted the principle that there is an implied warranty by the landlord that the leased premises are, or will be put, in a condition suitable for residential purposes. The underlying reason for the shift in attitude of the courts is recognition of the fact that the primary purpose of the modern residential lease is the provision of shelter. The reality of the modern residential lease is that the landlord sells the tenant a "package of goods and services." The fact that he conveys an estate in land is incidental to the modern residential tenant. Furthermore, with regard to heating, plumbing, electrical or structural defects, the ordinary residential tenant cannot be expected to have the knowledge, the capacity, or even the opportunity to make an adequate inspection and determine for himself the suitability of the premises for residential purposes. It is the landlord who has the expertise and opportunity to inspect and exercise real control over the premises; therefore, the landlord should have the burden of assuring the habitability of the premises. This view is also supported in §§ 5.1 and 5.5 of the Restatement, Second, Property (Landlord and Tenant). (See "Implied Warranty of Habitability", page 108.)

G. Illegal Use

As discussed above, there is authority for the position that where the tenant's use of the premises is expressly restricted to a particular purpose and the use for the particular purpose is illegal because of structural defects, the tenant may terminate or rescind the agreement. The reasoning of the courts is often framed in terms of failure of consideration or impossibility of lawful performance. Where the illegality involves "immoral" conduct, (e.g., gambling, prostitution, etc.), the lease is unenforceable. (See "Illegality and Frustration of Purpose", page 32.)

III. INTERFERENCE WITH THE TENANT'S POSSESSION AND USE OF THE PREMISES

A. Interference by the Landlord

The landlord may not interfere with the tenant's right to physical possession of the premises or interfere with the tenant's use and enjoyment of the premises. Where the tenant has been wrongfully ousted from the premises, he may recover possession by suit under the summary process statute or bring an action in ejectment. The tenant may also secure injunctive relief against the continued interference with his interests by the landlord, and may recover damages for breach of the landlord's covenant of quiet enjoyment. (See "Breach of Condition by Landlord—Covenant of Quiet Enjoyment", page 25.)

B. Interference by Third Parties

The prevailing rule is that the landlord is not liable for the unauthorized acts of third parties which interfere with the tenant's possession, use or enjoyment of the leased premises. The tenant must proceed directly against the wrongdoer. Of course, if the acts of interference of the third party are done at the direction of the landlord, the landlord will be liable. This latter view has been extended to cover instances where the landlord conveys his reversion with the knowledge that the purchaser intends to interfere with the tenant's leasehold interest.

There are several exceptions to the general rule which have received limited recognition.

1. Acts of Another Tenant

Often the interference will be caused by another tenant of the landlord. By the majority view, the landlord is not liable for the acts of his other tenants. This view is usually followed even though the acts of interference violate a covenant contained in all the leases; apparently on the rationale that the tenant has the capacity to protect his own interests (through the law of nuisance for example) and it is up to him to assert his rights. A small minority of cases has held that where the wrongful act is violative of a covenant contained in all of the leases, the failure of the landlord to take action to end the interference constitutes a breach of the landlord's covenant of quiet enjoyment. The underlying reasoning appears to be that the landlord is in a position to exercise control over the wrongdoer, and can more quickly and inexpensively stop the interference (e.g., by terminating the wrongdoer's lease).

Another exception to the rule has been recognized in some jurisdictions where the wrongful act is the lewd and immoral conduct of another tenant and the landlord has notice of such conduct. If the landlord allows the conduct to continue he will be held liable for breach of the covenant of quiet enjoyment. The exception is based upon public policy which disfavors such conduct. There are, however, a number of cases to the contrary.

2. *Criminal Acts of Third Parties*

Kline v. 1500 Mass. Ave. Apartment Corp., 141 U.S.App.D.C. 370, 439 F.2d 477 (1970), and several recent cases involving residential leases have held that the landlord has the duty to take reasonable steps to protect tenants from foreseeable criminal acts committed by third parties. Several theories have been espoused justifying the imposition of liability upon the landlord, including (i) an express or implied contractual duty; (ii) a duty to protect arising out of the nature of the landlord-tenant relationship, analogizing that relationship to the innkeeper-guest relationship; and (iii) a duty based upon the landlord's retention of control of the common areas.

Kline and its progeny emphasize several factors in deciding whether liability should be imposed on the landlord. The first factor is the degeneration of security arrangements subsequent to the letting. In *Kline,* the court's decision was significantly influenced by the fact that the security provided for the apartment complex had substantially degenerated between the time the tenant moved into the complex and the time she was assaulted in the hallway of her building. The court emphasized that the tenant had a reasonable and justified expectation that security measures taken by the landlord would not be reduced during the term. The court also held that a landlord has an implied obligation to take such protective measures as are within his reasonable capacity. The second factor is the causal connection between the defect and the criminal act. Thus, in Sherman v. Concourse Realty Corp., 47 A.D.2d 134, 365 N.Y.S.2d 239 (1975), a case involving a defective door lock, it was important that the tenant, attacked in a hallway just after entering the building, had actually closed the door after entering. The criminal then opened the door behind him and attacked the tenant. Third, the tenant must establish that the landlord was aware of the defect. In *Kline,* the landlord had actual notice of the dangerous conditions from the complaints registered with the landlord by the tenant. Where the dangerous condition is in a common area, the landlord may be held to have constructive notice of the condition arising out of his duty to inspect the common areas. Finally, the tenant must establish that the harm was foreseeable (e.g., that crimes of the same or similar character were a frequent occurrence in the area and the landlord knew or should have known of the situation).

The landlord is not an insurer of the tenant's safety. His duty is to take such protective steps as may be reasonably expected to lessen the risk of harm to the tenants. One test of the adequacy of the steps taken by the landlord is the standard of protection provided in apartments of a similar character in the community.

The recent cases are not unanimous; and there are recent decisions which follow the common law majority rule and reject the idea of imposing liability on the landlord for the wrongful acts of third parties. A number of rationales are put forth in support of majority rule including, among others, (i) the idea that the intentional criminal act of a third person is a superseding cause of harm to the tenant, (ii) the difficulty of determining the foreseeability of the criminal act, and (iii) judicial reluctance to modify traditional landlord-tenant concepts. A similar split of authority is found in recent cases involving commercial leases.

IV. THE EFFECT OF EMINENT DOMAIN (CONDEMNATION) PROCEEDINGS

A. Condemnation of the Entire Leasehold

In the absence of an agreement to the contrary, the overwhelming weight of authority is that where a condemnor takes a fee simple absolute in all the land covered by the lease, the lease terminates. The condemnor's acquisition of the leasehold and the reversion results in a merger which extinguishes the lease and the obligations of the parties thereunder.

It is universally recognized that the tenant is entitled to compensation for the interest in land taken from him. Virtually all jurisdictions have statutes governing the compensation to be paid in condemnation proceedings. Most of these statutes fall in one of three major categories: (i) statutes providing for a single ("lump sum") award equalling the value of the unencumbered fee; (ii) statutes which provide a separate award for the tenant, but limit the overall award to the value of the unencumbered fee; and (iii) statutes which provide that the compensation to be paid is the sum of the values of the separate interests, each interest being calculated separately. The result in "(iii)" of separately calculating the value of the interests of the landlord and tenant and awarding as compensation the sum of the two has also been reached judicially in a few jurisdictions.

In jurisdictions where the compensation to be awarded for the taking is the value of the unencumbered fee ("lump sum"), the amount awarded to the tenant is usually the net value of his leasehold interest. The net value of the leasehold interest is the present market value of the unexpired term less the rent reserved under the lease, which sum is reduced to present value. In addition, where the tenant is entitled to remove fixtures as against the landlord, the tenant is entitled to recover the value of any such fixtures taken by the condemnor.

B. Partial Condemnation

If only a portion of the leased land is taken, the weight of authority is that the lease is not terminated and the tenant remains liable for the payment of the full rent. An exception to this rule is recognized where the remaining portion of the premises is no longer susceptible to occupation for the purposes of the lease. Under such circumstances the tenant is permitted to terminate the lease.

Under the majority rule, there is no rent abatement following a partial taking. Instead, the tenant is awarded compensation in the sum of the full present market rental value of that portion of the leasehold premises which is taken. There is no deduction for unaccrued rent because the tenant remains liable for the full rent reserved under the lease. This rule has been criticized because it reduces the landlord's security for the payment of rent and imposes on the landlord the risk that the tenant will remain solvent and able to make the full rental payments throughout the unexpired balance of the term. Although in one sense the landlord has this risk in nearly all leases, the problem is more acute in this setting because the tenant is likely to expend the condemnation award and may later become insolvent. Under such circumstances, the landlord will not be able to collect the rent, and the land for which the award was substituted is no longer subject to repossession by the landlord.

The minority and better view is that there is a partial abatement of the rent when the lease continues after a partial condemnation. This view is also supported by § 8.1 of the Restatement, Second, Property (Landlord and Tenant). The landlord receives the full value of the premises taken less the net value of the leasehold interest of that portion of the premises taken, and thus, is not required to take the unsecured risk of the tenant's continued solvency. The tenant is compensated by the receipt of the net rental value of that portion of the leased premises taken by the condemnor, and, of course, there is a proportional abatement of the future rent.

Where all of the leased property is taken, but is taken for a period of time which is less than the unexpired term of the lease, the taking is treated as a partial taking and the lease does not terminate. The tenant remains liable under the lease, and is entitled to the condemnor's payment of compensation.

V. DUTY OF THE TENANT TO OCCUPY THE PREMISES

The weight of authority is that where the lease reserves a fixed amount of rent, there is no duty imposed upon the tenant to use or occupy the leased premises. Where the tenant's nonuser is responsible for the physical deterioration or destruction of the premises, the proper remedy for the landlord is an action for waste.

In leases where the rent payable is determined by production or a percentage of sales, the courts are generally willing to imply a covenant of use and reasonable effort. Such covenants are usually implied in oil and gas leases, and leases where the rental is based solely upon a percentage of sales. Where the lease provides for a percentage rental while also reserving a minimum rent, the authorities are split. Where the minimum rent approximates the fair rental value of the leased premises, a covenant of use and occupancy ordinarily will not be implied. Where the minimum rent is nominal, the percentage rent is deemed to be the primary compensation, and courts will imply a covenant of occupancy and use. For cases in between, a good rule of thumb is the higher the minimum rent, in relation to the anticipated total rent, the lower the likelihood a covenant of use and occupancy will be implied.

The landlord's remedies for breach of the covenant to occupy and use the leased premises are termination of the lease and damages. A few courts have granted specific performance or injunctive relief to the landlord. With regard to percentage leases, the amounts previously paid as rent will be used as a measure of damages. Where there is little or no rental history, proof of actual damages may be difficult or impossible. Under such circumstances, there is authority for the view that the landlord may use the fair rental value of the premises as a measure of damages.

CHAPTER V

REPAIRS AND IMPROVEMENTS

I. INTRODUCTION

This chapter will discuss the allocation of the duty to repair, express and implied, and tort liability for personal injury and property damage arising from defects existing on the leased property. The general rule under common law is that the landlord has no duty to repair the demised premises. The tenant's duty to repair is limited to making such repairs as are necessary to protect the leased premises from the elements. There are numerous exceptions to these general rules, and the parties may contractually modify their common law obligations to repair.

Personal injury and property damage often occur as a result of defects existing on the leased premises. When such injury or damage occurs it is important to remember that tort liability is generally said to be founded on possession and control of the premises and therefore, does not necessarily follow the duty to repair. As might be expected there are a number of exceptions to this rule, and the trend is to impose liability on the party with the duty to repair. Depending upon the rule followed, and the facts of the case, there are four possibilities with respect to tort liability: (i) the landlord is liable, (ii) the tenant is liable, (iii) the landlord and tenant are liable, or (iv) neither the landlord nor the tenant is liable.

II. THE DUTY TO REPAIR IN THE ABSENCE OF AN EXPRESS COVENANT TO REPAIR

Absent a contractual agreement between the parties, the general rule is that the landlord has no duty under common law to repair defects in the demised premises. The traditional rationale for the rule is founded upon the concept that the demised premises pass into the exclusive possession of the tenant. This right to exclusive possession extinguishes the right of the landlord to enter the premises, and therefore, his control over the premises. This lack of access and control consequently relieves him from the obligation to repair.

Tort liability is founded upon possession and control of the premises. Since the landlord is not in possession or control of the demised premises, he will not be liable for injuries suffered by the tenant or his invitees arising out of conditions which develop after possession has been transferred to the tenant. Further, since the doctrine of *caveat emptor* applies to tenants, as a general rule no liability is imposed upon the landlord to the tenant or his invitees for injuries arising out of defective conditions existing at the time of the lease.

There are several well-settled exceptions to the
rule that a landlord has no duty to repair. Where
a landlord leases different parts of a multi-unit
building to several tenants, the landlord has a duty
to maintain in a condition of good repair the common areas such as stairs, halls, walks, parking lots,
porches, balconies, and other similar areas over
which the landlord is deemed to have retained
control. Similarly, where latent defects exist on
the property at the time of leasing, or there is a
change in the condition of the premises between
the time the lease was executed and the time the
tenant was entitled to possession, or where property is leased for a purpose which involves the admission of the public, or the lease is a short-term lease
of a furnished dwelling, the landlord is obligated to
repair any defects existing at the commencement
of the term. (See "Fitness for Use," page 67.) The
rule has also been modified by statutes imposing a
duty to repair on the landlord in many jurisdictions; and in a significant number of recent cases
the courts have reassessed the "no duty to repair"
rule as it applies to residential leases, found it
wanting, and imposed a duty to repair on the
landlord under the doctrine of implied warranty of
habitability.

Under the common law majority view, when a
landlord defaults in his duty to repair (created by
express agreement or arising under one of the
exceptions noted above), the tenant's remedy is to
sue for damages. Because of the common law

theory of independence of covenants, termination
of the lease is usually not permitted. If, however,
the breach of duty is so severe as to constitute a
breach of the covenant of quiet enjoyment, the
tenant is also permitted to terminate the lease on
the theory that the landlord's conduct has constructively evicted the tenant. (See "Constructive
Eviction", page 26.)

Under the more recent residential lease cases,
if the landlord's default constitutes a breach of the
implied warranty of habitability, most courts
adopting the doctrine hold that in addition to the
aforementioned remedies, the tenant is also entitled to all of the usual contract remedies, including
rescission and specific performance. In addition,
the tenant has been granted rent abatement, and
has been permitted to withhold rent or, alternatively, to make the necessary repairs and deduct
the costs thereof from the rent due the landlord.
(See "Implied Warranty of Habitability—Remedies
of the Tenant", page 126.)

The tenant, as the party in possession and
control of the premises, has a duty not to commit
waste; i.e., he is under a duty to exercise reasonable care to protect the premises from the elements.
In fulfillment of his obligation the tenant is required to make minor repairs to the leased premises. However, the tenant's duty to repair does not
extend to repairs required by the destruction of the
premises, in whole or in part, by fire or other
casualty; nor is the tenant required to make re-

pairs necessitated by deterioration due to age or ordinary wear and tear except such repairs as may be necessary to avoid liability for waste.

The tenant's duty to repair, reasonable in the agrarian economy in which it arose, is inconsistent with the common practice in the modern urban residential landlord-tenant relationship. In the latter case the tenant, as a matter of ordinary practice, is not expected to make repairs. Further, with respect to residential leases, the legislative and judicial trend is to impose a duty to repair on the landlord. In the commercial setting, the common law relating to the duty to repair in the absence of a covenant remains substantially unchanged.

Where the tenant has the duty to repair and defaults in the performance of his duty, the landlord's remedy is to sue for damages. Again, the independent covenants doctrine precludes termination of the lease. However, most leases contain a right of entry (power of termination) clause which permits the landlord to reenter the premises and terminate the lease upon breach of any covenant by the tenant.

A. Duty of the Landlord to Repair the Common Areas

It is well settled in most jurisdictions that the landlord has a duty to maintain, repair and keep reasonably safe the common areas of a multi-unit building. Primus v. Bellevue Apartments, 241 Io-

wa 1055, 44 N.W.2d 347 (1950). The rule is founded on the theory that those portions of the premises used in common by the tenants do not
constitute a part of the premises demised to the
tenant, but rather remain in the possession and
control of the landlord. The landlord is treated in
a manner similar to that of a possessor who allows
visitors to enter for a purpose of his own. Thus,
the duty of the landlord extends to all persons
entering the premises pursuant to the normal and
expected use of the leased premises by the tenant.
The duty extends to the tenant, members of his
family, his employees, guests and invitees. To
avoid liability arising from injuries caused by defects of which the landlord has actual or constructive notice, the landlord must give a warning sufficient to enable avoidance of the risk of harm, or
repair the defect within a reasonable period of
time. The landlord is not an insurer, however;
thus, the standard of care imposed upon him is
only one of reasonable care.

1. *Common Areas Defined*

In general, entryways, hallways, passageways,
lobbies, stairs, elevators, approaches, yards, base-
ments, porches and all other portions of the premises maintained for the benefit of and use by the
tenants, or necessary for the tenants' reasonable
use of the demised premises, are deemed to be
areas over which the landlord retains control and
furnishes for the common use of the tenants. In
most jurisdictions there exists a rebuttable pre-

sumption that the landlord retains control over all areas of the premises which are not included in the individual leases and which are used in common by the different tenants. Primus v. Bellevue Apartments, supra. In many instances, the areas over which the landlord retains control are specifically set forth in the lease agreement, or collateral agreements between the landlord and tenant.

Often, the lease will not define the areas over which the landlord retains control and the question of control may become the central issue. Many close questions arise as to whether a particular area is part of the demised premises or part of the area over which the landlord has retained or reserved control. Where the lease agreement is silent, ambiguous or uncertain in defining the areas of the landlord's retained control, the question of control is one of fact. The manner in which the area in question has been used by the tenants is given great weight in determining whether the landlord has retained control over the area. Id.

The obligation of the landlord does not extend to portions of the premises which the tenant or his invitees are not reasonably expected to frequent, i.e., areas not deemed to be common areas; nor will the landlord be held liable for injuries arising out of an improper or unauthorized use of the premises by the tenant or his invitees.

2. *Landlord's Notice of Defect*

It is clear that the landlord will be liable for injuries arising out of his affirmative acts of negligence in the common areas. In the absence of an affirmative act of negligence on the part of the landlord, the landlord will be liable for injuries arising out of defects in the common areas only where he has actual notice of the defect, or by the exercise of reasonable care could have discovered the defective condition causing the injury.

The landlord's actual notice of the dangerous condition may be determined by the reasonable implications of the surrounding circumstances. For example, where a tenant notified the landlord that a portion of the porch was broken and in need of repair, the landlord was held to have notice of the defective condition of the entire porch, and therefore, was liable for injuries suffered when the tenant broke through the floor of another portion of the porch. Actual notice received by the landlord's agent is generally deemed to be adequate actual notice to the landlord.

In the absence of actual notice on the part of the landlord, the landlord may be held liable on the basis of constructive notice of the dangerous condition. The effect of the constructive notice rule is to impute to the landlord notice of the dangerous condition when the lack of actual notice is due to the landlord's own negligence in not discovering the condition. Peters Motors v. Poyner, 243 S.W.2d 893 (Ky.1951). In most cases, proof of the landlord's actual notice is not clear; therefore, the landlord's liability must rest on his constructive notice of the dangerous condition. Implicit in the constructive notice rule is the duty of the landlord to undertake reasonable inspections of the premises at reasonable intervals.

The duration and nature of the defect are important factors in determining the knowledge to be imputed to the landlord. In most instances the plaintiff will attempt to establish constructive notice by showing that the defect was obvious, and had existed for such a length of time that the landlord in the exercise of reasonable care should have discovered the dangerous condition and corrected it. This knowledge on the part of the landlord, coupled with the landlord's failure to repair within a reasonable period of time, will cause liability for injuries arising out of the dangerous condition to be imposed upon the landlord. Where the dangerous condition arises only a short period of time prior to the injury, the landlord has been held to be unable by the exercise of reasonable care to discover the dangerous condition.

Other factors are also considered in determining the knowledge to be imputed to the landlord; for example, it has been held that the natural tendency of wood to decay must be taken into account in determining whether knowledge of a defective railing will be imputed to the landlord.

3. Conduct of the Landlord After Notice of the Dangerous Condition

After the landlord has discovered the defect, the landlord will be given a reasonable period of time in which to correct the dangerous condition. Again, it should be noted that the landlord is not an insurer of safety, but rather is required only to exercise reasonable care in making the premises reasonably safe. Thus, in a few cases the landlord has been found to have actual knowledge of the condition causing the injury, but liability was not imposed because the landlord had no reason to believe the condition was unreasonably dangerous, or because the landlord had taken measures to make the condition reasonably safe.

4. Tenant's Notice of Defect

Where the plaintiff is someone other than the tenant, the tenant's notice of the defect will not relieve the landlord of liability. However, the tenant will also be subjected to liability when the plaintiff enters the premises with the consent of the tenant, and the tenant fails to warn the plaintiff of the dangerous condition.

5. Assumption of Risk—Contributory Negligence

The plaintiff's knowledge of the defective condition does not derogate from the landlord's obligation to maintain the retained areas in a safe condition. However, the plaintiff's conduct in light of such knowledge may subject him to the defenses of assumption of risk or contributory negligence. (See "Defenses of the Landlord", page 149.)

B. Areas Retained under the Landlord's Exclusive Control but Necessary to the Use of the Leased Premises

In addition to the landlord's duty to maintain the common areas in a safe condition, the landlord is also under a duty to maintain in a safe condition those portions of the premises retained under his exclusive control but necessary to the tenant's reasonable use and enjoyment of the leased premises. This rule generally applies to heating, plumbing and electrical systems, walls, foundations, roofs, and other areas essential to the use and enjoyment of the leased premises. The landlord's duty rests upon his control of these areas and the responsibility attending the possession of land generally. The landlord is not an insurer however, and his duty is limited to the exercise of due care in maintaining the retained premises in a safe condition. In the absence of the exercise of reasonable care, the landlord will be liable for any injuries arising out of dangerous conditions existing in the retained areas of which the landlord has actual or constructive knowledge.

The landlord's liability extends to the tenant, and all those on the leased premises with the consent of the tenant. The landlord's liability does not extend to personal injuries or property damage which occur on portions of the premises which the tenant and his invitees are not reasonably expected to frequent. For example, a tenant would not be expected to frequent other vacant apartments in a multi-unit apartment building, or a separate furnace room housing a central heating plant, and the landlord will not be liable for injuries occurring because of the tenant's unexpected presence in those locations.

1. Landlord's Notice of Defect

As is true with the landlord's liability for defects in the common areas, the landlord must have notice of the defect before liability will be imposed. The landlord is deemed to have actual notice of all defects of which he has actual knowledge, and constructive notice of all defects which he would have discovered by the exercise of reasonable care.

The landlord's actual knowledge can be imputed from his conduct; and the knowledge of a landlord's agent will be imputed to the landlord.

Absent actual notice on the part of the landlord, the landlord may be held liable on the basis of constructive notice of the defective condition. The effect of this rule is to impute to the landlord notice of the defect when the lack of actual notice is due to the landlord's own negligence in not discovering the dangerous condition. Again, implicit in the idea of constructive notice is the imposition on the landlord of an obligation to make reasonable inspections of the retained areas at reasonable intervals.

2. Conduct of the Landlord After Notice of the Dangerous Condition

After the landlord has discovered the dangerous condition, he will be given a reasonable period of time in which to effect the necessary repairs. The duty imposed on the landlord is the exercise of reasonable care to make the premises safe. Whether the landlord has exercised reasonable care in effecting the repairs in a timely manner is a matter of fact.

3. Assumption of Risk—Contributory Negligence

The plaintiff's knowledge of the defect does not derogate from the landlord's duty to maintain the retained premises in a safe condition. However, the plaintiff's conduct may subject him to the defenses of assumption of risk or contributory negligence. (See "Defenses of the Landlord", page 149.)

C. Repairs, Alterations and Improvements Required by Government Regulations

Often major, so-called "structural" repairs, alterations or improvements (e.g., widening stairs, rebuilding walls, installation of fire hoses and sprinkler systems, etc.) must be undertaken to bring the leased premises into compliance with local health and safety laws. Such structural changes are usually beyond the tenant's common law duty to repair and therefore, the tenant is under no duty to make such structural changes.

Gaddis v. Consolidated Freightways, Inc., 239 Ore. 553, 398 P.2d 749 (1965).

Where the tenant has covenanted to repair, the allocation of the costs of compliance will be determined by the nature of the required alteration or improvement and the reason the change is required. Where the change is required because of the particular use which the tenant is making of the premises, the tenant will ordinarily be required to bear the costs of the alteration or improvement. If the required repair is one which the tenant would ordinarily be required to make pursuant to his covenant to repair, the tenant will be required to bear the costs of such repair. Where the alteration or improvement is not one required by the tenant's particular use of the premises, nor one required to be made by the tenant under his covenant to repair, the burden of complying with the statutes and regulations will usually fall upon the landlord. Id.

The tenant may expressly covenant to make such repairs, alterations and improvements as may be required by government authority; however, where the lease provision is ambiguous with respect to the extent of the tenant's duty, the lease provision will be construed strictly in the favor of the tenant. The reason for preferring the tenant in such situations is that the structural changes are relatively permanent in nature and usually inure primarily to the benefit of the landlord. To force the tenant to bear the costs of the change would be to impose an unfair burden on him. The specific language of the lease provision may vary the results reached by the courts. Thus, an agreement by the tenant to comply with all laws relating to the maintenance and use of the property has been held not to impose upon the tenant the duty of making structural changes. A contrary position has been taken where the tenant agreed to comply with all laws and orders at his own expense and save the landlord harmless, or to make all improvements ordered by governmental authorities.

As might be expected, the results in different cases vary with the length of the balance of the term of the lease. Where the tenant holds possession under a long-term lease with a substantial amount of the term remaining, the courts appear to be more willing to impose the costs of structural changes on the tenant, apparently on the ground that the benefits from the changes will inure primarily to the tenant. Gaddis, supra.

· Absent an express agreement, the landlord has no duty to the tenant to make structural changes required by governmental authority. Where the tenant has no duty, the landlord also has no duty, and the structures are ordered vacated for noncompliance, the tenant's remedy is to consider the lease terminated. The tenant is not entitled to damages however, and if the tenant elects to make the alterations and improvements he cannot recover the costs thereof from the landlord.

D. Statutory Duty to Repair

The Industrial Revolution converted an essentially rural, agrarian society into the predominantly urban society we know today. The social and economic forces of this revolution coupled with the common law view of the lease as a conveyance of real property to which the doctrine of *caveat emptor* applied (and the covenants of which were generally deemed to be independent) produced a substantial number of large urban areas in which both the working and nonworking poor were housed in unsafe and unsanitary tenement houses. These tenants were without the economic leverage needed to improve their living conditions; and, except for a few cases in the very recent past, the courts demonstrated little willingness to modify these common law rules to give relief to the tenants. Thus, the burden of taking remedial action fell upon the various state and local governing bodies.

The somewhat narrow legislative response was to focus attention on the doctrine of *caveat emptor* by enacting housing codes which imposed upon the landlord a statutory duty to repair, with criminal or civil penalties for failure to repair. The universal *modus operandi* was for the state legislature to enact enabling legislation which allowed municipalities to enact a local housing code. Initially, it was common for housing codes to cover only multiple-unit buildings housing three or more families.

Today, however, many housing codes cover all residential dwellings.

The Federal Housing Act of 1954, as amended, (42 U.S.C.A. § 1451) requires all municipal recipients of urban renewal funds to have a "workable program . . . to eliminate and prevent the development or spread of slums and urban blight." One prerequisite for an acceptable "workable program" (initially administrative and now required by statute) is the enactment of a local housing code. As a result, over 5,000 communities have enacted housing codes.

Although the housing codes represent a step in the right direction, most of the codes have been criticized for setting standards which are too low to assure safe and sanitary housing for low income tenants. Additional criticism has been expressed because of the lack of uniformity (and thus the lack of a uniform standard of minimum habitability) among the various local housing codes.

1. *Criminal Sanctions*

Initially, the purposes of the housing codes were to be achieved through enforcement by public officials, and the imposition of criminal sanctions for code violations. The tenant was given no direct action against the landlord. Knowledge of a housing code violation was acquired through routine inspections of the structures or, more likely, from complaints made by tenants. Normal procedure then required the public official, usually a housing

inspector, to notify the landlord of the code violation.   If the violation was not remedied within a
reasonable period of time, additional acts, administrative and then judicial, were taken to compel
compliance.

Although the various housing codes provide for
jail sentences of up to 30 days and maximum fines
up to $500, enforcement of housing codes by way of
criminal sanction has proved to be an almost total
failure.   This failure is generally attributed to un-
derstaffing of the enforcement agencies, prolonged
delays at the judicial level, and the reluctance of
the courts to impose stiff penalties on landlords
found guilty of violating the housing codes.

2.   *Civil Sanctions*

The failure of criminal sanctions as a means of
obtaining compliance with local housing codes motivated the various state legislatures to authorize
the imposition of civil sanctions.   The reasoning
underlying the civil sanction is that it would impose economic costs for noncompliance on the landlord which would be greater than the costs of
complying with the housing code.   Although the
statutes vary, most civil statutes authorize one or
more of the following sanctions: (i) mandatory
injunctions requiring compliance with the housing
code, (ii) appointment of a receiver to collect the
rents and use them to make the necessary repairs,
(iii) cumulative civil fines, (iv) permit the necessary
repairs to be made by the government agency and
assess the costs of repair to the landlord, such costs

to be secured by a lien on the property, and (v) order the premises vacated until the necessary repairs have been made.

As is true with criminal sanctions, enforcement authority resides with public officials and as might be expected the enforcement agencies have not employed civil sanctions any more effectively than the criminal sanctions, and for the same general reasons. (See "Criminal Sanctions," above.)

3.   *Statutory Civil Sanctions Enforced by the Tenant*

The public agencies' ineffectiveness in enforcing housing codes through the imposition of criminal and or civil sanctions necessitated the creation of a method whereby tenants are enabled to enforce the provisions of a housing code. As a consequence, several states have enacted what may reasonably be referred to as "rent impairment" legislation. The statutes permit the tenant to take one or more of the following courses of action: (i) where, after notice, the landlord fails to make the requested necessary repairs within a reasonable period of time, the tenant may make the repairs and deduct the costs of the repairs from the rent; (ii) where the landlord fails to make the necessary repairs after receiving a notice of violation from a code enforcement agency, the tenant may withhold further rental payments; or (iii) where the landlord has received notice of a code violation from a code enforcement agency and has failed for a substantial period of time (e.g., 6 months) to make the necessary repairs, the rent will be suspended.

Although rent impairment legislation represents a significant step in the protection of residential tenants, each of the above remedies has its drawbacks. Most repair and deduct statutes limit the amount of repairs that a tenant can make; the limitation is usually to repairs the costs of which do not exceed one month's rent. The usual rent withholding statute has the disadvantage of requiring prior action by the various code enforcement agencies, agencies which have already proved their ineffectiveness. In addition, since the landlord will ultimately receive all of the rent withheld, there is less incentive for the landlord to make prompt repairs. The effectiveness of what is possibly the strongest sanction in the hands of the tenant, rent suspension, is reduced by the long period of time (often 6 months) which the tenant must wait before payment of rent is suspended. These disadvantages notwithstanding, one substantial benefit is afforded the tenant under rent impairment legislation: it allows the tenant to remain in possession while exerting economic pressure on the landlord to maintain the premises in a state of good repair.

4.   *Tort Liability Arising Out of the Statutory Duty to Repair*

a. Criminal Statutes. The criminal statutes discussed above shifted the obligation for maintenance of the demised premises from the tenant to the landlord without regard to the issue of which of them had control; but none of these statutes expressly created a cause of action for personal injury resulting from a violation of statute. However, once the legislatures imposed a statutory duty to repair, most courts were willing to take the next step and impose liability on the landlord for personal injuries and property damage arising out of his failure to repair. In Altz v. Leiberson, 233 N.Y. 16, 134 N.E. 703 (1922), the landlord was held liable for injuries suffered by a tenant when the tenant was injured by a ceiling which fell after the landlord had been notified of the defect and a reasonable period of time in which to effect the needed repairs had elapsed. In response to the landlord's claim that he was not liable because a landlord owed no common law duty to keep premises under the control of the tenant in good repair, the court said:

> "The legislature must have known that unless repairs in the rooms of the poor were made by the landlord, they would not be made by anyone. The duty imposed became commensurate with the need. The right to seek redress is not limited to the city or its officers. The right extends to all whom there was a purpose to protect." 134 N.E. at 704.

Most courts which have spoken to the issue have followed the lead of *Altz*.

A minority of jurisdictions refuses to impose liability on the landlord for injuries arising out of the landlord's failure to comply with a criminal housing code. A few courts reason that it is contrary to the legislative intent to construe a penal statute as giving rise to civil causes of action (in the absence of express statutory language creating such causes of action) where no such cause of action existed at common law or, that there was no legislative intent to abolish the common law rule of *caveat emptor* as it applies to tenants. Most courts following the minority view do so under the traditional theory that liability follows control, and, since the tenant is in possession and control of the premises, liability for injury to person or property will not be imposed on the landlord regardless of who has the duty to repair.

In jurisdictions following the majority view, the nature of the statute may be determinative of whether liability will be imposed on the landlord. In most jurisdictions, the landlord's liability may be founded upon a statute imposing a general duty to maintain the premises in good repair. In a few jurisdictions, liability will be imposed only where the landlord has been found to have violated a statute creating a specific duty of care. For example, in one jurisdiction there is authority for the position that violation of a specific regulation governing the installation of handrails may give rise to tort liability, standing side by side with another decision absolving a landlord from tort liability for violation of a general regulation requiring maintenance of the premises in good repair. In a few cases the courts have made a distinction between

statutes imposing a general duty of repair on the
landlord and so-called "safeplace" statutes; liability being imposed only under the latter statutes.
For example, one jurisdiction has held that liability may be imposed for violation of a statute requiring two escape exits from a work area, while also
holding that liability will not be imposed upon a
landlord for violation of a general statutory duty to
repair.

In the *Altz* case, the court stated that before a
cause of action will arise the landlord must have
actual or constructive notice of the defect. Virtually all courts have followed this rule. However,
when the housing code violation appears in the
interior of the demised premises which are under
the control of the tenant, the courts may find
themselves in somewhat of a dilemma in dealing
with the question of constructive notice. Where
the landlord reserves a right to enter, inspect and
repair the demised premises, and in fact has had
ample opportunity to discover and repair the defect, a few jurisdictions have held that the landlord
has constructive notice of the defect. In the absence of such a lease provision, the landlord's duty
to inspect is an open question. The only recorded
case to deal directly with the issue is Benjamin v.
Kimble, 43 Misc.2d 497, 251 N.Y.S.2d 708 (Sup.Ct.
1964). The court held that the statutory duty to
maintain the premises in good repair imposed upon
the landlord a duty to inspect the premises to
determine whether he is in conformance and com-

pliance with the law. The duty is limited to inspections at reasonable intervals. In *Benjamin,*
the landlord had owned the premises for a period
of three months. The complaint was dismissed,
the court holding that three months was not a
reasonable interval such as to impute constructive
knowledge of the defect to the landlord.

b. Civil Statutes. One form of civil statute
simply imposes civil sanctions for violation of criminal housing codes. It would seem that tort liability for injuries arising out of violation of such
statutes should follow the rules adopted by the
various jurisdictions for violation of criminal housing codes.

A second form of civil housing statute is repair
and deduct legislation. Such statutes impose a
duty to repair on the landlord (often a broader
duty than that imposed by the usual housing code),
and by analogy to tort cases arising out of violation
of criminal housing codes it might be expected that
a majority of courts would impose liability upon a
landlord for personal injury or property damage
arising out of the landlord's violation of a repair
and deduct statute. Such has not been the case.
In the leading case of Gately v. Campbell, 124 Cal.
520, 57 P. 567 (1899), a tenant sued the landlord in
tort under the California repair and deduct statute.
In denying the tenant relief the California Supreme Court held that "the only consequence of a
breach of the landlord's obligation is that the tenant may either vacate the premises or expend one

month's rent for repairs."   124 Cal. at 523, 57 P. at 568.

The narrow view taken by the California Supreme Court has been uniformly followed by other jurisdictions which have decided the question. This view has been taken even in jurisdictions (including California) which allow a plaintiff to bring a tort action for damages resulting from the landlord's violation of a criminal housing code. It is submitted that the better view is found in those cases allowing tort actions for violation of housing codes, and there is little reason to distinguish between criminal housing codes and repair and deduct statutes. To the contrary, it may be reasonably argued that repair and deduct statutes are a manifestation of legislative policy in favor of private, noncriminal enforcement of housing codes.

E. Implied Warranty of Habitability

1. *History and Development*

With the exception of a very early period in the development of the law of landlord and tenant (when the rights arising under a lease were characterized as contract rights), at common law, the rights of the landlord and tenant under a real estate lease developed in the field of real property law. A lease was considered a conveyance of an interest in land subject to the doctrine of *caveat emptor*. The landlord had no obligation to put the leased premises in a habitable condition prior to the commencement of the term, and no duty to

repair the premises if they later came into disrepair. These early common law concepts of the real
estate lease were probably well-suited to the agrarian economy in which they arose. At that time the
primary value of a lease was the land itself.
Dwellings which may have been included in the
leasehold were of secondary importance, of relatively simple construction, and readily repairable
by the typical farmer of that time.

A second significant factor in the development
of the common law of landlord and tenant is that
the fundamental concepts of the landlord-tenant
area of property law were established well before
the development of the concept of mutually dependent covenants in contract law. Thus, even if the
landlord expressly agreed to repair, the tenant's
covenant to pay rent was deemed to be independent of the covenant made by the landlord. Therefore, the landlord's breach of covenant did not
justify the tenant's nonpayment of rent. The tenant's remedy was an action for damages.

Recently, an increasing number of courts have
begun to reexamine the established common law
rules as they apply to residential tenancies in light
of modern conditions. The majority of courts
which have reconsidered the traditional common
law doctrines have found such doctrines wanting
and, accordingly, have made several major changes
in the common law of landlord and tenant. First,
the traditional common law rule holding that the
landlord has no duty to assure that the premises

are habitable at the inception of the lease or to maintain the leased premises in a habitable condition during the term of the lease was found to be obsolete, and an implied warranty of habitability imposing a duty to repair on the landlord has been adopted by these courts. Second, the courts have begun to emphasize the contractual aspects of the lease, rather than its characterization as a conveyance of an interest in property. As a result, courts adopting the implied warranty of habitability have also held that performance of the tenant's covenant to pay rent is dependent upon the landlord's performance of the implied covenant to repair and maintain the premises in a habitable condition.

Although most courts which have addressed the issue have adopted the implied warranty of habitability, several courts have refused to do so. In Posnanski v. Hood, 46 Wis.2d 172, 174 N.W.2d 528 (1970), the court implicitly found that the public policy arguments in favor of the implied warranty of habitability were not sufficiently compelling to justify abolishing the common law rule of *caveat emptor;* and then went on to hold that there was no legislative intent that the local housing code abrogate or modify the common law landlord-tenant relationship so as to create a contractual duty on the landlord to comply with the housing code. In Blackwell v. Del Bosco, 191 Colo. 344, 558 P.2d 563 (1976), the Colorado Supreme Court expressed the view that however desirable the adoption of the implied warranty of habitability might be, the implied warranty theory involves so many social and economic complexities that the issue of its adoption should be resolved by the state legislature—a body the court believed was more capable of resolving such complexities. In addition to the above jurisdictions, courts in Alabama, Florida, Idaho and Kentucky have refused to adopt the implied warranty of habitability. These jurisdictions represent the minority view with respect to jurisdictions which have considered the doctrine of implied warranty of habitability. The clear trend is toward adoption of the implied warranty of habitability.

Courts adopting the implied warranty of habitability have been influenced by a number of factors. The factual assumptions underlying traditional landlord-tenant law have, in large part, ceased to exist. The great majority of today's leases are for urban dwelling units and the tenant is no longer principally interested in the land itself. The expectations of today's residential tenant are well stated in the leading case of Javins v. First Nat. Realty Corp., 138 U.S.App.D.C. 369, 428 F.2d 1071 (1970):

> "When American city dwellers, both rich and poor, seek 'shelter' today, they seek a well-known package of goods and services—a package which includes not merely walls and ceilings, but also adequate heat, light and ventilation, serviceable plumbing facilities, secure windows and doors, proper sanitation and proper maintenance." 428 F.2d at 1074.

Further, because of the complexity of the modern dwelling, particularly apartment buildings, most tenants do not have the skill and expertise necessary to inspect the premises for major problems such as heating, plumbing, electrical or structural defects to see if the premises are reasonably fit for habitation; nor to repair such defects if they should arise during the term. In most instances, the tenants must rely upon the skill and expertise of the landlord. When the lease is viewed as the sale of a "package of goods and services", the tenant may reasonably expect the landlord to maintain the apartment in a habitable condition for the duration of the term of the lease. It is these expectations that the implied warranty of habitability recognizes and gives legal protection.

Several additional factors have influenced the courts which have adopted the implied warranty of habitability. Judicial dissatisfaction with the common law doctrine of *caveat emptor* has been manifested by the "furnished house", latent defect, and other exceptions to the common law rule that the landlord has no duty to repair the leased premises. The widespread enactment of housing codes is evidence of legislative dissatisfaction with *caveat emptor,* although the more recent explosion in the enactment of local housing codes may be more accurately described as a response to the federal government's carrot and stick approach to urban renewal under the Housing Act of 1954, as amended, 42 U.S.C.A. § 1451. The rapid rise in population generally, and urban population in particular, has produced a severe shortage of low-cost housing, particularly in urban areas, and created a substantial disparity in bargaining power between landlord and tenant. Racial and class discrimination in housing and the use of standard form leases (which have become contracts of adhesion), coupled with the shortage of rental housing, have eliminated competition in the rental housing market and placed most tenants in a "take it or leave it" position with respect to their ability to bargain with the landlord for express covenants of repair or habitability. Further, having characterized the lease as a "package of goods and services", several courts have gone on to hold that products liability principles should be applied to the landlord-tenant relationship. The landlord, like the commercial businessman, has a better opportunity and greater capacity to inspect and maintain the premises; and today's urban tenant, like consumers of other goods, relies on the implied representation of the landlord that the premises are and will remain habitable for the duration of the term. Each of these factors has to some degree influenced the courts which have adopted the implied warranty of habitability.

A substantial number of courts have held that the existence of a local housing code requires that a warranty of habitability be implied in leases of all dwellings covered by the code. The theory is that the relevant portions of the housing code are impliedly incorporated into and become a part of the lease agreement, thus creating private rights in the tenant. As stated by the court in Javins, ". . . by signing the lease the landlord has undertaken a continuing obligation to the tenant to maintain the premises in accordance with all applicable law." 428 F.2d at 1081. The reasons given for the implied incorporation of the statutory provisions vary. Some courts read statutory provisions into a contract for the purpose of providing a remedy for one party for damages caused by a second party's illegal conduct. Although there may be little factual support for their position, some courts read statutory provisions into contracts on the rationale that the essence of the statutory provisions would have been included in the contract by the parties had they not thought that it was unnecessary to include such provisions because of the existence of the statute. Other courts simply state that the common law doctrine that the landlord has no duty to repair is totally inconsistent with the legislative policy established by the housing code.

Finally, it is important to distinguish between those cases which have founded implied warranty of habitability upon the public policy considerations described above and those which have based it upon housing codes, because the underlying foundation of the warranty may affect the scope of the warranty and the standard of habitability to be applied in a particular case.

2. *Procedure for Raising Implied Warranty of Habitability*

Breach of the implied warranty of habitability may be the basis of an affirmative cause of action for damages and other contractual remedies by the tenant. Procedurally, however, breach of the implied warranty most often arises as an affirmative defense by the tenant to a summary possession action brought by the landlord. The following is a summary of a common scenario. First, the tenant notifies the landlord of the defective conditions. If the landlord fails to correct the defects within a reasonable period of time, the tenant stops paying rent until the repairs are made, at which time the duty to pay the contract rent resumes. (See "Rent Abatement and Withholding", page 131.) If the landlord brings an action to evict the tenant for nonpayment of rent, the tenant will raise the defense of breach of the implied warranty of habitability. During the pendency of the action and upon application by the landlord, the court may enter a protective order requiring the tenant to pay into court all rent coming due after entry of the order. (See "Protective Orders", page 137.) If the tenant proves his defense, the finders of fact must determine the reasonable rental value of the premises in their defective condition. The tenant is given a reasonable period of time in which to pay this sum to the landlord, and such payment precludes eviction. Any monies paid into court under a protective order will be distributed in accordance with the judgment. If the landlord prevails he will

receive the entire fund; if the tenant proves his
defense he is entitled to recover the excess over the
reasonable rent owed to the landlord.

3. *Scope of the Implied Warranty of Habitability*

The decisions are not in complete agreement
regarding the scope of the implied warranty of
habitability; however, there are several areas of
general agreement. It is generally agreed that the
implied warranty of habitability applies to written
and oral leases. The warranty of habitability is
implied in both long and short term leases. The
implied warranty of habitability requires the landlord to put the premises in a habitable condition at
the commencement of the lease and to maintain
the premises in a habitable condition throughout
the duration of the lease. (It should also be noted
that housing code violations existing at the inception of the lease may also give rise to the defense of
illegality on behalf of the tenant. See "Illegality
and Frustration of Purpose—Leases Which Violate
Housing Codes", page 38.) For the tenant to have
a valid claim, the defect must affect the demised
premises, the common areas used by the tenant, or
facilities retained under the exclusive control of
the landlord but necessary for the tenant's use and
enjoyment of the leased premises. With the exception of the above areas of general agreement, there
appears to be no consensus of opinion with regard
to the scope of the implied warranty of habitability.

a. Leases in Which the Warranty of Habitability Will Be Implied. There is a split of opinion as to whether the implied warranty of habitability should be restricted to leases of dwelling units in multiple-unit apartment buildings, or extended to encompass all residential leases, or extended further to include commercial leases. When the implied warranty of habitability is based upon a housing code, the provisions of the code will determine the dwellings to which the warranty will be extended. Many housing codes apply only to multiple-unit buildings and the warranty is limited accordingly; other housing codes, and consequently the implied warranty of habitability, extend to all dwellings. In jurisdictions which base the implied warranty of habitability upon public policy considerations (or analogy to products liability theories), there is no good reason why the implied warranty of habitability should not be implied in all residential leases, and a significant number of cases have applied the doctrine to leases of single family houses.

Where the implied warranty of habitability is founded upon an existing housing code, it follows that the warranty will not be extended to cover commercial leases. On the other hand, where the warranty is based upon public policy considerations or products liability analogies, a reasonable argument may be made for the extension of the warranty to commercial leases, particularly small commercial enterprises which have little bargaining power. A few cases, by inference or dictum, have indicated that the implied warranty extends to cover commercial leases. However, there appears to be no case involving a commercial lease in which the decision was based upon application of the theory of implied warranty of habitability. To the contrary, several cases have expressly rejected extension of the implied warranty theory to encompass commercial leases.

b. Standard of Habitability—Breach of Warranty. Once again, it is helpful to differentiate between cases which have based the implied warranty of habitability on public policy considerations and those which have implied the warranty on the basis of existing housing codes. In the latter jurisdictions the standard of habitability is established by the provisions of the housing code. In jurisdictions which found the implied warranty of habitability on public policy considerations, the standard of habitability is established by the court. Each theory has its advantages and disadvantages.

In code based jurisdictions, because the warranty is based upon housing code provisions, there is greater certainty in determining whether a breach of the implied warranty of habitability has occurred. There are some disadvantages however. First, only substantial violations of a housing code constitute breaches of the implied warranty of habitability and the courts' decisions have not satisfactorily distinguished between substantial and *de minimus* violations of housing codes. Second, the quality of the housing codes varies from locale to locale. Some codes are very detailed and comprehensive, while others merely provide that the landlord is required to keep the premises "in good repair". Still others have been criticized for setting standards which are too low to assure a suitable living environment. Since the breach of warranty is determined by whether there has been a substantial violation of the housing code, the courts have little flexibility in establishing a standard of habitability. The problem is particularly acute for the tenant where the jurisdiction has a detailed housing code which does not proscribe the particular defective condition which has in fact, although perhaps not under the applicable statutes, rendered the premises uninhabitable. Finally, tenants who live in municipalities which have no housing codes would not be protected in jurisdictions where the implied warranty is based upon the existence of a housing code. In jurisdictions where the housing code provides in general terms that the landlord has a duty to keep the premises in good repair, there is little difference between the standard of habitability in such jurisdictions and the standard of habitability in jurisdictions which base the implied warranty on public policy grounds.

In jurisdictions where the implied warranty of habitability is founded upon public policy, the courts have great latitude in determining the standard of habitability and what defects in the premises constitute a breach of the warranty. The problem in such jurisdictions is that the courts have provided little guidance for determining the standard of habitability—most usually speaking in general terms of the landlord having an obligation to provide dwellings which are "fit and suitable" for human habitation. The Uniform Residential Landlord and Tenant Act provides some guidance in determining fitness and suitability. Section 2.104 of the Act requires the landlord to: (i) comply with all building and housing codes affecting health and safety; (ii) maintain the common areas in a safe and clean condition; (iii) maintain in safe working order all plumbing, heating, ventilating, air-conditioning, sanitary and other facilities and appliances supplied or required to be supplied by him; (iv) provide receptacles for the temporary storage and removal of garbage and other waste; (v) to make such repairs as are necessary to maintain the premises in a fit and habitable condition; and (vi) with certain exceptions, to provide hot and cold running water and reasonable heat. Whatever the standard of habitability may be, a substantial deviation is required before breach of the implied warranty occurs. Again, there is little satisfactory guidance for distinguishing between substantial and minor breaches of the standard of habitability.

Public policy based jurisdictions, while not restricted to the housing code standard of habitability, often look to housing code provisions for guidance in determining whether there has been a breach of the implied warranty of habitability. Substantial compliance with the local housing code is evidence of the habitability of the demised premises; a substantial violation of the housing code is evidence of a breach of warranty. However, neither the violation of, nor compliance with, the housing code provisions is necessarily dispositive of the issue of breach of warranty in a public policy based jurisdiction.

(i) "Goods and Services" Covered by the Implied Warranty. It is generally agreed that the implied warranty encompasses defects located in the demised premises and in the common areas such as stairs, hallways and yards. The implied warranty also covers defective facilities which are necessary to the tenant's use and enjoyment of his apartment, but which remain in the exclusive control of the landlord (e.g., central heating systems, plumbing, etc.).

The type of facility covered under the implied warranty should include any facility which, if defective, would constitute a threat to the health or safety of the tenant. Thus, heating systems, plumbing systems, electrical systems, light, ventilation, dangerous common areas and vermin infestation would all be matters covered by the implied warranty of habitability. Defects relating to these matters would be evidence of breach of warranty by the landlord.

(ii) Substantial or Material Defects Constituting a Breach of the Implied Warranty. The au-

thorities are in general agreement that to be actionable the breach of implied warranty must be substantial or material. Whether the defect is of such a substantial or material nature as to render the premises unsafe or unsanitary, and therefore unfit for human habitation, is a question of fact to be determined by the circumstances of each case.

There are several general tests which may be applied to determine the existence or nonexistence of materiality. Deprivation of any of the essential "goods and services" which make up the modern urban leasehold would be a substantial breach of the implied warranty. A residential tenant expects to be able to eat, sleep, and have the use of sanitary facilities in the demised premises. The tenant also expects to have safe and reasonable ingress and egress to and from the demised premises. Defects which substantially interfere with or constitute a deprivation of these essential functions constitute a substantial breach of the implied warranty of habitability.

The courts have identified several factors as being germane to the issue of materiality: (i) whether there has been a violation of the applicable housing code, (ii) the nature and seriousness of the defect, (iii) the effect of the defect, actual or potential, on the health and safety of the tenants, (iv) the length of time that the defect has persisted, (v) the age of the building, and (vi) the reserved rent. Mease v. Fox, 200 N.W.2d 791 (Iowa 1972). Although very helpful, it is clear the list is not an exhaustive one.

As might be expected, whether a specific element of the package of "goods and services" is an essential or merely an amenity is a matter which is resolved only with great difficulty. Many courts have quoted with approval the following excerpt from Academy Spires, Inc. v. Brown, 111 N.J. 477, 268 A.2d 556 (1970), wherein the court attempts to distinguish between bare living requirements and amenities:

> "[I]n a modern society one cannot be expected to live in a multi-storied apartment building without heat, hot water, garbage disposal or elevator service. Failure to supply such things is a breach of the implied covenant of habitability. Malfunction of venetian blinds, water leaks, wall cracks, lack of painting, at least of the magnitude presented here, go to what may be called 'amenities'. Living with lack of painting, water leaks and defective venetian blinds may be unpleasant, aesthetically unsatisfying, but does not come within the category of uninhabitability." 268 A.2d at 559.

No doubt there are those who will disagree with the value judgments of the court in Academy Spires. It is probably more accurate to state that the standard of habitability, and what constitutes a substantial breach of the implied warranty of habitability, is incapable of precise definition. Like obscenity, perhaps the most that can be said is that "I know it when I see it."

c. Landlord's Notice of Defect. Before a claim of breach of implied warranty can be properly asserted, the landlord must have notice of the defect. Where the defect exists at the inception of the lease, the landlord will be liable for all defective conditions of which he had actual or constructive notice. Implicit in the concept of constructive notice is the requirement that the landlord inspect the leased premises, common areas, and areas retained in his exclusive control but necessary to the use of the leased premises prior to the inception of the lease. If the circumstances are such that a reasonable inspection would not result in discovery of the defect, then actual notice of the defect is required before the landlord will be subject to the claim of breach of the implied warranty of habitability.

After the transfer of possession to the tenant, the tenant has the exclusive right to possession of the demised premises. The landlord has no right to enter the demised premises, and therefore has no duty to inspect the premises. The landlord's liability for defective conditions in the demised premises arising after the transfer of possession is limited to those defects of which he has actual notice. This requirement of actual notice imposes an affirmative duty on the tenant to inform the landlord of any defect in the demised premises. However, where the landlord has actual notice of the defect from some other source, such as formal notification of a housing code violation by public authorities, the tenant has no obligation to give the landlord a second warning. Where the tenant makes reasonable attempts (e.g., mailed notice) to give notice of the defect to the landlord, but is unable to contact him, the notice requirement is deemed to be satisfied.

With respect to defects located in the common areas or areas retained in the exclusive control of the landlord but necessary to the use and enjoyment of the demised premises, the landlord should be liable for all defects of which he had actual or constructive notice. Again, implicit in the idea of constructive notice is the requirement that the landlord make reasonable inspections of these areas at reasonable intervals. (See "Duty of the Landlord to Repair the Common Areas—Landlord's Notice of Defect", page 91).

In addition to notice, by the better view, the landlord must be given a reasonable period of time after receiving notice to make the necessary repairs. Chess v. Muhammad, 179 N.J.Super. 75, 430 A.2d 928 (1981). On the other hand, there is authority for the view that the landlord will be held strictly liable for breach of warranty even when the landlord is not at fault and has made a reasonable effort to correct the defects. For example, in Knight v. Hallsthammar, 29 Cal.3d 46, 171 Cal.Rptr. 707, 623 P.2d 268 (1981), the landlord purchased a building which had defects at the time of purchase. The court held that a breach of warranty existed for which the landlord would be liable, whether or not the landlord had a reasonable period of time in which to effect the repairs.

4. Remedies of the Tenant

Until recently, the tenant had only two remedies available to him for the landlord's breach of duty to repair. The tenant (i) could bring an action on the contract for damages against the landlord or (ii) where the landlord's breach of duty was so great as to constitute an interference with the tenant's right to the peaceful use and enjoyment of the demised premises, the tenant could terminate the lease, and consequently his liability for rent, under the doctrine of constructive eviction. (See "Constructive Eviction", page 26.) Although there is some authority for granting the tenant the remedy of specific performance, most courts will not grant such equitable relief. The remedies of the residential tenant have been greatly expanded in jurisdictions adopting the implied warranty of habitability.

Jurisdictions which have adopted the implied warranty of habitability have also adopted the view that the lease is primarily a contractual relationship with the tenant's duty to pay rent dependent upon performance by the landlord of his implied covenant to repair and maintain the premises in a habitable condition. In addition to the aforementioned remedies, breach of the implied warranty of habitability also permits the tenant to assert all other basic contract remedies (e.g., rescission, specific performance, etc.), thus giving the tenant a number of avenues to seek resolution of his grievances against the landlord. In addition, the courts have substantially expanded the remedy of rent abatement.

   a. Termination and Rescission. In general, to permit termination, a breach of contract must be material. In implied warranty of habitability cases the uncorrected defective condition must be substantial before a breach of the implied warranty occurs. Thus, breach of the implied warranty of habitability should provide the requisite materiality for grounds for termination of the lease agreement. The remedy of termination for breach of warranty is similar to a tenant's claim of constructive eviction. However, under the former, a tenant is entitled to declaratory relief prior to vacation of the premises. Further, although the cases are not clear on the issue, the decisions indicate that the wrongful conduct of the landlord which breaches the implied warranty justifying termination by the tenant may be lesser in degree than that which would justify a finding of constructive eviction.

   Once the right to terminate is established, the tenant must give the landlord notice of the termination in order for it to be effective. Although he has other remedies available to him for the landlord's breach of the implied warranty of habitability, the tenant remains liable under the lease until such time as the lease is terminated. In addition to giving the landlord notice of termination, once the termination is effective the tenant must vacate the premises.

Rescission goes beyond termination. The term implies a discharge of all unperformed duties and an undoing of those duties which the parties have performed under the terms of the contract so as to place the parties in a position as near as possible to the status quo at the time the contract was executed. In such circumstances rescission is closely analogous to the principles of restitution.

In order to rescind, the tenant must establish that the landlord has substantially failed to perform under the terms of the lease agreement. The landlord's breach of the implied warranty should be sufficient nonperformance to give the tenant the right to rescind. The tenant must also give the landlord notice of rescission and offer to restore to the landlord all benefits he has received under the lease. The offer of restoration includes a tender of all rent due and unpaid for any period prior to the landlord's breach of implied warranty and the reasonable rent for the premises during the period of breach. The tenant is entitled to a return of an amount equal to the difference between the contract rent and the value of the premises during the term of the breach. The tenant is also permitted to recover prepaid rent and security deposits. The net effect of the tenant's exercise of his right of rescission is similar to the result reached by an exercise of his rights to termination and retroactive rent abatement.

b. Repair and Deduct. A number of states have statutes which permit the tenant, after notice of the defect to the landlord and the landlord's failure to repair, to repair the defective condition and deduct the costs thereof from the contract rent due and payable to the landlord. Although such statutes are of some help to a tenant, the benefit is limited because the statutes are restricted with respect to the purposes for which such expenditures may be made (e.g., "essential services", water, gas or electric services), and/or are restricted in the amount which can be expended and deducted to a specific amount or an amount based upon a set formula, (e.g., one month's rent).

In the absence of a repair and deduct statute, several jurisdictions have held that the tenant may make needed repairs and deduct the costs of such repairs from the rent due and payable to the landlord. In the leading case of Marini v. Ireland, 56 N.J. 130, 265 A.2d 526 (1970), the Supreme Court of New Jersey stated:

> "If, therefore, a landlord fails to make repairs and replacements of vital facilities necessary to maintain the premises in a liveable condition . . . , the tenant may cause the same to be done and deduct the cost thereof from future rents." 265 A.2d, at 535.

To avoid the situation where both the landlord and the tenant independently arrange to correct the default, and perhaps to avoid compelling the landlord to contribute to improvements he may believe to be unwise, "[t]he tenant's recourse to such self-help must be preceded by timely and adequate

notice to the landlord . . . ." 265 A.2d, at 535.
The remedy of repair and deduct has the advantage of giving the tenant some assurance that the
premises can be restored to a habitable condition;
however, the assurance is limited by the fact that
the value of the repair cannot, as a practical matter, exceed the amount of the rent due under the
lease.

   c. Specific Performance. Should the tenant wish to remain in possession, specific performance of the implied warranty of habitability is one
remedy the tenant may pursue. The tenant's remedy at law, damages, must be inadequate before
the tenant is entitled to specific performance. In
many instances the damages which can be recovered by the tenant (e.g., recovery of 40% of all rent
paid) are not sufficient to put the premises in a
habitable condition if applied to that purpose. The
benefit of many repairs and improvements extend
for a period of time far beyond the balance of the
term of the typical residential lease, and it would
be inequitable to impose the burden of such repair
on the tenant. Further, while the measure of
damages may be relatively certain in any given
jurisdiction, the application of the measure in the
determination of actual damages is often no more
than the visceral reaction of the court to the facts
presented to it. It would seem then that quite
often damages will be both inadequate and uncertain, and that specific performance should be permitted.

There may be even more compelling reasons for permitting an action for specific performance by the tenant. The housing shortage existing in many urban areas of the country and the disparity of bargaining power between most landlords and tenants—factors underlying adoption of the implied warranty of habitability—mean that most tenants will not be able to improve their position by moving to another dwelling. The low-income tenant will be shoved from one dilapidation to another, rendering the remedies of termination and rescission meaningless and continuing the deprivation of the tenant of the one thing which he has bargained for in his lease, a habitable dwelling. In a more affirmative vein, allowing specific performance will facilitate implementation of the policy underlying the implied warranty of habitability and local housing codes—the maintenance of all dwelling units in a condition fit for human habitation.

d. Rent Abatement and Withholding. The courts generally agree that the landlord's breach of the implied warranty of habitability entitles the tenant to an abatement of rent for the duration of the breach. However, the tenant is required to pay the landlord the reasonable rental value of the premises for the period during which the breach existed. The courts hold differing opinions on how the abatement should be determined. There appear to be three significant rules to determine the measure of rent abatement: (i) the fair rental value rule, (ii) the difference in value rule, and (iii) the proportional value rule.

Under the fair rental value rule, the rent payable by the tenant is reduced to the fair rental value of the premises in their defective condition. The results obtained under this rule are equitable in situations where the landlord has made a particularly good bargain. However, the rule may lead to an unjust result where the tenant has made a good bargain.

Example: Suppose that at the time of the breach of the implied warranty the fair rental value of the premises is $175.00 per month in a habitable condition and $125.00 a month in their present defective condition. If the contract rent is $200.00 per month, an abatement to the fair rental value of $125.00 per month would appear to be equitable and would put pressure on the landlord to repair the premises. On the contrary, if the contract rent is $115.00 per month there would be no abatement because the fair rental value of the premises in their defective condition is $125.00. This result is clearly unjust from the tenant's perspective (he loses the benefit of his bargain), and creates no incentive in the landlord to repair the defective premises.

The difference in value rule is set forth in Mease v. Fox, 200 N.W.2d 791 (Iowa 1972):

> "Where there has been a material breach of implied warranty, tenant's damages shall be measured by the difference between the fair

rental value of the premises if they had been as warranted and the fair rental value of the premises as they were during occupancy by the tenant in the unsafe or unsanitary condition." 200 N.W.2d at 797.

Under this test the rent reserved in the lease is unimportant except as evidence of the fair rental value of the premises. Following the above example, the difference in value would be $50.00 and it becomes evident that the fairness of the result in any particular case depends upon the ability of the parties to bargain at the time the lease was executed. If the contract rent is $200.00 per month, the rent payable by the tenant for the defective premises would be $150.00 per month. The difference between the rent the tenant must pay and what the landlord could receive if he were to put the premises in a habitable condition and lease to another party is relatively small ($25.00), and therefore, places little pressure on the landlord to repair the premises. On the other hand, if the contract rent is $100.00 per month (a good bargain for the tenant), the difference in value would reduce the tenant's rent to $50.00 per month for the duration of the breach of warranty. This represents a substantially higher percentage reduction of the contract rent, and perhaps works an injustice on the landlord.

The proportional value rule appears to have been adopted in several cases and has been adopted by the American Law Institute as part of the

Restatement, Second, Property (Landlord and Tenant), which provides:

§ 11.1   Rent Abatement

If the tenant is entitled to an abatement of the rent, the rent is abated to the amount of that proportion of the rent which the fair rental value after the event giving the right to abate bears to the fair rental value before the event. Abatement is allowed until the default is eliminated or the lease terminates, whichever first occurs.*

Following the above example, under the proportional value rule the tenant would be entitled to an abatement of approximately 28.6% of the contract rent [$(175 - 125) \div 175 = .286$; $.286 \times 100 = 28.6\%$], and this percentage reduction would apply regardless of the amount of the contract rent. The proportional value rule has the advantage of preserving the bargain of the parties in the same proportion as it was at the inception of the lease and for this reason is perhaps the most equitable manner of determining the amount of rent to be abated.

A fourth possibility, the proportional area rule, which provides for abatement in the same proportion as the fraction of land of which the tenant is deprived, has been applied primarily in leases of agricultural land. Because some defects

* Copyright 1977 by The American Law Institute. Reprinted with the permission of The American Law Institute.

which cause breach of the warranty of habitability (e.g., a defective toilet) may not "deprive" the tenant of any fraction of the physical space demised, the rule does not appear to lend itself readily to application to residential leaseholds.

It may make little practical difference which rule is adopted by a particular jurisdiction. Proof of reasonable rental value is difficult at best; and normally requires the testimony of expert witnesses, usually real estate appraisers. The cost of such expert testimony is beyond the financial ability of most tenants. Further, there is serious doubt as to the validity and availability of statistical data relating to apartments which are leased and operated in a substandard condition. These data would normally be required to elicit meaningful expert testimony. Thus, the expense of expert testimony effectively precludes most residential tenants from producing expert testimony to support their claims of diminution in value, and there are serious questions about the validity of such testimony if introduced into evidence. Perhaps for these reasons, most courts have not required substantial amounts of evidence with regard to market value. Their decisions regarding reasonable rental value can best be described as a bare gut reaction to the limited evidence presented.

The realization of rent abatement may take several forms. If the tenant has paid the contract rent during a period of time in which the landlord was in breach of the implied warranty of habitabil-

ity, the tenant is entitled to sue for the excess he
has paid to the landlord. The court will establish
the amount of the abated rent for the period of the
landlord's default. The tenant may also obtain a
declaratory judgment that the landlord has
breached the implied warranty of habitability, and
that the tenant is entitled to a rent abatement.
Rent abatement is most often accomplished by the
tenant withholding rent payments, and subsequently raising the landlord's breach of the implied
warranty of habitability as a defense in the landlord's action to remove the tenant for nonpayment
of rent.

Courts adopting the implied warranty doctrine
generally agree that rent withholding is an acceptable course of conduct on the part of the tenant.
In a summary possession action, if the court finds
that the entire rent obligation is extinguished by
the landlord's breach of warranty, judgment for
the tenant will be entered by the court. If it is
determined that the tenant is only entitled to a
partial abatement, the tenant will be given an
opportunity to pay the abated rent due and owing
and remain in possession of the premises. If the
tenant fails to pay the abated rent, judgment for
possession will be entered for the landlord.

(i) Rent Withholding Statutes. In some jurisdictions rent withholding is authorized by statute.
Most of these statutes require that the tenant
deposit the rent which is due and owing into a
private escrow account, with the court, with a

court-appointed receiver, or with a public agency. Most statutes also permit the escrowed money to be used to repair the premises. The disadvantage of such statutes is that most do not provide for a return to the tenant of the amount of rent which should have been abated because of the defective condition of the premises.

(ii) Protective Orders. In the absence of a rent withholding statute, the withholding of rent by the tenant subjects the landlord to the real possibility that the tenant will be unable to pay the back rent in the event that judgment is rendered in favor of the landlord. To guard against this possibility, the landlord is entitled to apply to the court for a pretrial protective order requiring the tenant to pay the contract rent into court. The monies so deposited are disbursed in accordance with the judgment of the court. In Bell v. Tsintolas Realty Co., 139 U.S.App.D.C. 101, 430 F.2d 474 (1970) the court stated that such protective orders are not favored and should be permitted ". . . only in limited circumstances, only on motion of the landlord, and only after notice and an opportunity for hearing on such a motion." 430 F.2d, at 479. To be entitled to the order the landlord must show a clear need for such protection. In determining the landlord's need the court should consider:

> ". . . the amount of rent alleged to be due, the number of months the landlord has not received even a partial rent payment, the reasonableness of the rent for the premises, the

amount of the landlord's monthly obligations
for the premises, whether the tenant has been
allowed to proceed *in forma pauperis,* and
whether the landlord faces a substantial
threat of foreclosure."   430 F.2d, at 484.

If a landlord demonstrates the requisite need, the
court should then balance the need of the landlord
against the apparent merits of the tenant's defense
to determine if the protective order should be is-
sued; and if so, whether the payment into court
should be the contract rent or a lesser amount.
The Bell court's approach appears to be a successful attempt to balance the interests of the landlord
and the tenant.

Where judgment is rendered in favor of the
landlord and the tenant appeals the decision, the
landlord will most likely request a protective order
pending the appeal.   Again, the landlord must
establish the need for protection.   However, once
the need is established the court is more likely to
issue a protective order pending appeal than it is to
issue a pretrial protective order.   There are several
reasons to view the landlord's request more favorably pending appeal.   First, unlike prejudgment security deposits, post-judgment security deposits are
not unusual.   Second, since judgment at the trial
court level has been rendered in favor of the landlord, it is reasonable to presume that the tenant's
defense was invalid.

(iii) Turnover Orders.   In addition to a protective order, the landlord may also request disburse-

ment of the security deposit to himself *pendente lite.* In Cooks v. Fowler, 148 U.S.App.D.C. 245, 459 F.2d 1269 (1971), the court, by way of dictum, indicated that the landlord might be entitled to the funds deposited by the tenant pursuant to a protective order. The court placed three conditions upon such disbursements: first, there must be a hearing after due notice to the tenant; second, the landlord is only entitled to receive that portion of the escrow funds which he can demonstrate that he will have a clear right to at the end of the litigation; and third, the landlord must be in dire need of the funds.

Following the lead of Cooks v. Fowler, the District of Columbia Court of Appeals, noting the landlord's need for income, recently upheld an order permitting pre-trial disbursement of part of the deposited rent to the landlord. Dameron v. Capitol House Associates Ltd. Partnership, 431 A.2d 580 (D.C.App.1981). Dameron is unusual in that the suit involved the validity of a rent increase granted by the local rent control board. Only the rent increase was being challenged; and since there was no dispute as to the original rent, i.e., the landlord had a clear right to it, the court held that the disbursement was permissible and within the trial court's discretion. Although the result in Dameron is reasonable on its facts; under more common factual settings, disbursement of escrowed funds to the landlord under the conditions set forth in Cooks v. Fowler may lead to an unreasonable risk of harm to the tenant.

There are several reasons for denying disbursement of the escrowed funds to the landlord *pendente lite*. Entitlement to the escrowed rent payments is the fundamental issue being litigated. The escrow of the rent payments protects the landlord against his greatest risk—the tenant's inability to pay should the landlord prevail in the action. Finally, if the landlord proves dire need, to disburse the funds to the landlord would force the tenant to take the risk of the landlord becoming insolvent and unable to reimburse tenant should the tenant's defense of breach of implied warranty of habitability prevail (a strong likelihood considering the "dire need" established by the landlord). Although denying a request for a turnover order may cause the landlord some financial hardship, a protective order will secure the payment of rent to the landlord if he prevails in the suit. On the other hand, a turnover would leave the tenant without security for repayment of the funds turned over to the landlord in the event the tenant prevails in the litigation. Under the circumstances, perhaps the better view is to deny the landlord any disbursement of the escrowed funds *pendente lite*.

e. Damages. In addition to rent abatement, the tenant is entitled to recover his incidental and consequential damages, including property damage and related economic losses arising out of the landlord's breach of the implied warranty of habitability. If the tenant vacates the premises prior to the expiration of the lease, he is entitled to recover the net value of the lease for the unexpired term. The amount to which the tenant is entitled is the present value of the difference between the fair rental value of the premises in a habitable condition and the contract rent for the balance of the term of the lease.

5. *Landlord's Defenses to the Implied Warranty of Habitability*

The landlord has two defenses to an action for breach of the implied warranty of habitability. The first defense, one which appears to need no discussion, is that the tenant will be denied relief when the defect is caused by the tenant's unusual or malicious use of the premises. The second defense is waiver of the implied warranty by the tenant. In jurisdictions which base the implied warranty of habitability on the provisions of a housing code, the courts generally have not permitted the tenant to waive it. This is consistent with the general view that public policy will not allow an individual to waive the protection that a statute is designed to give him. Javins v. First National Realty Corp., 138 U.S.App.D.C. 369, 428 F.2d 1071 (1970).

When the implied warranty is based upon public policy, the courts have usually held that the warranty may be waived or disclaimed; a view which is consistent with the theory that the lease is primarily contractual in nature. The waiver may be express, or implied from the conduct of the tenant (e.g., taking possession of leased premises which have obvious defects). The harshness of the waiver rule has been softened by several exceptions. There is no valid waiver (i) if the defect constitutes a substantial violation of the housing code, (ii) if there is a housing shortage which seriously limits the tenant's ability to obtain other standard housing, (iii) if the landlord promised to make the needed repairs and failed to do so, or (iv) if under the circumstances the waiver is unconscionable.

The tenant's right to waive certain remedies may be expressly governed by statute; for example, several state statutes permit the tenant to waive his statutory right to rent abatement. The better view is found in the Uniform Residential Landlord and Tenant Act § 1.403, which provides that any agreement by the tenant to waive his remedies under the Act is unenforceable.

6. *Tort Liability for Breach of the Implied Warranty of Habitability*

Characterization of the lease as a conveyance of land and the doctrine of *caveat emptor* are the foundation upon which the common law built the landlord's immunity from tort liability for injuries resulting from defects existing on the demised premises. Courts which have adopted the implied warranty of habitability have done so by characterizing the lease as a contract rather than a conveyance of land and abolishing the doctrine of *caveat emptor*. As might be expected, serious questions have been raised regarding continuation of the landlord's immunity from tort liability in implied warranty jurisdictions. The Supreme Court of New Hampshire is the only court of final review to directly decide the issue. In Sargent v. Ross, 113 N.H. 388, 308 A.2d 528 (1973), the court held that since it had discarded the underpinnings of landlord tort immunity by adopting the implied warranty of habitability in an earlier case, it would bring the other half of landlord-tenant law up to date by imposing on landlords the duty to ". . . exercise reasonable care not to subject others to an unreasonable risk of harm." 308 A.2d at 534.

The holding in the Sargent case appears to be the better view, and in the past few years a number of courts have followed its lead and logic. To hold otherwise would require a court which has adopted the implied warranty doctrine to take the somewhat inconsistent positions that a tenant can withhold rent (and exercise other remedies) for the landlord's failure to perform his duty to repair, but cannot recover in tort for personal injuries or property damage resulting from that same failure to repair. Imposition of tort liability would also further encourage the landlord to maintain the premises in a habitable condition. Finally, imposition of liability on the landlord is consistent with the majority view, supported by the Restatement, Second, Torts § 357 (1965), which imposes liability on the landlord for personal injuries and property damage arising out of the landlord's breach of an express covenant to repair.

Undoubtedly, a number of courts will follow the more traditional view that tort liability follows control, and absolve the landlord of tort liability for breach of the implied warranty on the grounds that the tenant has exclusive possession and control of the demised premises and the implied covenant to repair is not sufficient to transfer control back to the landlord.

F. Retaliatory Eviction

The doctrine of retaliatory eviction is simply another aspect of the recent evolution in landlord-tenant law. As noted above, there has been a substantial legislative and judicial effort to improve the quality of housing for low and moderate income tenants. This effort is evidenced by the widespread adoption of housing codes and residential landlord-tenant legislation, and the growing judicial adoption of the doctrines of illegality and implied warranty of habitability. Predictably, the assertion of these new rights by tenants has been met by retaliatory conduct on the part of many landlords. This conduct has usually taken the form of refusal to renew leases, termination of periodic leases, and/or exhorbitant rent increases. Under the traditional common law, a landlord could assert any rights he had against the tenant, or alter the particular landlord-tenant relationship in any facially legitimate manner. Until recently, the motives for the landlord's conduct were unquestioned. With a few narrow exceptions (e.g., racially motivated termination of a lease; and this exception is very recent), a landlord could, upon proper notice, terminate a periodic tenancy for any reason or for no reason at all. The doctrine of retaliatory eviction modifies the traditional common law view by stating that facially legitimate actions taken by the landlord may be illegal if taken with a retaliatory motive.

Edwards v. Habib, 130 U.S.App.D.C. 126, 397 F.2d 687 (1968), was the first case to recognize retaliatory eviction as a defense to a summary possession action. In Edwards, the tenant reported certain housing code violations to the proper authorities. In response to these complaints, the landlord gave the tenant a thirty day notice to quit, and upon the tenant's failure to vacate the premises began a summary possession action. The court held that if the termination was motivated by the tenant's complaints to the authorities, the eviction would be barred.

There are several theories underlying the doctrine of retaliatory eviction. First, effective enforcement of housing codes contemplates and depends upon private (tenant) reporting of code violations. To allow the landlord to evict the reporting tenant would reduce the effectiveness of housing codes and undermine the public policy evinced by such legislation. Similar arguments are made in support of the doctrine retaliatory eviction in jurisdictions where the public policy is manifested by judicial adoption of the implied warranty of habitability. Another theory, discussed but not decided in Edwards, is that the grant of summary possession under retaliatory circumstances constitutes state action in violation of the tenant's rights of free speech and to petition her government. Most courts deciding the latter issue have held that the landlord's retaliatory action is purely private conduct; Weigand v. Afton View Apartments, 473 F.2d 545 (1973).

Although the doctrine of retaliatory eviction has been widely accepted, the parameters of the concept have not been well defined. The scope of tenant conduct which will be protected, what landlord conduct is prohibited, and issues of burden of proof are all areas in which there is no general agreement. Many states have enacted legislation recognizing the defense or doctrine of retaliatory eviction. The statutes vary in scope, but most specifically set forth the tenant activities protected, the landlord activities prohibited, and allocate the burden of proof.

1. Conduct of the Landlord and Tenant

Generally, it may be said that the tenant will be protected with regard to actions taken in the pursuit of obtaining a habitable dwelling. A much narrower view was taken by the court in Dickhut v. Norton, 45 Wis.2d 389, 173 N.W.2d 297 (1970). In Dickhut, the court held that in order to have a valid defense the tenant must show that the code violation did in fact exist, the landlord knew of the violation and the tenant's complaint, and the complaint was the landlord's sole motive for terminating the lease. Less restrictive decisions have protected the tenant who withheld rent asserting that the dilapidated condition of the premises violated the implied warranty of habitability or made the lease illegal. Robinson v. Diamond Housing Corporation, 463 F.2d 853 (1972). Tenants have also been protected when opposing zoning changes supported by their landlords, when such opposition was motivated by the fear of loss of the residential tenancy if the zoning change was approved. On the other hand, there is significant authority for the view that the defense of retaliatory eviction will not be recognized where the lease terminated is a commercial one.

The prohibited landlord conduct is what one might expect. The list includes: exhorbitant rent increases, and other significant alterations in the terms of the lease; refusal to renew a lease; termination of a periodic tenancy; and threats of eviction. It is possible for the above landlord actions to be legitimate, and therefore, the real issue is the motivation of the landlord. This in turn raises the issues of who has the burden of proof and what standard of proof is required.

2. Burden of Proof

In Dickhut v. Norton, supra, the court held that the burden of proof was on, and remained with, the tenant. Since the thing to be proved, motivation, is subjective, and only the landlord can truly have actual knowledge of his motivation, this is an onerous burden to impose on the tenant.

Other courts have held that any unexplained "retaliatory action" following some protected tenant activity gives rise to a presumption of retaliatory eviction. See Robinson v. Diamond Housing Corporation, supra. Once the tenant establishes a *prima facie* case, the landlord has the burden of proving nonretaliatory motive. This is also the position taken by statutes governing retaliatory eviction.

Three standards of proof have been adopted by the courts. Again, the narrowest position is to be found in Dickhut v. Norton. There the court held that retaliation had to be the sole motive in order for the tenant to have a valid defense. At the other extreme, several courts in interpreting statutes governing retaliatory eviction have held that the landlord must prove that his conduct was totally devoid of retaliatory motive. Parkin v. Fitzgerald, 307 Minn. 423, 240 N.W.2d 828 (1976). Mixed motives will not save the landlord; apparently, even if his predominant motive is legitimate. The more reasonable middle ground was adopted in Robinson v. Diamond Housing Corporation, supra. There the court said the test was whether retaliation was the dominant motive (the "causative factor") in the landlord's conduct.

There are additional unresolved issues, most relating to timing. For example, how long after the protected tenant activity can the defense be raised; and at what point will the presumption of retaliation come to an end? After the tenant has successfully raised the defense of retaliatory evic-

tion, how long must the landlord wait before he
can recover possession of the premises? Statutes
governing retaliatory eviction cover these problems
to varying degrees. There is a paucity of case law
on these issues, and what there is is unsatisfactory
in analysis and result.

3. Remedies

The issue of retaliation usually arises as a
defense to an action of summary possession
brought by the landlord. Where the landlord's
retaliatory conduct takes a form other than the
attempted eviction of the tenant, injunctive relief
may be granted; e.g., an exhorbitant rent increase
may be enjoined. The tenant may also recover
damages for any harm suffered as a result of the
landlord's wrongful conduct.

G. Defenses of the Landlord to Tort Liability

1. Express Assumption of Risk

The above discussion of the landlord's duty to
repair points out that there is a substantial area
within which the landlord can be held liable for
personal injuries and property damage arising out
of the defective condition of the leased premises
and areas retained under the control of the landlord. A landlord may protect himself against the
losses arising from such liability by carrying the
appropriate type of insurance. The cost of such
insurance may be borne by the landlord, thus
decreasing his net return from the leased property.

Alternatively, the lease can expressly provide that the tenant shall pay the cost of such insurance, or, the landlord may charge a higher rent which takes into account the cost of such insurance. The latter alternatives increase the tenant's cost for the leased premises and make leasing more difficult for the landlord. From the landlord's perspective the problem is how to relieve himself of liability without decreasing the net rent or increasing the difficulty of letting. Many landlords attempt to solve the problem by inserting in the lease a covenant in which the tenant agrees that the landlord shall not be liable for personal injury or property damage arising from the condition of the premises. As a supplement to such exculpatory clauses, or in lieu thereof, leases often contain a covenant whereby the tenant agrees to indemnify the landlord for any such liabilities imposed upon the landlord. Usually, exculpatory clauses are broadly worded so as to encompass both personal injury and property damage, but often they will be limited in their application to property damage or willful acts of the landlord.

There is a split of authority with respect to the validity of exculpatory clauses. The decision of any particular court will depend upon its resolution of the conflict between the constitutionally guaranteed freedom of contract and the desirability of protecting and preserving the rights and duties arising under tort law. Most courts have upheld the validity of exculpatory clauses on the theory that such clauses are not contrary to public policy because the landlord-tenant relationship is not a matter of public interest, but relates exclusively to the private affairs of the parties. Miller v. A & R Joint Venture, 97 Nev. 580, 636 P.2d 277 (1981). The courts in these cases view the parties as standing on equal terms and believe that they should have full freedom to contract as they please.

A minority of jurisdictions holds exculpatory clauses to be void as violative of public policy. This view is founded upon the ideas that exculpatory clauses are not purely the private affairs of the parties, and that to uphold such clauses would sanction the immunization of landlords from liability for personal injuries sustained by their tenants arising from the landlord's own negligence, thus destroying the benefits obtained from the concept of negligence and the standards of affirmative duty imposed upon landlords for the protection of their tenants. McCutcheon v. United Homes Corporation, 79 Wash.2d 443, 486 P.2d 1093 (1971).

Even in jurisdictions which recognize the validity and enforceability of exculpatory clauses, the clauses are not favored by the courts and as a consequence are strictly construed. Most such courts also hold that exculpatory clauses will not be effective to absolve a landlord from liability for personal injury and property damage arising out of the landlord's fraudulent, reckless or intentional misconduct; and some, distinguishing between active and passive negligence, hold that liability will be imposed upon a landlord for active negligence despite the existence of an exculpatory clause in the lease. In addition, most courts hold that exculpatory clauses do not affect the landlord's liability to third parties, including the minor children of the tenant, lawfully on the premises. Such third parties are not parties to the contract and therefore, are not bound by its terms. Vernon Fire & Casualty Company v. Graham, 166 Ind.App. 509, 336 N.E.2d 829 (1975).

Recently, there has been a legislative and judicial trend in the direction of invalidating exculpatory clauses. At least 19 states have statutes invalidating exculpatory clauses in leases. Some statutes apply only to those portions of the premises retained in the control of the landlord, while others also include the leased premises within their coverage.

An increasing number of courts have exhibited a readiness to void exculpatory clauses on a case by case basis when it is apparent that the landlord and tenant were in unequal bargaining positions at the time the lease was executed. In these jurisdictions, exculpatory clauses have been held void in public housing leases, the classic example of unequal bargaining power, and in leases between private parties. There is also increasing support for the position that a residential lease is not purely a private matter, and that exculpatory clauses contained in such leases must yield to the public interest. McCutcheon v. United Homes Corporation, supra. The probability of a court adopting such a view is enhanced where the jurisdiction has enacted a housing code, where there is a substantial housing shortage in the area, or where the clause is contained in a standard form lease used by most landlords in the area.

Although some cases may be found where exculpatory clauses in commercial leases have been voided in situations where the landlord and tenant were in unequal bargaining positions, most courts have hesitated to void exculpatory clauses in commercial leases.

2. *Implied Assumption of Risk and Contributory Negligence*

Implied assumption of risk and contributory negligence, separate and distinct defenses of the landlord, often overlap and a great many courts fail to clearly distinguish between the two, or simply confuse them. Traditionally, the defense of implied assumption of risk arises in situations where the plaintiff (usually the tenant, his family, guests or invitees) has knowledge of the danger and voluntarily encounters it. Contributory negligence arises in situations where the plaintiff's conduct falls below that of the reasonable man with regard to (i) discovering the risk, (ii) the manner in which the risk is encountered, or (iii) encountering the risk when it is clearly unreasonable in relation to the benefit attempted to be obtained by the plaintiff.

In most jurisdictions both defenses are available to the landlord in an action for damages arising out of the defective condition of the demised premises. Where successfully raised, the defenses are usually a complete bar to recovery by the plaintiff. A number of jurisdictions have adopted the comparative negligence theory. In these jurisdictions contributory negligence reduces the amount the plaintiff may recover but does not automatically act as a total bar to recovery by the plaintiff. In addition, a few comparative negligence jurisdictions have held that assumption of risk merely reduces the amount which the plaintiff may recover, rather than acting as a complete bar to recovery. Other jurisdictions have held that implied assumption of risk is abolished on the ground that it no longer serves a useful purpose. The argument is that where the plaintiff knows of the risk and reasonably assumes it, the landlord owes no duty of care to the plaintiff, or, if there is such a duty, no breach of duty has occurred. Alternatively, the plaintiff is contributorily negligent if he knows of the danger and unreasonably encounters it.

Where the tenant's action is based upon the landlord's violation of a statutory duty to repair, the landlord will usually be permitted to raise the defenses of implied assumption of risk and contributory negligence. Since it is against public policy to permit a person to waive statutory rights, an express assumption of risk of harm from the landlord's violation of a statutory duty to repair would be invalid. However, the law also expects a tenant to exercise reasonable care in looking out for his own safety, and it is on this ground that most courts hold that the defenses of implied assumption or risk and contributory negligence may be raised by the landlord. An exception to this general rule is made for statutes which are intended to protect the plaintiff against his inability to protect himself. Housing codes usually have not been construed to be this type of protective statute, and therefore, the landlord may avail himself of the defenses of implied assumption of risk and contributory negligence despite the existence of a housing code.

a. Implied Assumption of Risk. The defense of implied assumption of risk usually arises where the plaintiff and defendant enter into a relationship in which there is a known risk to the plaintiff and the plaintiff knows that the defendant will not protect him against said risk; or in situations where the plaintiff knows of a danger created by the negligence of the defendant, but nonetheless voluntarily encounters the danger.

In order to successfully raise the defense of implied assumption of risk, the defendant must establish that the plaintiff knew and understood the danger, and freely and voluntarily elected to encounter it. It is not enough that the plaintiff know the facts which give rise to the danger, he must also understand the danger itself. Age, experience and mental capacity are all factors to be considered in determining the plaintiff's comprehension of the risk encountered. Therefore, the test for assumption of risk, at least in theory, is one of subjective intent. However, there are certain dangers which any reasonable person is held to understand; for example, ice on exterior stairs, or water on a waxed floor. To the extent this latter standard is applied, the test may be more accurately described as objective rather than subjective.

The election to encounter the known danger must be completely free and voluntary. The intentional encountering of a known risk is not necessarily evidence of the plaintiff's consent to subject himself to such risk. Where the tenant objects to some perceived danger on the premises, but deliberately encounters such danger after assurances by the landlord that the condition is safe or will be remedied, the tenant will not be deemed to have assumed the risk; assuming, of course, that the reliance on the landlord's assurance was reasonable. Further, where the plaintiff has no reasonable alternative to encountering the known danger he will not be held to have assumed the risk. For example, if there is only one reasonable exit from an apartment building, the tenant will not be held to have assumed the risk of the landlord's negligent maintenance of the hallway leading out of the building.

The tenant's actual or constructive notice of the dangerous condition will not relieve the landlord of liability to the tenant's guests and invitees who have no knowledge of the existing defect. However, the tenant's knowledge, coupled with his failure to give adequate warning of the dangerous condition, may subject the tenant to liability to third parties on the premises with his consent. Under such circumstances both the landlord and the tenant will be liable to the injured third party.

The courts are divided on the question of the right of a tenant's child to recover damages for injuries arising out of a dangerous condition of which the tenant has knowledge. Where liability is imposed upon the landlord, it is based upon the landlord's duty to maintain the premises in a reasonably safe condition, as set forth above. Where liability is denied it is frequently stated that the primary duty of reasonable care in the protection of children from dangers in the common areas rests with the parents, and the parents' contributory negligence will be imputed to the child.

b. Contributory Negligence. Contributory Negligence arises in situations where the plaintiff's conduct falls below that of the reasonable man with regard to (i) discovering the risk, (ii) the manner in which the risk is encountered, once the risk is discovered, or (iii) when the risk is clearly unreasonable in relation to the benefit attempted to be obtained by the plaintiff. Most courts hold that the plaintiff is barred only when his negligence has been a substantial factor in causing the resulting injury. Under the minority view, any negligence, however slight, on the part of the plaintiff will bar the plaintiff's cause of action.

Not every encountering of a known danger constitutes contributory negligence on the part of the plaintiff; for example, a plaintiff may not be contributorily negligent for walking through a common hallway under a ceiling known to be defective when the hallway is the only means of access to the plaintiff's apartment. The defendant's claim of contributory negligence may be unavailing where the plaintiff exercises reasonable care in encountering the known danger. For example, it has been held that a tenant was not contributorily negligent for using the front steps to her apartment house, known to her to be defective, since she exercised reasonable care in using the steps. Generally, it may be said that the reasonableness of the plaintiff's conduct will be determined by balancing the risk encountered against the benefit sought by the plaintiff. Where the risk is great and the benefit to be obtained is slight, the defense of contributory negligence may bar recovery by the plaintiff.

III. EXPRESS COVENANT TO REPAIR

A. Covenants Made by the Tenant

It is common for the lease to contain provisions expressly allocating the duty to repair. Where the duty is imposed upon the tenant, it usually takes the form of a general covenant to repair in which the tenant agrees to repair, or to maintain the premises in good repair. In the absence of an express agreement to the contrary, a general covenant to repair requires the tenant to repair all defective conditions arising after commencement of the lease, regardless of the cause of the defect. Damage arising from ordinary wear and tear is usually expressly excluded, as is damage caused by the elements, acts of God, or the wrongful acts of a stranger.

A general covenant to repair does not require the tenant to put the premises in a better condition than when received; but it is important to distinguish between a general covenant to repair and a covenant "to put in repair", or to deliver the premises in good condition at the end of the lease. The latter two covenants obligate the tenant to put the premises in a good state of repair whatever their condition at the commencement of the lease. A covenant to redeliver the leased premises to the landlord in as good a condition as when received is merely a covenant to repair.

Breach of covenant is a question of fact. In determining whether there has been a breach, it is important to consider the age and type of construction of the building, its condition at the beginning and at the end of the term, the use for which the premises were demised, and any exceptions contained in the covenant to repair.

A general covenant to keep the premises in repair imposes a continuing duty on the tenant to make repairs as they become necessary. Where no

time is specified for performance of the tenant's
covenant to repair, there is authority for the view
that prior to the termination of the lease the
landlord has no cause of action for damages for the
tenant's breach of covenant to repair unless the
landlord can establish that the tenant's failure to
make prompt repairs injures the landlord's reversionary interest. Other courts hold that the tenant's failure to make the necessary repairs within
a reasonable time will subject him to an action for
damages prior to the expiration of the lease.

When the tenant's breach of covenant to repair occurs during the term, and the landlord has
an immediate cause of action, the measure of damages is the injury to the landlord's reversion, not
the costs of repair. National Bank of Detroit v.
Estate of Voight, 357 Mich. 647, 99 N.W.2d 504
(1959). If the action is brought after the expiration
of the lease, the measure of damages is the costs of
repair. Corbett v. Derman Shoe Co., 338 Mass.
405, 155 N.E.2d 423 (1959). In addition, the landlord may recover any special damages arising from
the tenant's failure to repair.

1. Destruction of the Premises

Often a lease will contain a general covenant
to repair by the tenant, but will contain no express
provisions regarding the obligations of the parties
in the event of the total destruction of the premises. Although the building situated on the demised premises may be the principal subject matter of the lease, the great weight of authority holds

that destruction of the building does not terminate the lease. The theory is that the lease is a conveyance of an interest in land, the purchase price of which the tenant has agreed to pay in installments, and although the building has been destroyed, the tenant still retains his interest in the land. (See "Termination of the Lease—Destruction of the Premises", page 43.)

In addition, most courts hold that a general covenant by the tenant to repair, or maintain or keep the premises in repair, imposes on the tenant an obligation to rebuild in the event that the premises are completely destroyed, unless the cause of destruction is within the scope of an express exception to the duty contained in the lease. Chambers v. North River Line, 179 N.C. 199, 102 S.E. 198 (1920). The obligation to rebuild imposed on the tenant by a general covenant to repair exists whether the destruction is caused by storm, flood, fire, inevitable accident, or the act of a stranger. Upon the probable ground that the term "repair" contained in a lease would not reasonably be construed to mandate the reconstruction of all, or substantially all, of the demised premises in the event of their destruction without fault on the part of the tenant, a substantial minority of courts holds that a general covenant to repair does not require reconstruction of the premises by the tenant in the event of their destruction. Anderson v. Ferguson, 17 Wash.2d 262, 135 P.2d 302 (1943). Further, it is unlikely that courts which have adopted the implied warranty of habitability will construe repair clauses in residential leases as requiring reconstruction of the premises in the event of their destruction. Several states have modified the majority rule by statute.

B. Covenants Made by the Landlord

A covenant by the landlord to repair may be contained in the lease, or may be made after the tenant has taken possession. It may be written or oral. In order for a subsequent promise by the landlord to be enforceable, or utilized as grounds for the imposition of tort liability, the plaintiff must prove that it is supported by consideration. It should be noted that a reservation by the landlord of the privilege to enter and make repairs of the leased premises is not a covenant to repair. It merely gives the landlord the option to make repairs, and is not sufficient to create a duty to repair.

Where the agreement is made prior to the tenant taking possession, the landlord is under a duty to inspect the premises before delivering them to the tenant and to make such repairs as are necessary to put the premises in good repair. With respect to defects arising after the tenant takes possession, the general rule is that the landlord is under no duty to inspect the leased premises unless he expressly agrees to do so; therefore, the tenant is obligated to give the landlord notice of such defects. However, the duty to inspect may be implied from the terms of the agreement, the circumstances surrounding the agreement, or the subsequent conduct of the parties.

The traditional common law view is that a general unqualified covenant to repair by the landlord imposes upon the landlord the duty to rebuild if the premises are destroyed by storm, flood, fire, inevitable accident, or the act of a stranger. However, a limited covenant to repair, such as a promise to keep the roof and exterior walls in good repair, will not be enlarged to impose a duty to rebuild upon the landlord. Further, an exception has been made when the leased premises are a small part of a larger building, the duty to rebuild being denied in such circumstances.

Contrary to the older common law view, there is substantial recent authority for the view that a general unqualified covenant to repair by the landlord does not impose a duty on him to rebuild the leased premises in the event of their destruction. A landlord retains a long-term capital interest in the building, and for this reason the argument for rebuilding is stronger against a landlord who agrees to repair than a tenant who promises to repair; nevertheless, imposition of an obligation to rebuild does not seem to be a reasonable construction of the word "repair". This appears to be the better view, and is consistent with the fact that most persons using the term "repair" do not contemplate reconstruction of a totally destroyed structure.

1. Remedies of the Tenant

The landlord's default in the performance of his covenant to repair does not relieve the tenant of the tenant's duty to pay rent. This result is a direct consequence of the common law doctrine of independence of covenants. However, if the landlord's failure to repair renders the leased premises untenantable, the tenant, upon abandoning the premises, may treat the lease as terminated under the doctrine of constructive eviction. (See "Constructive Eviction", page 26.) Further, in jurisdictions which have adopted the implied warranty of habitability, there seems to be no good reason why the tenant's duty to pay rent should not be treated as dependent upon the landlord's performance of his covenant to repair. The landlord's failure to repair would justify the tenant's nonpayment of rent, and constitute a good defense to an action by the landlord for possession of the leased premises. (See "Implied Warranty of Habitability", page 108.)

Upon default in the landlord's promise to repair, there are several options open to the tenant who is unwilling to terminate the lease. Where the defects are minor, the tenant's usual course of action is to make the repairs and sue the landlord for the costs. If major repairs are required the tenant has the option of making the repairs and recovering the costs from the landlord, or bringing an action for damages against the landlord. When the action is for damages, the measure of damages is the difference between the value of the premises in the condition in which they were contracted for and the fair rental value in their defective condition. In addition, lost profits, to the extent they are susceptible of being ascertained with reasonable certainty, and other losses, reasonably supposed to have been within the contemplation of the parties at the time the agreement was executed, may be recovered by the tenant.

Where the repairs are extensive and expensive, there is some authority for the view that the tenant may maintain an action for specific performance of the landlord's covenant to repair; apparently on the ground that the damages remedy is inadequate.

2. Liability of the Landlord for Personal Injury and Property Damage

There is a fairly even division of authority as to whether the landlord may be held liable to the tenant, and his guests and invitees, for personal injuries or property damage caused by conditions resulting from a breach of the landlord's covenant to repair. The traditional common law view, adhered to by about half the jurisdictions deciding the issue, takes the position that breach of the landlord's covenant to repair creates no liability in tort. Sheppard v. Nienow, 254 S.C. 44, 173 S.E.2d 343 (1970). This view is founded on the theory that liability flows from possession and control of the premises and, in the landlord-tenant situation, it is normally the tenant who has the exclusive possession and control of the premises. The cove-

nant to repair does not transfer sufficient control
back to the landlord to impose tort liability upon
him.

Under the traditional view, the remedy for
breach of the landlord's covenant to repair is a
contract action for damages. Since third parties
have no privity of contract with the landlord, he
has no liability to them. Suit can be brought only
by the tenant, and the tenant may only recover
damages which were within the contemplation of
the parties at the time the agreement was executed. Whether particular property damage is within
the contemplation of the parties is a matter of fact
to be determined by the circumstances of each
particular case. If the property damage is not
within the contemplation of the parties, the tenant's remedy for the landlord's breach of covenant
is limited to recovery of the cost of repair or the
diminution in the rental value of the premises.

Where the property damage is within the contemplation of the parties, but the damaged property is owned by a third party, many courts hold that
the tenant is entitled to indemnification from the
landlord for any claim the tenant is obligated to
pay to the third party. However, there is authority to the contrary.

The trend, and the better view, supported by
Restatement, Second, Torts § 357 (1965), and Restatement, Second, Property (Landlord and Tenant)
§ 17.5 (1977), is to impose tort liability on the
landlord for personal injury and property damage

resulting from his failure to exercise reasonable care in the performance of his covenant to repair. Several reasons have been given for imposing liability upon the landlord. First, the landlord has agreed to keep the premises in repair and the tenant is likely, and entitled, to rely upon the landlord's premise. Such reliance induces the tenant to forego repairing conditions which may be dangerous to himself and others on the premises with his consent. Second, the landlord's retention of the reversionary interest coupled with his contract to repair may be construed as a retention or resumption of the duty (by analogy to that of an owner and possessor) to maintain the premises in a safe condition. The landlord's duty extends to the tenant and all those on the premises with his consent, express or implied.

In cases where the covenant is to make specific repairs, or to make repairs directly related to the tenant's personal safety, or where the covenant is to maintain the premises in a condition of safety, liability for injuries to person and property will usually be imposed on the landlord.

3. *Notice of the Defect*

The tenant's exclusive possession of the premises puts him in the best position to discover defective conditions on the demised premises, and therefore, the tenant is required to give the landlord notice of such defects if liability is to be imposed. Further, the tenant's right to possession and control precludes the landlord from entering the premises, and therefore, he is under no duty to inspect the demised premises unless there is an express agreement that he do so. Even where the landlord has undertaken the duty to inspect, he will not be held liable for personal injuries or property damage resulting from latent defects which could not be discovered by a reasonable inspection of the premises.

IV. NEGLIGENT REPAIRS

Although the general rule is that the landlord has no duty to repair the leased property and is not liable for injuries or property damage arising from defects in the demised premises, virtually all jurisdictions agree that where the landlord attempts to make repairs and fails to exercise reasonable care in making such repairs he is liable for any personal injuries resulting from his negligent conduct. Youngset, Inc. v. Five City Plaza, Inc., 156 Conn. 22, 237 A.2d 366 (1968). The rule applies whether the repairs are made gratuitously or pursuant to an express or implied covenant to repair. Id. The landlord's liability is not based upon the landlord-tenant relationship, but rather is imposed by the unreasonable risk of harm to others created by the landlord's affirmative conduct. A similar rule exists with respect to improvements, as distinguished from repairs, made by the landlord.

The majority of decisions imposing liability on the landlord involve situations where the attempted repair has worsened the condition, making it more dangerous, or has created a deceptive appearance of safety causing the plaintiff to rely to his subsequent harm. There are a few cases, now supported by the Restatement, Second, Torts § 362 (1965), and Restatement, Second, Property (Landlord and Tenant) § 17.7 (1977), which hold that liability will be imposed upon the landlord for negligent repairs only if the negligence results in a worsened condition or the premises are left looking deceptively safe. A greater number of courts hold that the duty of the landlord is to exercise reasonable care in making repairs and impose liability on landlords for negligent repair whether or not the negligence makes the condition worse or makes it look deceptively safe. In the latter jurisdictions, the plaintiff needs only to prove that (i) the landlord attempted to make the repairs, (ii) the defect was not corrected, (iii) prudent work would have eliminated the defect, and, of course, (iv) there is a causal connection between the negligent conduct and the harm.

The courts are also in general agreement that the landlord's liability extends to the tenant, his family and all others on the premises with the consent of the tenant.

A. Massachusetts Rule

A different rule is applied in Massachusetts with respect to gratuitous repairs made by the landlord. In Massachusetts if the landlord negligently repairs gratuitously, he is liable only for gross negligence and only to the person with whom

he made the gratuitous agreement to repair.   If
the negligence of the landlord results in the death
of the party with whom he made the gratuitous
agreement to repair, the landlord is subject to
liability for ordinary as well as gross negligence.
The Massachusetts Rule does not appear to have
been followed in any other jurisdiction.

B. Knowledge of the Tenant

Where the tenant knows of the landlord's negligence, or in the exercise of reasonable care should
have discovered the negligence, the landlord often
escapes liability for injuries to the tenant.   This
result can be reached on one of three theories.
There is authority for the view that the tenant's
reliance on the landlord's proper repair is the basis
of liability, and thus, is an indispensable requisite
to the imposition of liability on the landlord for
negligent repair.   Where the tenant knows, or
should have known, of the landlord's negligent
repair, no such reliance is possible and recovery
will be denied.   Where prior to the accident the
plaintiff has no knowledge that the landlord has
made repairs, no reliance is possible and liability
will not be imposed on the landlord.   For similar
reasons many courts hold that the landlord is not
liable for negligent repairs made prior to the tenant's occupancy.   In addition to the "no reliance"
defense, the defenses of contributory negligence
and assumption of risk may also be available to the
landlord.   (See "Defenses of the Landlord," page
149.)

Under the majority view, third persons are not barred from recovery by the tenant's knowledge of the landlord's negligent conduct. However, where liability is based upon the deceptive appearance of the premises and the tenant has knowledge of the landlord's negligent conduct, some courts hold that the landlord will not be liable to injured third parties; apparently on the theory that the knowledge of the tenant is imputed to third parties on the premises with the tenant's consent.

C. Landlord's Use of an Independent Contractor

Where the landlord hires an independent contractor to effect repairs on the premises and the contractor is negligent in making such repairs, the weight of authority holds that the landlord will be liable for personal injury and property damage resulting from the contractor's negligent repairs. The authorities are virtually unanimous in this view when the work is done pursuant to an express covenant to repair, or is done on that part of the premises retained in the control of the landlord. The landlord remains liable on the theory that his duty of due care is nondelegable. There is a split of opinion where the repairs are done gratuitously on the leased premises, with those jurisdictions denying liability apparently doing so on the ground that the landlord was not discharging a duty in hiring an independent contractor to do the work, and thus, the nondelegable duty rationale would be inapplicable.

D. Effect of Transfer of the Parties' Interest

Transfer of either the landlord's or the tenant's interest does not affect the landlord's liability for negligent repairs. The landlord's duty extends to all those on the premises with the consent of the tenant, and where the tenant transfers his interest, in whole or in part, the assignee or sublessee is on the leased premises with the consent of the tenant and therefore, is within the protected class. Since liability is founded upon the negligent conduct of the landlord, a transferee of the reversionary interest would not be liable for the wrongful acts of his predecessor in interest. Finally, having created the dangerous condition by his own negligent conduct, a landlord may not absolve himself of potential liability simply by transferring his reversion.

V. LIABILITY FOR INJURY TO PERSONS AND PROPERTY OUTSIDE THE LEASED PROPERTY

The general rule is that a possessor of land is liable to third parties for personal injuries and property damage occurring outside the land but caused by structures or other artificial conditions existing on the land. In the absence of an express covenant to repair, a landlord is not liable to third parties outside the leased premises for injuries to the person or property caused by dangerous conditions on the leased property when the dangerous conditions arise after the tenant takes possession of the premises. As the party in possession and control of the premises, the tenant will be liable for such injuries. However, when the dangerous condition causing the injury arises prior to the lease but the injury occurs after the transfer of possession to the tenant, both the landlord and the tenant will be liable to the injured third party. The landlord's liability is founded upon his failure to correct the dangerous condition while the leased property was under his full control, and the tenant's liability is founded upon his control of the premises at the time the injury occurs.

Where the dangerous condition arises from purely natural causes, the courts generally refuse to hold owners or possessors of land liable for personal injury or property damage occurring outside the property by the dangerous condition existing on the property; apparently on the theory that activity is essential to liability, or, alternatively, on the ground that one has no obligation to take affirmative action to protect others. However, if any person has contributed significantly to the creation of the dangerous condition, liability will be imposed.

> **Example:** L owns land on a hillside on which a number of large rocks are naturally, but precariously located. A previous tenant attempted to terrace the land to use it for agricultural purposes, and in the process loosened the soil around the rocks. L leases the land to T. Subsequently the rocks break loose, roll

down the hill and injure several motorists on an abutting public road. L is subject to liability to the motorists.

The risk to persons outside of the leased property from artificial conditions usually occurs in one of three situations: (i) the building as constructed is inherently dangerous no matter how it is maintained and used; (ii) a usually safe structure is dangerous because of disrepair; or (iii) a building which is safe if not used becomes unreasonably dangerous if used or if used in a particular manner. Where the building is dangerous only if used or used in a particular manner, the landlord is not subject to liability unless use of the structure or the particular use of the structure was contemplated by the parties at the time the lease was executed.

There is one major exception to the "natural condition" rule. In urban areas the possessor of land is under a duty to exercise reasonable care, including inspection, to prevent personal injury and property damage resulting from the dangerous condition of trees located on his land; the theory apparently being that the risk of harm resulting from the concentration of people is so great that it is reasonable to impose a duty of due care on the possessor.

In addition to the above exception, there is at least one case holding that the occupier of land has a duty, arising solely from his possession, to manage his property in a manner which will eliminate the risk of harm to persons off the premises arising from a natural condition existing on the land. Sprecher v. Adamson Companies, 30 Cal.3d 358, 178 Cal.Rptr. 783, 636 P.2d 1121 (1981). Again, the basis of liability is negligence. The test to be applied is whether in the management of the property, the possessor has acted as a reasonable person under all of the circumstances.

A. Dangerous Conditions Antedating Transfer of Possession to the Tenant

As mentioned above, the landlord will be liable to third parties for personal injuries and property damage occurring outside the leased property as a result of dangerous conditions on the leased property if the dangerous conditions antedate the transfer of possession to the tenant. Granucci v. Claasen, 204 Cal. 509, 269 P. 437 (1928). It is generally agreed that the landlord must have actual or constructive notice of the condition before liability will be imposed. However, the doctrine of *res ipsa loquitur* has been applied in some jurisdictions, and a few courts appear to impose strict liability upon the landlord.

The idea of constructive notice reflects the imposition upon the landlord of a duty to inspect the premises during the period of his control over the premises. However, the landlord's failure to make a reasonable inspection will subject him to liability only if such an inspection would have disclosed the dangerous condition which caused the injury. In addition to actual or constructive notice

of the condition, the landlord must be given a
reasonable period of time in which to eliminate the
dangerous condition before liability will be imposed.

Since the landlord's liability is founded upon
his failure to correct the dangerous condition when
the property was under his full control, the landlord will not be absolved of liability merely because
the tenant knew of the dangerous condition or
should have discovered it after taking possession.
Also, the landlord's liability does not negate that of
the tenant, as possessor, and the injured party may
recover against either the landlord or the tenant.

1. *Covenant by the Tenant to Eliminate the Dangerous Condition*

By the majority view, a promise by the tenant
to eliminate the dangerous condition or to indemnify the landlord from liability to third persons for
injuries arising out of such dangerous conditions
will not relieve the landlord of his liability to
injured third parties. On the other hand, the
tenant's promise does entitle the landlord to recover from the tenant any damages the landlord is
required to pay to said third parties. A few cases
hold that the tenant's promise to eliminate the
dangerous condition or indemnify the landlord ab-
solves the landlord from further responsibility for
correcting the defect; therefore, he has no liability
for injuries to third parties arising out of the
dangerous condition. This view is subject to at
least two criticisms. First, a promise to indemnify

should not, and ordinarily does not, absolve a tortfeasor of liability; otherwise all insured persons would be free of liability. Second, the rule permits a nonrecourse delegation of a positive duty, conduct not usually permitted.

2. *Sublease*

Where the tenant subleases the property he will be subject to liability as a landlord on the same basis that liability has been imposed on owner-landlords. Thus, it is possible that the landlord, tenant and subtenant may all be liable for personal injury and property damage to third parties outside the leased property resulting from the dangerous condition existing on the leased property. If the dangerous condition predates the original lease, the owner-landlord and the tenant-sublandlord would be subject to liability for their respective failures to eliminate the dangerous condition while the leased property was under their control, and the subtenant would be liable as a possessor.

B. Effect of the Landlord's Covenant to Repair

The weight of authority holds that if the landlord covenants to repair or maintain the leased premises in a safe condition and breaches his covenant, he will be liable for injuries to persons and property outside of the leased property caused by dangerous conditions on the property which performance of his covenant would have eliminated. Lommori v. Milner Hotels, Inc., 63 N.M. 342, 319

P.2d 949 (1957). Retained control is the basis of
liability; the landlord's retention of a reversionary
interest coupled with his agreement to repair is
construed as retention of control over the demised
premises. Id. The idea of control is at best a
fiction; and perhaps it would be more accurate to
say that these factors manifest an intent by the
landlord to retain or reassume some of the duties
that a possessor of land has to third parties. Some
courts hold that an agreement whereby the landlord merely retains the right to inspect the demised premises and make such repairs as he deems
necessary is sufficient to impose liability upon the
landlord.

In order for liability to be imposed upon the
landlord, the landlord must have actual or constructive notice of the defect and have had a reasonable time in which to effect repairs. Where the
dangerous condition arises prior to the lease, most
courts appear to assume the landlord has knowledge of the condition. When the defect arises after
the transfer of possession, there is a split of authority as to whether the landlord must be given actual
notice of the defect, or if he has a duty to inspect
the premises to ascertain their condition. Some
courts impose liability on the landlord if in the
exercise of reasonable care he could have discovered the defective condition in time to repair it,
while others appear to require that actual notice
be given to the landlord.

A few courts have denied recovery against the
landlord on the ground that a breach of contract

creates no right of action in one who is not a party to the agreement.

The landlord's covenant to repair or maintain the premises in a safe condition does not absolve the tenant of his liability to third parties injured as a result of the dangerous condition existing on the leased premises. As the possessor of the demised premises, and the person in actual control of the premises, the tenant retains his liability for injuries resulting from dangerous conditions on the property and he may not avoid liability by his contract with the landlord. Third parties suffering personal injury or property damage from the dangerous condition may recover against either the landlord or the tenant. Where the landlord has notice of the dangerous condition, and an opportunity to repair the defect, it would appear that the tenant is entitled to indemnification for any damages he is obligated to pay because of the landlord's failure to repair.

C. Landlord Under a Statutory Duty to Repair

Where an obligation to repair is imposed upon the landlord by statute or administrative regulation, the weight of authority is that the landlord will be liable to third parties outside the leased premises for personal injuries or property damage resulting from his failure to comply with the statutory or regulatory obligation. Moretti v. C.S. Realty Co., 78 R.I. 341, 82 A.2d 608 (1951). Most courts considering the issue follow the view that violation of the statute or regulation is negligence per se.

A minority of courts holds that violation of a statute or regulation cannot be the basis for imposing tort liability upon the landlord. The arguments most often put forth in support of the minority view are (i) that there was no legislative intent to abolish the doctrine of *caveat emptor* or, (ii) more traditionally, that tort liability follows control and possession of the premises and shifting the burden of repair to the landlord is not sufficient to constitute retention of control by the landlord. A few courts have denied recovery on the theory that the statute or regulation was not intended for the benefit of persons off the leased property.

The landlord is subject to liability only for dangerous conditions of which he has actual notice, or which he could have discovered in the exercise of reasonable care; and the landlord must be given a reasonable period of time in which to effect the necessary repairs. A major factor to be considered in determining what defects are reasonably discoverable by a landlord is his disability to inspect leased premises under the exclusive control of the tenant.

The landlord's statutory duty to repair the dangerous condition does not absolve the tenant of his duty to third parties outside the leased property. Third parties suffering personal injury or property damage as a result of dangerous conditions on the property may recover against either the landlord or the tenant.

D. Activities Conducted on the Leased Premises After Transfer of Possession

Generally, liability is imposed on the landlord for personal injury and property damage to persons outside of the leased property caused by the activities of the tenant on the leased property when such activities involve an unreasonable risk of harm to others and are engaged in with the consent or knowledge of the landlord. The required consent or knowledge may be express, or implied from the surrounding circumstances. Where the landlord does not consent and reasonably would not have contemplated the activity of the tenant, there is no liability.

Where the requisite unreasonable risk and consent or knowledge are present, the landlord's liability encompasses harm arising from the activities of the tenant or a subtenant, and the activities of a licensee, invitee or employee of the tenant or subtenant. However, unreasonable risks which are the result of the tenant's failure to take normal precautions to avoid harm to third parties will not impose liability on the landlord unless he was aware that the tenant would not engage in the activity in a reasonably cautious manner. Further, the landlord's consent to, or knowledge of, one dangerous activity does not permit the imposition of liability for harm caused by other unauthorized activities of the tenant.

The limited authority on the issue indicates that the landlord may not relieve himself of liability by transferring his reversionary interest. Where the reversionary interest is conveyed, the transferee will not be liable for the tenant's dangerous activities unless he had full knowledge of the unreasonable conduct at the time of transfer.

VI. CHANGES IN THE CONDITION OF THE DEMISED PREMISES— RIGHTS AND DUTIES OF THE TENANT

It is usual for the physical condition of the premises to change during the term of the lease. The most common change in condition is the ordinary wear and tear which occurs from the normal and reasonable use of the premises by the tenant. Other changes in the demised premises occur as a result of alterations and/or annexations to the leased premises by the tenant, the removal of valuable minerals from the subsurface of the leased premises, the removal of trees and other plants from the surface of the leased premises, and physical changes caused by strangers and acts of God. The tenant's rights and obligations vary with the source and character of the physical change, as developed below.

A. Physical Changes Due to Acts of a Stranger or Acts of God

In virtually all jurisdictions, historically and under the present law, the tenant is not liable if the leased property is damaged by an act of God (lightning, flood or windstorm) or by an accident in which the tenant is not at fault unless the tenant expressly assumes such liability in the lease; for example, where the leased building adjoins another and in the process of demolishing the adjoining building the adjoining wall of the leased building is damaged by a third party, the tenant is not liable for such damage. In the absence of such an agreement the tenant's duties are to use reasonable diligence to protect the leased property and avoid the commission of waste.

Although the reasons have never been well articulated, the earlier decisions imposed liability on the tenant for damage to the demised premises resulting from the fault of a stranger. Some writers have suggested that unlike the situations of unavoidable accident or act of God, imposition of liability on the tenant was not unfair because the tenant could recover in turn from the wrongdoing third party. Others have suggested that liability is imposed because the possibility of collusion between the tenant and the stranger is so great that the tenant should be made an insurer of the demised premises against such harm. In a number of jurisdictions the case authority follows this common law view. However, such cases are old and of doubtful wisdom. The rule has been rejected by the Restatement of Property § 146 (1936) with respect to life tenants, and today it is unlikely that a court would impose liability on a tenant for damage to the leased premises caused by the act of a stranger in the absence of an express covenant whereby the tenant assumes such liability.

B. Ordinary Wear and Tear and Voluntary Alterations to the Leased Property Made by the Tenant

In the absence of a provision expressly setting forth the use to be made of the premises by the tenant, the tenant is entitled to make any use of the premises which is reasonable in light of the surrounding circumstances. The location of the demised premises, its physical characteristics and past use are all factors relevant in determining what uses are reasonable under the circumstances.

1. Alterations by the Tenant

The exact state of the law regarding the tenant's right to make alterations to the demised premises is unclear. Ordinarily, the landlord is entitled to have the leased premises returned at the end of the term in the same condition as when leased, ordinary wear and tear excepted. Thus, most courts take the view that a tenant may not materially alter the premises without the landlord's consent. Many courts following this view also hold the tenant liable for waste for any material alteration even though the change substantially increases the value of the land; presumably, the measure of damages is the cost of restoring the premises to their original condition. Others take the view that to constitute actionable waste, the alterations must decrease the value of the reversion and be of such a material and permanent nature that restoration of the leased premises is virtually impossible. A few courts have gone so far as to hold that the demolition of buildings located on the demised premises does not constitute actionable waste where such conduct is clearly beneficial to the estate of the landlord and the existing structure is economically obsolete.

The minority and better view is that in the absence of an agreement to the contrary, the tenant is permitted to make such alterations as are consistent with and reasonably necessary for the tenant's reasonable use of the leased premises. To be permissible the alterations must meet two preconditions: (i) the alteration must relate to a reasonable use being made of the premises by the tenant, and (ii) the alteration must be reasonably necessary for the tenant's utilization of the leased premises. The minority position is supported by the Restatement, Second, Property (Landlord and Tenant) § 12.2 (1977) which also provides that, where possible, the tenant must restore the leased premises to their former condition at the end of the term unless such restoration would be unreasonable in light of the probable future use of the property.

Courts which ordinarily deny or severely restrict the tenant's right to make alterations tend to relax their application of the rule in cases involving life tenancies and long term leases. A few jurisdictions have statutorily modified the common law rule against alterations by permitting the tenant to make alterations under certain, specified conditions; for example, if the alteration: (i) is one the owner would be likely to make, or (ii) will not depreciate the value of the reversion, such alterations will be permitted. Such statutes usually require the tenant to post security for damage which may occur to the reversion.

2. Ordinary Wear and Tear

The most common physical change in the leased premises is deterioration from wear and tear from the ordinary use of the premises. Ordinary wear and tear is expected by the parties to the lease and, in the absence of an agreement to the contrary, the tenant is entitled to the use of the premises without incurring liability for reasonable wear and tear. However, it should be remembered that the tenant does have an obligation not to commit permissive waste; that is, he has a duty to make such repairs as are necessary to keep the demised premises "wind and water tight" to prevent damage to the premises from the elements.

> For example, suppose the tenant leases a small office building for a period of five years. If the carpet in the office building becomes worn and threadbare from the ordinary use of the premises as an office, the tenant is not be liable for such damage. If the roof to the building should develop a water leak caused by normal deterioration of the roofing material, the tenant is not liable for such damage to the roof. However, the tenant is required to take reasonable steps to protect the interior of the building from damage which might be caused

by water leaking through the roof, and his
failure to take such steps will result in him
being liable for permissive waste. The latter
obligation would most likely require the tenant to repair the roof.

The basis of liability is the tenant's duty to repair,
and liability is measured by the injury to the
landlord's reversionary interest resulting from the
tenant's failure to perform his duty.

C. Waste

In the absence of an express provision governing the use or uses to be made of the leased
premises, the implied intent of the parties will
govern.   As a general rule the tenant will be
entitled to use the premises for any purpose which
is reasonable in light of the surrounding circumstances, and the landlord impliedly consents to acts
by the tenant which are reasonably necessary to
effectuate his reasonable use of the demised premises.   However, any unprivileged conduct on the
part of the tenant that causes permanent and
substantial injury to the landlord's reversion constitutes waste.   Thus, the tenant is considered to
have committed waste to the extent that he exceeds the express or implied limitations on his
right to use of the demised premises (e.g., cutting
timber), or violates a concomitant duty arising out
of his leasehold interest (e.g., the tenant's limited
duty to repair), and such conduct results in permanent and appreciable damage to the landlord's
reversion.

The landlord may expressly authorize the tenant to do and perform certain acts which in the absence of such an agreement would constitute waste. A conveyance "without impeachment for waste" is the broadest authorization that the landlord can grant short of conveying the fee, and such a conveyance gives the tenant a free hand in his use of the premises. However, even where the leasehold is granted without impeachment for waste, the tenant is not entitled to perform wanton, malicious or unreasonable acts with respect to his use of the demised premises. Such conduct is generally characterized as equitable waste and will be enjoined by a court of equity.

In determining whether waste has been committed, a substantial majority of jurisdictions adopts what is called the functional approach to the law of waste. Stated simply, this theory provides that an act of the tenant constitutes waste only when it diminishes the landlord's reversionary interest. Whether the landlord's reversionary interest has been diminished is a matter of fact, and depends upon the normal rights attributed to the conveyance of a leasehold, any additional rights and interest intended to be conveyed to the tenant by the landlord, and the rights and interest intended by the landlord to be reserved unto himself.

The landlord's action for waste must be distinguished from actions arising from the tenant's breach of covenants contained in the lease. It is well settled that the parties may agree that the tenant's use of the demised premises will have a greater or lesser scope than would be the case in the absence of such an agreement, except, of course, where such agreement violates public policy. Where the landlord imposes restrictions on the use of the demised premises, such restrictions are categorized as restrictive covenants, and the violation of such covenants by the tenant constitutes a breach of contract rather than the commission of waste. In such cases, the landlord's remedy is in contract rather than in tort.

1. Conduct of the Tenant Constituting Waste

a. Cutting Timber. The majority of cases dealing with the issue of what constitutes waste have involved the cutting of timber. The early cases in this country adopted a test of "good husbandry". It was said that the cutting of trees was not waste unless permanent injury was done to the reversion. At the time of these decisions clearing land of timber in order that it could be used for agricultural purposes substantially increased the value of the land. Thus, most courts held that cutting trees did not constitute waste.

Today most courts have adopted a reasonable use standard; that is, the tenant is limited to the reasonable use of the land in light of the purpose for which it is leased. Where land is leased for agricultural purposes, the tenant is entitled to cut trees on the leased property only when necessary to effectuate the agricultural purpose of the lease.

This appears to be consistent with the functional approach. A minority of courts continue to follow the view that any injury to the reversion constitutes waste, and uses value as the test for determining whether there has been an injury. In these cases any act which decreases the value of the land injures the reversion and therefore constitutes waste; however, if cutting the timber increases the value of the land the tenant is not liable for waste.

Where the cutting of trees might otherwise constitute waste, the tenant is entitled to cut a reasonable number of trees for use on the leased premises for purposes of building and maintaining necessary fences, for use as firewood, and to make necessary repairs to the leased premises to avoid liability for permissive waste. This common law right of the tenant is known as the right of estovers. The tenant is also entitled to take timber to make repairs when he has an express obligation to repair or when the landlord has the obligation to repair and fails to do so.

Modern practice is to hire an expert to make the necessary repairs and purchase lumber from one who sells it in the ordinary course of business. In recognition of this practice most courts hold that when the tenant has the right to cut timber for use in making repairs, he also has the right to sell the standing timber and use the proceeds to pay the costs of materials and labor necessary to complete the repairs.

In a few instances the question has been whether cutting timber was the specific reasonable use for which the premises were leased. In such cases discerning the intent of the parties is the real issue. Although the question is a difficult one there is authority for the view that where the land is purchased for its standing timber or where the primary value of the land is the standing timber located thereon, the tenant is entitled to commercially cut the timber. The limited use which can be made of the land is evidence of the intent of the parties, and the logging operation is seen as reasonable in light of the surrounding circumstances.

b. Removal of Valuable Minerals by the Tenant. In the absence of an agreement to the contrary, the removal of coal, oil, gas or other valuable minerals from the subsurface of the leased property by the tenant constitutes waste; the theory is that the value of the reversion is permanently reduced by the removal of such minerals. There is one major exception to this rule under the common law—the open mine exception. Under the majority view, if the removal operation was in existence at the time the lease was executed, the tenant is entitled to continue the removal of the subsurface minerals. The intent to allow the tenant to remove the minerals is inferred from the existence of the mining operation. However, the tenant is not entitled to open new mines or wells, and his operation of the existing mine or well is limited to an operation which is within the bounds of sound business practice for the removal of the particular substance.

c. Permissive Waste. Except as it may have been modified by the adoption of the implied warranty of habitability, the great weight of authority holds that the tenant has a duty to make minor repairs to keep the leased premises wind and water tight. Although there is no clear definition of the scope of this duty, the tenant generally has no duty to repair or rebuild structures destroyed, without fault of the tenant, in whole or in part, by fire or other casualty, nor to reconstruct a structure whose useful life has come to an end through ordinary wear and tear and the passage of time. The duty most often involves the repair of roof leaks, the replacement of broken windows and doors, etc., which repairs are necessary to prevent the elements from damaging the interior of the building. Damage arising from the tenant's failure to perform his duty constitutes permissive waste for which the tenant is liable.

d. Equitable Waste. It is not unusual for a landlord to convey a leasehold with a provision which enlarges the usual estate of the tenant, or contains a provision that the conveyance is "without impeachment of waste". At law, the words "without impeachment for waste" are construed to mean that the tenant is not liable for waste, and in effect give the tenant a free hand with respect to his use of the demised premises. At an early date the equity courts developed the rule that despite such a lease provision the tenant would be liable for wanton, malicious or unreasonable conduct which resulted in permanent and substantial injury to the reversion. Such conduct is commonly referred to as equitable waste. The test for whether the conduct of the tenant is permissible or constitutes an actionable wrong is whether his actions are those which a reasonable owner of the fee might perform.

It is unclear whether an express provision absolving the tenant from liability for equitable waste will be upheld by the courts. Such a provision may be contrary to public policy.

2. *Effect of a Covenant to Repair*

Generally, a covenant to repair by the landlord will not be construed as authorization for the tenant to engage in conduct which would otherwise constitute waste. A covenant to repair ordinarily covers repairs made necessary by ordinary wear and tear or damage from causes not the fault of the tenant, but the covenant to repair will not be enlarged so as to encompass acts of waste by the tenant.

Where the tenant covenants to repair the scope of his duty will depend upon the language of the covenant and the construction usually placed on such covenants by the court. For example, the majority view appears to be that a general covenant of repair obligates the tenant to repair damage caused by third parties or non-man-made forces. However, the tenant's breach of covenant would give the landlord an action for breach of contract rather than an action in tort for waste. (See "Express Covenants to Repair—Covenants Made by the Tenant", page 158.)

3. *Effect of an Assignment or Sublease*

While the tenant retains possession of the leased property, he is liable for all acts of waste committed by himself or third parties on the property with his consent or at his behest. Where the tenant assigns the lease, he has no liability for any improper changes in the condition of the leased premises occurring subsequent to the assignment. The assignee is liable to the landlord for such waste.

Where the tenant sublets rather than assigns, there appears to be no good reason why the landlord should not have a cause of action against the subtenant for acts of waste committed by the subtenant. This is the general rule and the landlord is entitled to damages and injunctive relief for waste committed by a subtenant. In addition, since the tenant continues to have privity of contract and privity of estate with the landlord and, so far as the landlord is concerned, is the party entitled to possession, the tenant is also liable to the landlord for any unauthorized physical changes in the condition of the leased property caused by the subtenant.

4. Statute of Limitations

There is a division of opinion on when the statute of limitations begins to run against the landlord in an action for waste. Most courts hold that the statute of limitations begins to run when the unauthorized physical change in the leased premises occurs. A substantial minority of courts holds that the statute of limitations does not begin to run until the landlord discovers, or should have discovered, the tenant's acts of waste. This view appears to take into consideration the fact that the landlord does not have possession and control of the leased property, and therefore, is usually in a poor position to discover acts of waste committed by the tenant. A third view, followed in Kentucky, distinguishes between voluntary and permissive waste. In Kentucky, with respect to voluntary waste, the statute of limitations begins to run when the act of waste is committed. With respect to permissive waste, the statute begins to run at the termination of the leasehold estate.

5. Remedies of the Landlord

The landlord's usual remedies for the tenant's acts of waste are to sue for damages and/or seek injunctive relief. Where the action is for damages, the measure of damages is usually the reduction in the fair market value of the property resulting from the tenant's unauthorized acts of waste. However, damages are often measured by the cost of repair or reconstruction of the damaged proper-

ty, and when the waste is the result of unauthorized removal of part of the demised premises (e.g.,
timber, minerals, etc.) courts are inclined to award
damages measured by the value of the property
taken. Almost one-half of the states have statutes
which provide for the recovery of double or treble
damages in an action for waste.

The universal rule is that a court of equity will
enjoin the commission of waste. Today, most
courts hold that injunctive relief is permissible
even in the absence of allegations that the plaintiff's remedy at law is inadequate or that the
plaintiff will suffer irreparable harm in the absence of injunctive relief. Although most cases
involve injunctions to restrain affirmative acts of
waste, the language of the decisions indicates that
the courts are willing to grant mandatory injunctions in appropriate circumstances. In addition to
injunctive relief, the landlord is also entitled to an
accounting where appropriate; for example, where
the tenant has removed minerals from the leased
property, the landlord is entitled to an accounting
for net profits made by the tenant.

The initial difficulty of the landlord is discovering the conduct (or lack thereof) resulting in the
waste. In the absence of an agreement to the
contrary, the general rule is that the landlord is
not entitled to enter the demised premises during
the term of the lease to determine their condition
or to make needed repairs. The rule is an out-

growth of the tenant's right to exclusive possession and applies even when continued disrepair will result in waste. Under the minority view the landlord may enter and repair to prevent waste. It should be noted that the landlord's right to enter and repair to prevent waste may prove to be a hollow one if the jurisdiction also follows the general rule that the landlord has no right to inspect the demised premises to determine their condition, and if the statute of limitations begins to run at the time the waste was committed.

Virtually all jurisdictions appear to follow the common law rule that the landlord is not entitled to terminate the lease because of the commission of waste by the tenant. However, the impact of the rule is slight because most leases reserve a right of entry (power of termination) which permits the landlord to terminate the lease in the event the tenant commits waste, and at least twenty states have statutes which permit termination of the lease as a remedy for waste.

It should be noted that a tenant at will is not liable for permissive waste. The reason usually given is that it is unfair to impose the burden of repair on a tenant at will when his estate may come to an end at any time at the whim of the landlord. Further, the ability to terminate the lease at will provides adequate protection of the landlord's reversionary interest. The commission of voluntary waste terminates a tenancy at will and the tenant at will becomes liable for damages in an action for trespass.

D. Fixtures

A fixture is perhaps best defined as a former chattel which by reason of its annexation to or association in use with land is so connected with the land that a disinterested third party would consider the former chattel to be a part of the subject realty. Fixtures should be distinguished from accessions because some fixtures are removable by the tenant, whereas accessions are not removable. A fixture is a chattel which retains its separate identity in spite of its annexation to the realty (e.g., a furnace), whereas where the chattel is so annexed as to lose its separate identity (e.g., bricks, nails and lumber which become part of a building) the issue is one of accession.

In the United States most courts hold that whether a chattel becomes a fixture is a matter of the intent of the parties. The intent test was first proposed in the leading case of Teaff v. Hewitt, 1 Ohio St. 511 (1853), in which the Ohio Supreme Court stated that there were three criteria for determining whether a chattel had become a fixture. The first of these criteria required that there be an ". . . actual annexation to the realty, or something appurtenant thereto." Usually physical annexation to the land is required but in certain circumstances the relationship between the chattel and the land, or the use to which the land is put, is such that the chattel will be deemed to be constructively annexed to the realty. For example, the storm windows and doors of a house will normally pass to the purchaser of the land even though the storm windows and doors were removed and in storage at the time of the conveyance.

The second criterion is that the chattel be appropriated ". . . to the use or purpose of that part of the realty with which it is connected." Generally, where the chattel is so necessary or convenient to the use of the land on which it is located that a disinterested third party would regard it as a part of the realty, then the chattel will be regarded as a fixture (e.g., a hot water heater in a home, or the seats in a theater).

The third criterion is that it be ". . . the intention of the party making the annexation to make the article a permanent accession to the freehold. . . ." The intent is not the subjective intent of the party making the annexation, but rather the objective intent as manifested by his conduct and the surrounding circumstances; as the *Teaff* court stated: ". . . this intention being inferred from the nature of the article affixed, the relation and situation of the party making the annexation, and the purpose or use for which the annexation has been made."

1. *Tenant's Right to Remove Tenant Fixtures*

Most commentators and a good many courts espouse the view that all tenant fixtures should be treated alike and that the primary consideration for determining whether a fixture is removable by the tenant is a matter of the intention of the tenant. However, there are a substantial number of decisions which classify tenant fixtures into three categories: Trade fixtures, agricultural fixtures, and domestic fixtures (including ornamental fixtures). The result in a number of cases appears to be affected by this categorization of the fixtures at issue in the litigation.

a. Trade Fixtures. Fixtures which the tenant attaches to the leased premises for the purpose of carrying on his trade or business are generally referred to as "trade fixtures" (e.g., built-in suit racks in a men's clothing store). The courts decided at an early date that a tenant is entitled to remove his trade fixtures from the leased premises. The tenant's right of removal may be justified on one of several grounds: (i) that it is unfair to allow the benefit of such fixtures to inure to the landlord who has contributed nothing to them (it may be argued that this reasoning should be equally applicable to other fixtures); (ii) that it was not the intention of the tenant to make a permanent accession to the freehold (perhaps because of the particular use made of the fixture by the tenant, and the assumption that he will want to use the fixture in his business even if he moves to a new location); or (iii) that there is an implied agreement that the tenant may remove his fixtures.

Not every fixture is removable and a distinction is made between trade fixtures (removable) and fixtures which generally improve the demised premises (not removable). The cases demonstrate that the line is not easily drawn. For example, a tenant has been denied the right to remove heating equipment where the equipment was installed for the general purpose of heating the premises; while on the other hand, it has been held that the tenant may remove heating equipment which was installed for the particular needs of the tenant in his trade and business. In the latter instance the heating equipment was held to be a removable trade fixture.

Another distinction is the severability of the chattel from the leased property. Where a chattel is so annexed to an existing structure that it becomes an integral part thereof, the general rule is that the fixture is not removable but rather becomes a part of the landlord's realty. For example, where a commercial tenant constructed a balcony in the leased building, it was held that the balcony became the property of the landlord at the end of the term. On the other hand, the trend and majority view is that buildings constructed by the tenant can be removed by the tenant if they were constructed for the purpose of advancing his trade or business.

In sum, it cannot be said with certainty that any particular chattel attached to the leased premises by the tenant can be removed by him; the intent of the parties making the annexation will be determinative, and thus, it is advisable to cover the matter in the lease. Distinctions such as the ones discussed above are merely devices used to determine the intent of the parties.

b. Agricultural Fixtures. A few early cases distinguished between trade fixtures and fixtures annexed to property leased for agricultural purposes, holding that the tenant was entitled to remove trade fixtures, but that he was not entitled to remove agricultural fixtures. There appears to be no valid reason for this distinction and today the great weight of authority treats agricultural fixtures in the same manner as trade fixtures.

c. Domestic Fixtures. Domestic fixtures may be generally described as annexations made by residential tenants to improve the comfort, convenience or aesthetics of the demised premises. In general, the right to remove domestic fixtures seems to be more restricted than the tenant's right to remove trade or agricultural fixtures. There are few decisions directly on point, but such decisions as exist tend to distinguish between attachments which fulfill some particular personal need of the tenant and attachments which tend to improve the leased premises generally. The tenant is generally denied the right to remove fixtures which fall in the latter category. For example, in one case a tenant was held to be entitled to remove a chandelier (aesthetics), while in another the right to remove an oil furnace was denied (a general improvement).

d. Limitations on the Tenant's Right of Removal.

(i) Character of the Annexation. Most courts hold that where the fixture is so annexed to an existing structure that it cannot be removed without substantial damage to the leased premises the fixture may not be removed by the tenant. It becomes a part of the realty of the landlord. It may be argued that the tenant should be allowed to remove any fixture so long as he is willing to restore the premises to their original condition. It is submitted that the damage that removal of the fixture would cause to the leased premises should be viewed as merely another factor to be considered by the court in determining the objective intent of the tenant, rather than an absolute bar to removal where tenant is willing to restore the premises to their original condition. Such a rule has not been adopted by the courts.

(ii) Time Limitations. Where the tenant's term is for a fixed period, the tenant is usually required to remove his fixtures by the end of the term or lose the ownership thereof to the landlord. An exception exists when the tenant holds over temporarily with the acquiescence of the landlord. In such cases his right to remove fixtures continues during the holdover period.

Where the tenant surrenders his leasehold prior to the expiration of the term leaving his fixtures on the leased premises, the general rule is that the right to remove fixtures ends with the surrender and ownership vests in the landlord.

When a term for years is prematurely terminated by the landlord for breach of condition by the tenant, the decisions are divided with regard to the tenant's right to remove fixtures that are on the premises at the time his possession comes to an end. Some courts follow the general rule and hold that ownership of the remaining fixtures resides in the landlord. Other courts allow the tenant a reasonable time after termination of the lease in which to remove the fixtures.

If the lease in question is one for an indefinite term (e.g., a periodic tenancy or tenancy at will), the tenant will be given a reasonable period of time after termination of the lease in which to remove tenant fixtures from the demised premises. The reason for this rule is that, unlike a term for years which comes to an end at a fixed point in time, the tenant under a lease for an indefinite term is unable to determine the termination date of the lease and it would be an undue hardship on such tenants to require forfeiture of their right to remove fixtures because of the termination of such leases, at least where the termination is at the landlord's behest. It should be noted that this reasoning also applies to the term for years lease which is prematurely terminated by the landlord, and supports the rule which gives the tenant a reasonable period of time for removal of fixtures under such circumstances. What constitutes a reasonable time is a matter of fact to be determined by the circumstances of each particular case.

CHAPTER VI

TRANSFERS BY THE LANDLORD AND TENANT

I. INTRODUCTION

After the execution of a lease the interests of the parties may generally be described as a term (for years, periodic or at will) held by the tenant, and a reversion (to which the right to receive rent and benefits under the lease attaches as an incident thereto) held by the landlord. In the absence of a contractual agreement or statutory provision to the contrary, the interests of the landlord and the tenant are freely alienable, in whole or in part.

There is one major exception to this general rule. Inherent in the nature of a tenancy at will is the fact that it may continue only so long as both parties will its continuance. An attempt by the landlord or the tenant to transfer their respective interests is usually construed as a manifestation that the transferor no longer desires the continuance of the tenancy. As a result, a transfer or attempted transfer by the landlord or the tenant of their respective interests results in a termination of the tenancy at will. Although an assignment by the tenant at will can confer no rights on the assignee as against the landlord, there is authority for the view that such an assignment is valid as between the tenant and his assignee. There is also authority for the view that as between the landlord and tenant, the tenant at will can make a valid sublease (as distinguished from an assignment) of his interest; apparently on the theory that the tenant continues to recognize his tenancy in the sublease situation.

Many states have statutes which modify the tenant's common law right to transfer his leasehold interest, and which set forth certain formalities for the transfer of the tenant's interest in the leased property.

II. TRANSFERS BY THE TENANT

Except for a tenant at will, in the absence of a covenant or statutory provision to the contrary, a tenant may transfer all or any part of his interest in the demised premises. In the absence of a statute, no particular formalities are required for a valid assignment of the tenant's leasehold interest. However, the recording acts of a particular jurisdiction may require that the assignment be recorded in order to be valid against third parties, and the Statute of Frauds may require that the assignment be made in writing.

To this rule of free alienability there is one well recognized exception. Where the rents and other benefits expected to be derived under the lease by the landlord depend upon the special skills and expertise of the tenant, the tenant is not entitled to assign the lease without the consent of the landlord. The usual situation involves a lease in which the rent is reserved as a percentage of the tenant's production, profits or sales. Such a lease is said to create a personal relationship of trust and confidence between the landlord and the tenant so as to preclude any assignment by the tenant without the consent of the landlord. The existence of this implied covenant against assignment may be denied where the lease also reserves a substantial minimum rent; the large minimum rent negates the implication of reliance and therefore, the implied covenant against assignment also. Where the transfer of the tenant's interest does not deprive the landlord of the special skills he bargained for, there is no good reason to restrict the tenant's right to transfer his interest. For example, where agricultural land is leased for one year on a crop sharing basis and the crop has been harvested and marketed, the tenant should be entitled to assign the balance of his term since the landlord will not be deprived of the special farming skills for which he bargained.

A. Assignment and Sublease Distinguished

The characterization of the tenant's transfer as a sublease or assignment will have substantially different legal consequences. In general, if the transfer is characterized as a sublease the original landlord-tenant relationship continues unabated and the tenant becomes the landlord of his subtenant. The tenant remains directly liable to the landlord for breach of the lease covenants. Since there is neither privity of contract (there being no contractual relationship between the landlord and the subtenant) nor privity of estate (privity of estate usually exists only when all of the tenant's estate is transferred, as will be developed below) between the original landlord and the subtenant, they ordinarily will not have direct actions one against the other for breaches of the covenants contained in the original lease.

If the tenant's transfer is characterized as an assignment, the assignee stands in the place of the tenant, and the assignee and the original landlord are in privity of estate and are liable to one another with respect to the covenants in the original lease which run with the land. (See "Effect of Transfers by the Landlord or the Tenant—Covenants Running With the Land", page 229.) The original tenant is not absolved of his liability under the lease, however. The tenant's privity of contract with the landlord continues and the tenant in effect becomes a surety with respect to liability for damages arising out of the assignee's breach of any covenant contained in the original lease.

In determining whether the tenant's transfer constitutes a sublease or an assignment as against the landlord, most courts hold that if the tenant conveys the entire balance of his term, retaining no reversionary interest therein, the transfer will be construed as an assignment; but, if the tenant retains a reversionary interest in the original

leasehold, the transfer will be construed as a sublease. Jaber v. Miller, 219 Ark. 59, 239 S.W.2d 760
(1951). Under the minority view, if the tenant
reserves a right of entry (power of termination)
and additional rent, the transfer will be construed
as a sublease in spite of the fact that the tenant
purports to transfer his interest for the balance of
the term. A similar result has been reached where
the tenant extracts from the transferee additional
covenants not found in the original lease. In such
cases, the tenant is said to have reserved a "contingent reversionary interest".

The requisite reversionary interest which must
be reserved to create a sublease may be of any
duration—a week, a month or a day—and therefore, it is a simple matter for the tenant and his
transferee to structure the transfer in a manner
calculated to give the desired characterization to
the transfer.

Where the tenant transfers an undivided share
of the demised premises for the balance of the
term, or where the tenant transfers his entire
interest in a physical portion of the demised premises for the balance of the term, the great weight of
authority holds that the transfer is a partial assignment rather than a sublease. A transfer by
the tenant of a physical portion of the demised
premises for a period less than the balance of the
term is construed as a sublease.

Although the decisions are divided, there is
authority for the view that regardless of the rule

followed in determining the assignment-sublease issue between the landlord and the transferee, as between the tenant and his transferee a particular transfer will be treated as a sublease if that is the intent of the parties. Thus, a given transfer may be treated as an assignment in determining the rights and duties of the landlord and transferee against one another, and as a sublease with respect to the rights and obligations of the tenant and his transferee against one another.

B. Covenants Against Transfer of the Tenant's Interest

Without dissent, the courts uphold covenants by the tenant which prohibit the assignment or sublease of all or any part of the demised premises without the consent of the landlord. Segre v. Ring, 103 N.H. 278, 170 A.2d 265 (1961). The courts also uphold covenants which provide for forfeiture of the leasehold as a penalty for the tenant's breach of the covenant against transfer. This restraint on alienation is usually justified on the ground that the landlord as the owner of the reversion, and in the interest of protecting his reversion, is entitled to exercise his judgment with respect to the character and financial responsibility of the person who will be entrusted with the possession and use of the subject land. A few jurisdictions have statutes which prohibit transfer of the tenant's interest without the consent of the landlord.

The tenant's transfer in violation of a covenant against transfer is valid as between the tenant and his transferee, subject, of course, to the remedies which the landlord has for the tenant's breach of covenant. Although the landlord may have reserved a right of entry (power of termination) for breach of covenant, the lease continues until the landlord takes affirmative steps to terminate it.

Although the covenants against transfers are universally held to be valid, as a restraint on alienation they are also universally frowned upon by the courts. As a result, covenants against transfer are strictly construed against the landlord and in favor of the tenant. For example, under the majority view, a covenant against assignment without the consent of the landlord does not prohibit the tenant from subleasing the demised premises. DeBaca v. Fidel, 61 N.M. 181, 297 P.2d 322 (1956). Further, except for leases where the expectations of the landlord are closely tied to the special skills of the tenant, covenants against transfer will not be implied, nor will a landlord be permitted to establish an oral agreement restricting the tenant's right to transfer where the balance of the lease is in the form of a written agreement. The courts have also demonstrated a great willingness to find the necessary consent, or a waiver of such consent, from the landlord's conduct. For example, the landlord's knowledge of an assignment coupled with his acceptance of rent from the assignee is usually construed as consent to the assignment, or as a waiver of the required prior consent. Hendrickson v. Freericks, 620 P.2d 205 (Alaska 1980).

As might be expected, the courts' narrow construction of covenants against transfer has resulted in a great deal of litigation focused on the question of whether a particular transfer falls within the spirit and letter of a particular covenant against transfer, and therefore, within the operation of such covenant.

1. Breach of Covenant

Whether a covenant against transfer has been breached by the tenant is a matter of fact. The landlord must show that the tenant's conduct is violative of both the spirit and the letter of the restrictive covenant in order for the tenant to be held liable. The universally strict construction of such covenants requires that great care be taken in their drafting. As noted above, a covenant against assignment does not prohibit a tenant from subleasing the demised premises. Similarly, it has been held that the execution of a contract to assign the lease, or the tenant's declaration of himself as trustee for another, does not constitute breach of the covenant against transfer. The reason given is that only legal, as distinguished from equitable, assignments are prohibited. The following is a partial list of actions by the tenant which may or may not constitute breach of a covenant against assignment.

a. Reassignment to the Original Tenant. Where the tenant has previously assigned his leasehold interest with the consent of the landlord, most courts hold that the existence of a covenant against assignment without the consent of the landlord does not require the assignee to obtain the consent of the landlord prior to reassigning to the original tenant. The rationale for this rule is that the landlord consented to take the tenant for the full term in the original lease, and therefore, his consent to the reassignment is unnecessary.

b. Cotenancy, Partnership and Corporate Tenants. If two or more persons lease land as tenants in common, a covenant against assignment without the consent of the landlord is generally construed to prohibit an assignment of the interest of one cotenant to the other cotenant; apparently on the ground that each cotenant has a separate interest, and the covenant applies separately to the interests of each cotenant. Further, taking in additional cotenants is also deemed to be a breach of the covenant not to assign.

The addition or withdrawal of a general partner is usually held not to be violative of the covenant against assignment where the leasehold interest is held by a partnership. Similarly, where the tenant is a corporation, a change in the share ownership does not constitute a breach of the covenant against assignment. In such cases, the partnerships and corporations are treated as entities separate and distinct from their partners or share-

holders. To the extent that such "entity" treat-
ment is legally recognized, the rule seems justified.

   c. **Leasehold Mortgages.** In jurisdictions
where the execution of a mortgage merely creates
a lien against the mortgaged property, the rule is
well settled that the tenant's mortgage of his leasehold does not constitute a breach of the covenant
against assignment. In the so-called "title states,"
i.e., states in which the execution of a mortgage
has the effect of transferring the title of the mortgagor to the mortgagee, there is a split of authority. The probable majority view is that the execution of the mortgage does not constitute a breach of
the covenant against assignment. This can perhaps be justified on the ground that the tenant's
rights under the leasehold are essentially those of
possession and use; rights which are usually expressly "regranted" to the tenant in a leasehold
mortgage. On the other hand, the mortgage is a
transfer of the tenant's legal interest in the demised premises, and as such, supports the minority
view that execution of a leasehold mortgage without the landlord's consent constitutes a breach of
the covenant against transfer.

   In jurisdictions permitting leasehold mortgages, if the tenant defaults in payment of the
mortgage and the leasehold is sold pursuant to a
foreclosure sale, the majority view is that the
forced sale does not constitute a breach of the
covenant against assignment. This would seem to
be a necessary conclusion since to hold otherwise

would create the anomalous situation of validating
the mortgage while denying its enforcement by the
mortgagee. The view is sometimes justified on the
ground that the foreclosure sale constitutes an
involuntary assignment, and therefore, is not violative of a general covenant against assignment.
(See "Involuntary Assignments", below.)

   d. Involuntary Assignments. A general
covenant against assignment is usually construed
to apply only to voluntary transfers, with the result that involuntary transfers and transfers occurring by operation of law are outside of the operation of such a covenant. Although the landlord is
still forced to allow someone into possession without his consent, the courts nevertheless require
express language in the lease to avoid this result;
doubtless a reflection of the policy of strictly con-
struing covenants restraining alienation of land.
Thus, a covenant against assignment is not violated by the sale of the tenant's leasehold interest
upon execution of a judgment against the tenant.
Further, the weight of authority is that a breach of
the covenant against assignment has not occurred
where the tenant's interest is transferred in a
bankruptcy or involuntary insolvency proceeding.
The transfer is by operation of law, and the rule
applies whether the bankruptcy proceeding is voluntary or involuntary. Similarly, on the theory
that receivers are not assignees and acquire no
title by their appointment, the appointment of a
receiver for the tenant and his subsequent adop-

tion of the lease do not constitute a breach of the covenant against assignment. On the other hand, the tenant's assignment of his leasehold for the benefit of creditors is usually construed as a breach of the covenant against assignment. Although the tenant may be financially pressed, and the assignment is in the interest of both the landlord and the tenant, such an assignment is not compelled by law and thus is characterized as voluntary, and requires the consent of the landlord.

2. The Rule in Dumpor's Case

In the absence of a statute to the contrary, where the lease contains a covenant against assignment without the consent of the landlord and the landlord gives his consent to an assignment by the tenant, the apparent majority rule is that further assignments of the leasehold may be made without the consent of the landlord. This rule is referred to as the Rule in Dumpor's Case, and there is authority for the view that the rule will be followed even though the covenant purports to bind the "tenant and his assigns". Most courts attempt to justify the rule on the ground that the covenant is entire and indivisible. In jurisdictions which follow the Rule in Dumpor's Case, the landlord may protect himself against further assignment by imposing, as a condition to his first consent, an agreement that no further assignment shall be made without the landlord's consent.

The rule has been severely criticized, even by those jurisdictions which have adopted it, and a minority of jurisdictions have refused to adopt the rule on the ground that it does not comport with "logic, reason or common sense." Many courts which ordinarily follow the rule hold that where the covenant purports to bind the tenant and his assignees, the consent of the landlord is required prior to the subsequent reassignment. The courts' displeasure with the rule has also resulted in a number of exceptions. Thus, most courts hold that the rule does not apply to covenants against subleases; and there is authority for the view that the rule does not apply in cases of implied waiver, as distinguished from cases where the landlord has given his express consent to the first assignment.

3. *Landlord's Consent Unreasonably Withheld*

Where the lease covenant provides that the tenant shall not assign without the consent of the landlord, and nothing more, the weight of authority is that the landlord may capriciously and arbitrarily withhold his consent, or condition his consent in any manner that he chooses. In what appears to be a successful attempt to balance the courts' general disapproval of restraints on alienation and the landlord's valid concern about the character and financial responsibility of persons who may be placed in possession and control of the leased property, a substantial minority of cases holds that the landlord's consent may not be unreasonably withheld. This view is now supported by the Restatement, Second, Property (Landlord and Tenant) § 15.2 (1977).

It is quite common for the covenant against transfer without the consent of the landlord to also provide that the consent of the landlord shall not be unreasonably withheld. Whether the landlord's conduct is unreasonable or reasonable is a matter of fact. With respect to unreasonableness, it has been said that consent which is withheld ". . . without fair, solid and substantial cause or reason . . ." is unreasonable. In determining reasonableness, most courts apply the prudent man test; thus eliminating consideration of personal tastes or preferences. Some of the factors considered in determining the acceptability of the transferee are the personal character and financial responsibility of the transferee, the nature of his proposed use and its suitability for the demised premises, and the legality of the proposed use. Some courts have held that the standard which was applied to the original tenant is the one which should be applied in determining the acceptableness of the proposed assignee, and that the failure of the landlord to accept a proposed assignee who meets such standards is unreasonable.

"Tenant-shareholders" in cooperative apartment buildings find themselves in the somewhat unique position of being part owners of the corporate landlord and having their right of occupancy tied to their shareholder status. The lease of the tenant-shareholder usually contains a covenant that there can be no assignment of his stock or his leasehold interest without the consent of the remaining shareholders. Such covenants have generally been upheld on the ground that the other tenant-shareholders have a direct and substantial interest in the social acceptability of those who will be living in close proximity to them, and in the financial responsibility of those who must bear part of the costs of operating the cooperative.

Where the landlord's consent is unreasonably withheld the tenant may seek specific performance or damages for the landlord's breach of his covenant not to unreasonably withhold his consent to assignment. The tenant may also seek declaratory relief, and as a practical matter may assign without the consent of the landlord and defend against the landlord's suit to terminate the lease and evict the tenant or his assignee.

4. *Waiver*

Covenants against transfer are made for the benefit of the landlord and may be waived by him. The waiver may be express or may arise by implication from the conduct of the landlord.

With regard to implied waiver, the landlord's acceptance of rent from the transferee with knowledge of the transfer is the most common act of waiver committed by landlords; however, any course of conduct which may be reasonably construed as the landlord's acquiescence in the assignment or sublease is sufficient to constitute a waiver. For example, failure to object to a voidable transfer within a reasonable time and permitting the transferee to make repairs and improvements on the demised premises have been held to be conduct constituting a waiver of the breach of covenant against transfer.

There is also authority for the view that under certain circumstances general principles of estoppel will prevent the landlord from nullifying a transfer violative of a covenant against assignment or sublease.

5. *Remedies of the Landlord*

The landlord normally reserves a right of entry (power of termination) for breach of the material covenants contained in the lease. Thus, the landlord may terminate the lease for the tenant's breach of covenant against transfer. The landlord may also recover damages or obtain injunctive relief against a threatened transfer.

III. TRANSFERS BY THE LANDLORD

After the conveyance of a leasehold interest, the landlord's remaining interest in the land is a reversion which carries with it the right to receive the rents and other benefits reserved under the lease. The landlord's reversion, or any part thereof, is freely alienable and a transfer of the reversion will not terminate the lease nor deprive the tenant of his rights thereunder. The transferee of the reversion takes subject to the tenant's leasehold interest if he has actual or constructive notice of the lease. If there is no such notice, and the lease is subject to the recording acts, the transferee takes free of the tenant's interest and may terminate the lease. However, a few jurisdictions have held that a transfer of the landlord's reversion without stipulations protecting the tenant's leasehold interest constitutes a wrong to the tenant for which he may recover damages from the landlord. For example, it has been held that a landlord must protect the tenant's rights under a valid oral lease where the transferee of the reversion has no notice of the tenancy.

Except for tenancies at will or leases where the landlord only has a life estate, the death of the landlord does not terminate the lease. The reversion passes to his heirs or devisees, as the case may be, subject to the rights of the tenant. A tenancy at will terminates with the death of the landlord because his death brings to an end the mutual will of the parties that the tenancy continue. Where the landlord only has a life estate, the lease terminates with his death because the landlord cannot convey an estate which will endure for a longer period than his own.

A. Restraints on Alienation

The generally accepted view is that covenants running in favor of the tenant restraining alienation of the reversion are invalid. Section 15.1 of the Restatement, Second, Property (Landlord and Tenant) (1977), takes the view that restraints on alienation of the landlord's reversion are valid when the special skills and expertise of the landlord are necessary in order for the tenant's expectations under the lease to be fulfilled. However, only one case has been found upholding a restraint on alienation of the landlord's reversion in favor of the tenant.

B. Lease in Reversion

The landlord may convey his entire reversionary interest in all or a physical part of the demised premises, or he may convey his entire reversionary interest for a fixed period of time, or he may simply transfer his right to receive rents or other benefits under the lease. When the landlord executes a second lease the term of which is to commence at the end of the term of the first lease, the conveyance is generally referred to as a lease in reversion. If the second lease is to commence on a specified date after the expiration of the first lease, the second tenant's right to possession begins on that date regardless of any premature termination of the prior lease. If the second lease provides that the term shall commence with the expiration of the prior lease, then the second lease becomes effective upon the termination of the prior lease regardless of the time or reason for the termination of the first lease.

C. Concurrent Leases

The landlord may execute, to a third party other than the first tenant, a lease of all or part of the physical premises demised to the first tenant for periods of time which are concurrent, in whole or in part, with the term of the first lease. Such leases are referred to as concurrent leases. If the second lease conforms to the formal requirements of a conveyance of a reversion, the second tenant becomes the landlord of the first tenant with the right to receive the rent and other benefits under the first lease for the duration of the concurrent terms of the two leases. The second tenant also bears the burdens of any covenants running with the land. (See "Covenants Running with the Land—Partial Transfers", page 237.)

D. Mortgage of the Reversion

The effect of the mortgage on the landlord's reversionary interest depends upon whether the particular jurisdiction follows the title, intermediate or lien theory with respect to mortgages. In "title" jurisdictions a mortgage is construed as a conveyance of the mortgagor's interest to the mortgagee. In such jurisdictions the mortgagee becomes the landlord and, absent an agreement to the contrary, is entitled to the rents from leases executed prior to the mortgage.

In "lien" states, the mortgagee obtains no ownership or possessory rights prior to default by the mortgagor (and usually none are obtained prior to foreclosure and sale) and therefore, the landlord-mortgagor's rights as against the tenant remain unchanged.

In the so called "intermediate" states, although the title technically passes to the mortgagee, the landlord-mortgagor retains the right to possession of the mortgaged land (absent any default under the mortgage) and to the rents and profits issuing therefrom. In such jurisdictions the landlord-tenant relationship would remain unchanged by the landlord's mortgage of the leased premises.

IV. EFFECT OF TRANSFERS BY THE LANDLORD OR THE TENANT—COVENANTS RUNNING WITH THE LAND

A. Assignments by the Tenant

During the tenant's occupancy of the leased property he is generally considered to hold by both privity of estate and privity of contract. When the tenant assigns his lease his privity of estate with the landlord, and his liability founded thereon, come to an end. However, in the absence of a novation or express release by the landlord the tenant remains liable to the landlord on the promises made in the lease based upon his privity of contract.

By virtue of the assignment, the tenant's assignee obtains the estate of the tenant and privity of estate immediately arises between the assignee and the landlord. The net effect of the transfer on the assignee is that the assignee acquires the benefits and suffers the burdens of the lease covenants which run with the land so long as he holds the leasehold estate. (See "Covenants Running with the Land", page 229.) Since the liability of the assignee to the landlord is based solely on privity of estate, reassignment of the leasehold interest will end the assignee's liability under the lease for breaches occurring after the reassignment. The assignee, of course, remains liable for all breaches which occur during his possession.

After an assignment of the tenant's interest, both the tenant (on the basis of privity of contract) and the assignee (on the basis of privity of estate) are liable to the landlord for violation of the covenants in the lease which run with the land. J.E. Martin, Inc. v. Interstate 8th Street, 41 Colo.App. 203, 585 P.2d 299 (1978). The tenant and the assignee are both primarily liable to the landlord and the landlord may elect to sue one or the other or both. As between themselves, the assignee is primarily liable and the tenant is secondarily liable; the tenant's status being analogous to that of a surety.

An assignee under an implied assignment stands in the same position as an assignee who acquires the leased premises under a written assignment. Thus, an implied assignment arising out of possession of the leased property forms a sufficient basis for the running of the benefits and burdens of the lease covenants to the assignee.

If, in addition to taking an assignment, the assignee also expressly agrees to assume the covenants of the main lease, he also becomes liable to the landlord on the basis of privity of contract.

The assignee's reassignment of the leasehold will terminate his liability founded upon privity of estate, but will not terminate the liability founded on privity of contract.

B. Sublease by the Tenant

The execution of a sublease merely creates a landlord-tenant relationship between the tenant in the original lease and his subtenant. No direct relationship between the landlord and the subtenant arises; and since there is no privity of estate or privity of contract between the two, ordinarily neither of the parties has a direct right of action against the other for violation of lease covenants which run with the land.

Although the landlord cannot sue the subtenant directly for breach of a lease covenant, the landlord is not without remedy. First, where the landlord has reserved a right of entry (power of termination) for breach of covenant, the landlord may terminate the main lease for breach of any of the covenants contained therein, and the sublease will be extinguished with the termination of the supporting main lease. Second, equity will allow the landlord to enforce against a subtenant a restrictive covenant of which he has notice, and the landlord is also entitled to enjoin the subtenant from committing waste. With respect to unpaid rent, the landlord has no direct cause of action against the subtenant, but in many jurisdictions he is entitled to impress a statutory lien against the subtenant or levy distress upon the subtenant's

chattels which are located on the demised premises. (See "Landlord's Lien", page 279, and "Distress for Rent", page 284.) In addition, where the
tenant is insolvent, by the prevailing view the
landlord is entitled to assert an equitable lien on
the rent due under the sublease in preference to
the other creditors of the tenant.

C. Transfer of the Landlord's Reversion

The landlord's conveyance of his reversion terminates the privity of estate between the landlord
and the tenant. With the exception of breaches
which occur prior to transfer, the landlord's right
to enforce the benefits of covenants and agreements made by the tenant which run with the land
ceases, and the benefits of such covenants vest in
the transferee of the reversion on the basis of his
privity of estate with the tenant. Bedwick v.
Mecham, 26 Cal.2d 92, 156 P.2d 757 (1945). On the
other hand, the conveyance of the reversion does
not release the landlord of his obligations under
the lease because he remains in privity of contract
with the tenant. R.H. Macy & Co. v. Fall River,
323 Mass. 624, 83 N.E.2d 880 (1949). The landlord
and his transferee are both primarily liable to the
tenant for breach of covenant. Thus, where the
tenant is entitled to some benefit under a covenant
in the lease (e.g., a right to have the landlord
repair the leased premises) and there is a breach of
that covenant, the tenant may sue the landlord,
the landlord's transferee or both. As between
themselves, the transferee is primarily liable and

the transferor-landlord is secondarily liable, the latter being treated in a manner analogous to a surety.

D. Covenants Running with the Land

A covenant running with the land may be generally described as a contractual agreement the subject matter of which is so inextricably bound up with the land that a court is willing to hold that the assignees of the covenantor (the party making the promise) and the covenantee (the party to whom the promise was made) are bound by the obligations and entitled to the rights created by the contract. There are two foundations for the rights and obligations which arise under a covenant running with the land. First, a covenant is primarily a contract which creates contract rights in the covenantee and imposes contract duties on the covenantor. Second, the covenant is also a real covenant, i.e., it is directly related to the land, and as a consequence the duties (burdens) of the covenantor attach to his estate and run with the estate to the covenantor's transferees. Similarly, the benefit of the covenant attaches to the covenantee's interest in the leased property and runs with his estate to his subsequent transferees. In this second situation liability is said to be founded upon the privity of estate which arises out of the landlord-tenant relationship.

In analyzing running covenant problems several things should be kept in mind. First, although one must determine what rights and obligations were created by the contract, the primary issue is whether the assignees of the covenantor and the covenantee are bound by the obligations or entitled to accept the benefits created by the original contract. Second, the running of the benefit and the burden of a particular covenant should be analyzed separately. It is not unusual to find a covenant in which the burden will run and the benefit will not, or vice versa.

There are four prerequisites for the running of a covenant, or more accurately the running of the benefit or burden of a covenant: (i) generally, the covenant must be in writing; (ii) there must be an intent that the covenant run; (iii) there must be privity of estate between the litigants; and (iv) the subject matter of the covenant must touch and concern the land.

1. *Writing*

If under the applicable statute of frauds the lease is required to be in writing, then all covenants which are a part of the lease must also be in writing to be enforceable as covenants running with the respective estates of the landlord and tenant. If an oral lease is created, the term of which falls within the exception to the applicable statute of frauds, the lease is generally enforceable. Since the lease itself is enforceable there would appear to be no good reason why the oral covenants contained in the lease should not run with the respective estates of the landlord and tenant.

2. Intent that the Covenant Run

Spencer's Case, 5 Co. 16a, 77 Eng.Rptr. 72 (1583), established several fundamental rules relating to running covenants which remain with us to this day. The first proposition in Spencer's Case declared that if the covenant pertained to a thing *in esse,* the covenant runs with the land and binds the assignee. The second proposition in Spencer's Case declared that if the covenant pertains to a thing which is not *in esse* at the time of the demise but rather pertains to a thing to be built subsequently, the covenant does not bind the assignee unless the language of the covenant expressly purports to bind assignees. The effect of the two resolutions is that where the covenant pertains to a thing which is in existence and located on or connected with the demised premises, the presumed intention of the parties is that the covenant will run; and in the absence of such existence, the presumed intent is that the covenant will not run. For example, it is presumed that the parties intend that the benefits and burdens of a covenant to repair an existing building will run to their respective assignees. On the other hand, where the lease contains a covenant to maintain and repair a barn which is to be constructed six months after the commencement of the lease, the presumed intent of the parties is that the covenant is personal, i.e., the covenant will not run unless an express intent to bind assignees is contained in the words of the covenant. No particular words are necessary to express the parties' intent that the covenant run;

however, the word "assigns" is generally accepted as providing the requisite intent and in a number of cases the absence of the word "assigns" has been fatal to the running of a covenant.

The founding of presumed intent on the basis of the existence or non-existence of the subject matter of the covenant has been harshly criticized by a number of courts, and the idea of determining presumed intent on the basis of such distinction has been rejected in several jurisdictions. The more recent cases tend to avoid this mechanical distinction and apply a general test of intent, which intent may be garnered from the four corners of the lease. An intent to run is often inferred when the covenant substantially concerns and affects the use and enjoyment of the demised premises.

3. *Touch and Concern*

The most significant proposition in Spencer's Case was the one which established the "touch and concern" requirement:

> ". . . but although the covenant be for him and his assigns, yet if the thing to be done be merely collateral to the land and doth not touch or concern the thing demised in any sort, there the assignee shall not be charged."

This language is generally construed to mean that the benefit or burden of a covenant will not run unless the subject matter of the covenant is connected with or relates to the respective estates of the covenantor and covenantee in the demised premises.

A number of tests, none completely satisfactory, have been espoused for determining whether the subject matter of a covenant touches and concerns the land. Perhaps the best and most practical of these is a proposal which requires a court to determine the effect of a particular covenant on the parties' rights, powers, privileges and immunities with respect to the demised premises. Where they are decreased, the burden touches and concerns the land; where they are increased, the benefit touches and concerns the land.

Covenants which touch and concern the land can be broken down into three general categories. The first of these is covenants for the payment of money, the most common of which are covenants to pay rent and covenants to pay taxes. Into the second category fall those covenants which require or prohibit the doing of some act which affects the physical condition of the premises. Included in this second category are covenants by a tenant not to remove trade fixtures and covenants to repair. The final category involves covenants which relate to the duration of the lease. Included in this category are covenants providing for the termination of the lease upon the happening of a specified event and options to extend or renew the lease. As can be seen from the foregoing, most covenants which ordinarily appear in leases satisfy the touch and concern requirement. Other specific covenants, not mentioned above, which are generally held to run are: (i) covenants to provide services, such as heat, water, electricity, etc.; (ii) covenants not to assign or sublease without the consent of the landlord; and (iii) options to purchase.

4. Privity of Estate

The general rule is that a person cannot incur liability under a contract unless he is a party thereto. The obligations arising under a contract are personal in nature and privity of contract must exist before liability will be imposed. One well recognized substitute for privity of contract is privity of estate.

"Privity of estate" is the term used to declare that two parties have a relationship with respect to a particular parcel of land. There are two kinds of privity of estate, mutual (or continuing) privity of estate and successive privity of estate. Successive privity of estate is said to arise when one person transfers an interest in land to another. For example, where A transfers all of his interest in Blackacres to B, successive privity of estate is said to arise between A and B. Mutual privity of estate is said to exist where two or more persons have a continuing simultaneous interest in the same parcel of land. In the landlord-tenant relationship; mutual privity of estate exists because of the continuing relationship the landlord (reversion) and the tenant (leasehold) have in the land.

As noted above and discussed further below, a sublease by the tenant does not create privity of estate between the landlord and the subtenant. (See "Sublease by the Tenant", page 227; and "Partial Transfers", page 237.)

5. *Transfer of the Covenantee's Entire Estate*

The covenantee of a covenant running with the land is entitled to enforce the covenant on the basis of his privity of contract or his privity of estate with the covenantor. Upon transfer of his entire estate, the privity of estate between the covenantee and the covenantor is extinguished and privity of estate arises between the covenantee's transferee and the covenantor. Further, the covenantee's contract rights are deemed to have been impliedly transferred with his leasehold. As a result, the covenantee has no right of action for breaches of covenant arising after the transfer of his interest. Breaches which occurred prior to the transfer give rise to a personal cause of action in the covenantee which remains with him unless it is expressly assigned to his transferee.

6. *Transfer of the Covenantor's Entire Estate*

As noted above, prior to transfer, the obligations of the covenantor are based upon both privity of contract and privity of estate. A transfer of the covenantor's entire estate extinguishes the privity of estate between the covenantor and the covenantee, and creates privity of estate between the covenantor's transferee and the covenantee. The covenantor has no liability, founded on privity of estate, for breaches which occur after the transfer. However, the general rule is that a person may not unilaterally relieve himself of his contract obligations and therefore, the covenantor remains liable in contract for breaches which occur after the transfer. The covenantor and his transferee are both primarily liable to the covenantee. With respect to each other, the transferee is primarily liable and the covenantor is secondarily liable, the covenantor being treated as a surety.

The liability of the covenantor's transferee is based upon his privity of estate with the covenantee. In the absence of an express assumption of the lease covenants by the covenantor's transferee, reassignment of the leasehold will terminate his liability for breaches occurring after the reassignment. This termination of liability has been upheld even where the transfer was for the express purpose of preventing further liability, or where the second transferee was insolvent. However, where the first transferee's reassignment is a sham and he retains the beneficial use and enjoyment of the leased property, the sham assignment will not relieve him of liability.

Where the covenantor's transferee assumes and agrees to perform the covenants of the original lease, privity of contract arises between the covenantor and his transferee. In the event the covenantor becomes liable for subsequent breaches of covenant, the covenantor may sue his transferee on the basis of their contract rather than rely on his suretyship remedies, and reassignment by the assuming transferee will not relieve him of liability.

In jurisdictions which recognize third-party beneficiary contracts, the covenantee is deemed to be the third-party beneficiary of the assumption agreement between the covenantor and his transferee. Thus, there arises both privity of estate and privity of contract between the covenantee and the covenantor's transferee. Under such circumstances, reassignment by the covenantor's transferee will not relieve him of his contractual liability to the covenantee for future breaches of covenant. Even in jurisdictions which do not recognize such third-party beneficiary contracts, there is authority for the view that where a covenantee-landlord expressly consents to an assignment by the covenantor-tenant and the assignment contains an express assumption by the transferee, the covenantee-landlord is deemed to be a party to the contract and entitled to enforce the covenants against the covenantor-tenant's transferee.

7. *Partial Transfers*

Where the landlord transfers all of his interest in a physical part of the leased property, to the extent the benefits and burdens running to the reversion are apportionable, they will be divided in the same proportion into which the reversion was divided by the landlord's partial transfer. The same rule is applied where the tenant transfers all of his interest in a physical part of his leasehold estate.

In cases where an undivided interest in an entire estate is transferred (either the leasehold or the reversion), privity of estate arises in the transferee and he becomes jointly and severally liable with his "cotenants" (e.g., tenants in common) for the breach of all covenants which burden his estate. The transferee is also entitled to enforce the benefits of all covenants running to his estate, but he is usually required to join all "cotenants" in any action to enforce the covenant.

If the tenant subleases the premises, the subtenant is not in privity of estate with the landlord and therefore, the subtenant acquires no rights and suffers no liabilities on the covenants contained in the main lease. The original tenant remains in privity of estate with the landlord because of his failure to transfer all of his interest, remains liable for any breach of covenant, and is entitled to enforce the benefit of the covenants contained in the main lease.

A situation similar to that of the sublease situation arises where the landlord executes a second, concurrent lease of the same premises. The results in such cases have differed substantially from the results in cases involving a sublease. The tenant in the second lease is usually held to be the landlord of, and in privity of estate with, the tenant in the first lease; and the benefits and burdens which attach to the reversion under the first lease are said to pass to the second, concurrent tenant. This result may be justified on the ground that the concurrent lease interposes the concurrent tenant between the landlord and the first tenant. The benefits of the landlord under the first lease are impliedly assigned to and enforceable only by the concurrent tenant. An exception exists for benefits which attach to the reversionary interest held by the landlord after execution of the concurrent lease—such benefits remain with the landlord's retained reversionary interest. The landlord remains liable, in a manner similar to a surety, on the burdens of covenants contained in the first lease.

8. *Duration and Waiver*

a. Express Covenants. If the lease contains an express provision with respect to the duration of a covenant, that provision will control. In the absence of such a provision, the duration of a covenant is generally determined by the nature of the covenant. Where the covenant is a continuing one (e.g., a covenant to repair), capable of multiple breaches, the duration of the covenant coincides with the term of the lease. Where the covenant is entire, i.e., a covenant capable of only one breach, the covenant terminates when the breach occurs.

A breach of covenant may be waived by the party entitled to the benefit of the covenant. Such waiver may be express, or implied from the conduct of the party. The covenantee's waiver of one breach does not terminate the covenant, nor does it imply waiver of subsequent breaches by the covenantor.

b. Implied Obligations. A number of landlord-tenant obligations arise independently of any express agreement between the parties (e.g., the landlord's duty to maintain and repair the common areas). Liability in such cases is said to rest on the privity of estate which exists between the landlord and the tenant. Since these obligations are based solely on privity of estate, the duty remains only so long as the party upon whom the duty is imposed remains in privity of estate with the intended beneficiary.

There is a split of opinion on the issue of whether rights acquired under such implied obligations may be waived. Some courts hold that waiver is permissible, while others refuse to entertain a defense of waiver on the grounds that such waivers are contrary to the public policy underlying the implied obligation. (For example, see "Landlord's Defenses to the Implied Warranty of Habitability", page 141.)

9. Covenants Not to Compete

Promises by the tenant that he will not use the demised premises in a manner which will compete with the business of the landlord conducted on other property, or with the business of a third party holding under the landlord and conducted on such other property, are usually held to be valid. Similar promises made by the landlord not to operate or lease any land owned or otherwise controlled by him for a business which competes with the tenant's business are also usually held to be valid. Such covenants are deemed to be an essential part of the lease and the covenantee is entitled to termination of the lease, damages and/or injunctive relief for breach of covenant by the covenantor.

Although usually upheld, such covenants are sometimes found to be invalid as unlawful restraints on trade. A promise not to compete may be invalid because it is too broad in scope, i.e., it may proscribe the covenantor's conduct for too long a period of time or too large a geographical area; or it may prohibit entry into businesses which do not conflict with that of the covenantee. The usual test is the reasonableness of the restraint. Where the covenant not to compete is overly broad, courts are often willing to reform the objectionable portion of the covenant in a manner so as to render the covenant valid and enforceable.

Example: L leases a building to T for 15 years to conduct an automobile repair business. L also agrees that he will not operate or lease any other land owned or controlled by him, within a 100 mile radius of the demised premises, for an automobile repair or jewelry business during the next 25 years. The promise is almost certain to be held invalid as overly broad. However, a court might "reform" the agreement by disregarding the overly broad portions and enforcing the remainder. Thus, the restriction against the jewelry business would be disregarded as not in competition with the covenantee's automobile repair business. The court may also determine that the restriction on L engaging in the automobile repair business is only enforceable for three years and only within a five mile radius of the demised premises. Such a resolution gives T reasonable protection against L's potential competition, but does not unduly restrain trade.

Where a covenant not to compete is found to be invalid and the court is unwilling to reform it, most courts hold that not only the covenant, but the entire lease is invalid and unenforceable on the theory that the covenant is essential to the tenant's use and enjoyment of the demised premises.

Since covenants not to compete do in fact restrain trade, they are generally frowned upon by the courts and as a consequence are narrowly construed. For example, a promise by a landlord that he personally would not engage in business competition with the tenant has been held to be unenforceable against his successors in title. Similarly, an agreement not to lease land to a competing business has been held not to preclude the sale of land to a competitor. It is clear that great care must be exercised in drafting covenants not to compete.

a. Running of Covenants Made by the Tenant. The fundamental issue in the running of covenants not to compete is whether the benefits and burdens of the covenant touch and concern the respective estates of the parties. Where the tenant promises not to engage in a business which would be in competition with the landlord, the promise limits the purposes for which the tenant could otherwise use the leased property; therefore, the burden is deemed to touch and concern the leasehold, and will be binding on an assignee of the tenant. Although the promise may benefit the landlord personally, or benefit other land owned by him, the promise of the tenant does not appear to have any direct beneficial effect upon the reversion. As a result, the benefit does not touch and concern the reversion and is not enforceable by a transferee of the landlord's reversion.

b. Running of Covenants Made by the Landlord. Where the landlord promises not to engage in, or to permit third parties holding under him to engage in, any business which would be in competition with the tenant on other land owned or otherwise controlled by the landlord, the burden of the covenant clearly limits the personal activity of the landlord and may burden other land owned or controlled by him, but the covenant does not appear to have any direct effect on his reversion. Thus, the burden of the covenant does not touch and concern the reversion and is not enforceable against a transferee of the landlord's reversion.

The courts are divided on the matter of the running of the benefit with the leasehold. Some courts hold that the covenant merely enhances the business of the tenant, as distinguished from benefiting the leasehold or the use and occupancy of the land, and therefore, is personal to the tenant and does not run to an assignee of the tenant. Other courts view the covenant not to compete as enhancing the value of the leasehold and, accordingly, hold that the benefit touches and concerns the leasehold and passes to an assignee of the tenant's leasehold.

CHAPTER VII

EXTENSIONS, RENEWALS, AND OPTIONS TO PURCHASE

I. INTRODUCTION

Often, the occurrence or non-occurrence of a future event will make shortening or lengthening the term of the lease desirable to the landlord or the tenant, or perhaps both. Where such events are anticipated, it is not unusual to find an express provision in the lease empowering the landlord, the tenant, or both, to shorten or extend the term of the lease. Absent statutory provisions to the contrary (e.g., provisions in rent control statutes prohibiting shortening the term), the courts have not found such agreements objectionable. Thus, a provision permitting the landlord or the tenant to terminate the lease upon giving a stipulated notice (e.g., 60 days written notice) and clauses permitting the landlord or tenant to terminate the lease upon the happening or nonhappening of some specified event (e.g., a bar owner's loss of a necessary liquor license) have generally been upheld.

Occasionally a lease will confer on the landlord the power to prolong the duration of the lease; however, this power is usually given to the tenant. When the lease provides an option to extend the term of the lease, but does not state which party holds the option, the courts usually find that the option rests with the tenant.

II. EXTENSIONS AND RENEWALS DISTINGUISHED

The lease provision conferring on the tenant the power to lengthen the term of the lease will often refer to such power as an option to renew, or an option to extend the term. Theoretically, it can be said that the distinction between the two is that an option to renew contemplates the execution of a new lease, while in the case of an option to extend, the extension is viewed as part of the original term—the term being terminable by the tenant at the earlier stipulated date. With the exception of certain recording act problems discussed below, the distinction seldom has any practical affect on the rights of the parties. Nevertheless, a substantial minority of jurisdictions adheres to this distinction. In such jurisdictions, a lease for a term of three years with a power in the tenant to extend the term for an additional three years would be construed as a lease for a term of six years terminable by the tenant at the end of the first three year period. If the lease gave the tenant an "option to renew" rather than an "option to extend", the lease is viewed as being one for a term of three years which contemplates the execution of a second three year lease at the option of the tenant.

Under the majority view the problem is neatly finessed. The courts in these jurisdictions pay homage to the technical distinction between an extension and a renewal, but hold that whether the lease provision is an option to renew or an option to extend is a matter of intent to be determined by the surrounding circumstances. Didriksen v. Havens, 136 Conn. 41, 68 A.2d 163 (1949). Use of the words extension or renewal are evidence of such intent, but are not controlling. Id. Further, the courts in these jurisdictions usually presume that an extension was intended on the ground that ordinarily the parties to a lease do not intend to undergo the trouble and expense of executing a second lease.

A third view, adopted by several courts, holds that there is no practical distinction between extensions and renewals and therefore, refuse to recognize one. Liebowitz v. Christo,75 So.2d 692 (Fla. 1954). These courts view the conveyance as a lease for a term, the duration of which is measured by the original term and the authorized prolongations thereof with an option in the tenant to terminate the lease at the end of the original term.

In jurisdictions which consider the term of the lease to be the sum of the original term plus the possible extensions and renewals, a lease which otherwise would not need to be recorded may be brought within the purview of the various jurisdictions' recording statutes. For example, if a jurisdiction has a recording statute which requires that leases for a term of three years or more to be recorded, it is clear that a simple two year lease need not be recorded. If, however, the two year lease also contains an option to extend the term for an additional two years, the lease may be subject to the provisions of the recording statute. If the lease is not recorded, subsequent bona fide purchasers of the leased property who purchase without notice of the tenant's interest will acquire a claim of ownership which takes priority over the rights of the tenant. Leases that contain covenants which provide for the automatic renewal of the term in the absence of a valid notice of termination (covenants not favored by the court) have been known to suffer a similar fate.

III. CONSTRUCTION AND OPERATION OF RENEWAL AND EXTENSION PROVISIONS

Where the distinction between extension and renewal is recognized, it is often held that some overt act, such as the execution of a new lease or a formal extension of the existing lease, is necessary for a valid exercise of a power to renew. The tenant's exercise of his power of extension may be implied from his continued possession of the demised premises.

The power to extend or renew the lease may be conditioned in any manner that the parties see fit. The most common condition is that the tenant give the landlord prior notice of his intent to

exercise the option. The provision will normally
state the time and the manner in which the notice
must be given. If the lease contains no provision
specifying the manner in which the tenant's option
is to be exercised, the tenant may exercise his
option to extend or renew the lease by giving
written or oral notice of his election, and his election to extend may be implied from his conduct.
Nicklis v. Nakano, 118 Colo. 317, 195 P.2d 723
(1948). Where the lease specifies the time and
manner in which notice must be given, the weight
of authority holds that strict compliance with the
notice provision is required unless waived by the
landlord. A few cases can be found in which the
tenant was given equitable relief from a short
delay in giving notice where the harm to the landlord was slight and termination of the lease would
cause great hardship to the tenant.

If the landlord and tenant execute a second
lease, the terms of that lease govern the rights and
obligations of the parties. In the absence of such a
second lease, the rights and duties of the landlord
and tenant during a validly extended term are
fixed by the provisions contained in the original
lease, together with any modifications made by the
parties during the original term. Scirpo v. McMillan, 355 Mass. 657, 247 N.E.2d 368 (1969). There is
one major exception to this rule. A general covenant for extension or renewal of the term is usually construed as permitting only one extension or
renewal, and therefore, the tenant's exercise of his

right to extend or renew the term does not carry with it the right of further extensions or renewals.

Often a lease provision will empower the tenant to extend or renew the lease without specifying the period of renewal. Under such circumstances, the courts usually presume that the extension or renewal period is of the same duration as the original term.

It is not unusual to see a lease which purports to give the tenant a perpetual right of renewal. Such a lease is essentially a conveyance of a fee simple, and they have been so construed by some courts. Perpetual renewal clauses are not favored, and a lease will not be construed as granting a right of perpetual renewal unless the landlord's intent to do so is without doubt.

Although the term "first option" is confusing and often leads to litigation, a "first option" for a new lease is usually distinguished from an option to extend or an option to renew the lease. Where the lease contains an extension or renewal provision, the lease term is extended solely at the option of the tenant. Where the lease provides for a "first option", the provision is usually viewed as giving the tenant a priority in right should the landlord elect to lease the premises again.

IV. OPTIONS TO PURCHASE

A lease will often contain a provision giving the tenant an option to purchase the leased property. The option to purchase is merely an agreement whereby the landlord gives the tenant the right to purchase the reversion at a fixed price during a specified period. In brief, it is a continuing offer to sell. There is no obligation on the tenant to buy; the tenant merely has the right to buy if he so chooses.

To be valid, the price and terms of purchase must be definite and certain, and the agreement must be supported by valid consideration. The consideration for an option to purchase contained in a lease is generally considered to be the rent reserved in the lease. The purchase price must be fixed or readily ascertainable by some method set forth in the lease. A provision purporting to empower the tenant to purchase at a price to be agreed upon is usually held to be too indefinite and uncertain to be enforceable. However, there is authority for the view that in the absence of a fixed or readily ascertainable purchase price, the option should be construed as an offer to sell at a fair and reasonable price, usually the fair market value of the land. Where the purchase price is fixed, but the terms of payment are not set forth in the lease, most courts construe the provision as requiring the payment of cash at the time of closing. Curiously, the courts are divided where the lease provides that the terms of payment are to be agreed upon. One view is that the option provision is invalid because of indefiniteness and uncertainty. By the better view, the provision is construed as requiring "reasonable terms"; usually on the ground that the terms of payment are immaterial, particularly where the vendee tenders cash.

A lease provision conferring on the tenant an option to purchase is a covenant running with the land. The covenant is binding on a transferee of the landlord who takes with notice, and enforceable by an assignee of the tenant's leasehold estate.

A. Right of First Refusal Distinguished

Leases frequently contain provisions conferring on the tenant what is commonly referred to as a right of first refusal. This right, often called a first privilege, first refusal, or first option, does not give the tenant an absolute right to purchase the leased property, but rather gives him a preferential right to purchase in the event that the landlord elects to sell the property.

Whether an option to purchase or a right of first refusal is intended by the landlord is often unclear. Some jurisdictions construe the word "first", when used with first options, first refusals, etc., as creating a conditional option, i.e., a right of purchase conditioned upon the landlord's election to sell. Other courts take the view that the use of such language is not controlling, and attempt to discern the intent of the landlord from the four corners of the lease and the surrounding circumstances.

B. Duration of the Option

When the duration of the option is not speci-fied in the lease, the generally held view is that the duration of the option coincides with the term of the lease, and may be exercised at any time during the term. The option expires with the term of the lease. If after the expiration of the original term a new lease is entered into between the landlord and the tenant which omits all reference to the option to purchase, the tenant no longer has an option to purchase. Similarly, where the tenant holds over with the acquiescence of the landlord, the tenant is not entitled to exercise the option to purchase during the holdover period.

In addition to the option to purchase, the lease may also contain an option for renewal or exten-sion of the lease. Where the tenant exercises his option to renew or extend the lease, the weight of authority holds that the option to purchase is an integral and inseparable part of the lease and therefore, continues to be exerciseable during the extension or renewal period.

Any valid termination of the lease terminates the option to purchase which is a part thereof. The option to purchase expires with the normal expiration of the lease. Where the landlord reserves the right to prematurely terminate the lease upon giving some stipulated notice and exer-cises his right, or where the landlord exercises his right to terminate the lease because of the tenant's breach of covenant, the exercise of the right to terminate the lease also terminates the tenant's option to purchase. However, the mere breach of another covenant by the tenant usually does not result in termination of the option to purchase; the landlord must exercise his right to terminate the lease.

The landlord may waive, expressly or impliedly by his conduct, breaches by the tenant of other covenants in the lease. Such waiver precludes the landlord from terminating the lease for such breaches, thus preserving the lease and the tenant's option to purchase which is dependent thereon.

Often the issue is whether the option to purchase and the lease are a single agreement or are independent agreements. The results in the cases depend upon the intent of the parties as garnered from the four corners of the lease and the surrounding circumstances. When the option to purchase and the lease are supported by an indivisible consideration (e.g., the rent), the option and the lease are said to be a part of a single agreement, and when the lease falls the option to purchase must fall with it. In cases where the option to purchase and the lease are construed as independent, breach of the lease conditions and covenants and the subsequent forfeiture of the lease have no effect on the tenant's rights under the option to purchase.

C. Effect of Exercise of the Option to Purchase

The tenant's exercise of his option to purchase is nothing more than an acceptance of the landlord's continuing offer to sell. Upon the proper exercise of the option to purchase, a valid enforceable contract for the sale of real property arises. Further, the tenant's exercise of the option to purchase terminates the landlord-tenant relationship and a vendor-vendee relationship arises in its place. In the absence of an agreement to the contrary, this termination of the lease terminates the parties' obligations thereunder, including the tenant's duty to pay rent. The agreed upon purchase price is presumed to cover the conveyance and any intermediate use of the premises by the tenant-vendee.

By the weight of authority, the contract for the sale of the demised property gives rise to an equitable conversion of the ownership with the result that the tenant-vendee is treated as the owner of the land and a debtor of the vendor. The landlord-vendor is treated as a secured creditor in a manner analogous to a mortgagee. This is particularly true where the vendee is in possession of the subject property. This equitable conversion has a substantial effect on the rights of the parties. For example, by the majority view, the vendee bears the risk of loss arising out of the destruction of the premises which occurs after the execution of the contract of sale, but prior to the actual transfer of the vendor's title. Similarly, but more favorably to the tenant, it has been held that a tenant is entitled to the compensation paid in a proceeding for the condemnation of the property—the tenant, of course, being required to pay the vendor the purchase price under the contract of sale.

A few courts have adopted the view that the equitable conversion relates back to the time that the option was given. Accordingly, after the tenant's exercise of the option to purchase, his rights (such as the right to receive the compensation paid for a partial condemnation of the property) relate back to that date; usually the date the lease was executed. Most jurisdictions refuse to apply the doctrine of relation back.

CHAPTER VIII

RENT AND SECURITY

————

I. RENT DEFINED

Rent is a normal incident of the landlord-tenant relationship. Rent may generally be defined as the compensation paid to the landlord in return for the tenant's right to possess and use the demised premises. The compensation may be in the form of money, chattels, or services rendered to the landlord by the tenant. Taxes, special assessments, utilities and other specified readily ascertainable sums paid by the tenant will be treated as rent if such is the intent of the parties as manifested by the language contained in the lease.

Although rent is a normal incident of the landlord-tenant relationship, the relationship may be created without any duty on the part of the tenant to pay for the possession and use of the premises if such is the express intent of the parties.

The tenant's obligation to pay rent is a contingent one which becomes absolute upon the tenant's use and enjoyment of the demised premises for a specified rental period. Prior to becoming due, unaccrued rent is usually classified as real property—an incorporeal hereditament, i.e., a right without physical substance, but issuing out of the substance of real or personal property (e.g., rent issues from the land). When rent becomes due and payable under the terms of the lease (accrued rent), it is generally considered to be merely a debt of the tenant owed to the landlord, a chose in action disconnected from the land.

II. DUTY TO PAY RENT

Ordinarily, the lease contains a provision which specifies the amount of rent to be paid and the time and manner of the payment. This provision is usually in the form of an express agreement by the tenant to pay the reserved rent. The language used to create the covenant is important. A few cases have held that a lease which states that it is "subject to" or will "yield and pay" some particular rental does not constitute an express covenant to pay rent, but rather gives rise to an implied covenant which does not run with the land. However, the tenant will be liable for the reasonable value of the use of the land.

Occasionally, the parties will fail to include a provision specifying the rent reserved under the lease. A great many states have statutes which provide that in the absence of an express agreement to pay rent, the tenant's possession and use of the property gives rise to an obligation to pay the reasonable value of the possession and use of the premises. The standard applied in determining reasonable value is the fair market rental

value of the demised premises. Virtually all jurisdictions hold that an implied agreement to pay the
reasonable rental value arises even in the absence
of such statutes.

An express covenant to pay a specified rent is
a covenant which runs with the land. The tenant's assignee will be liable on such a covenant
because of his privity of estate with the landlord,
and the tenant will remain liable for any default in
the payment of rent because of his privity of contract with the landlord.

In the absence of an express covenant to pay
rent, the tenant's obligation to pay the reasonable
value of his possession and use of the premises, an
obligation imposed by statute or decision, rests
solely on the tenant's privity of estate with the
landlord. National Bank of Commerce v. Dunn,
194 Wash. 472, 78 P.2d 535 (1938). The tenant's
transfer of his entire interest in the leasehold
estate terminates his privity of estate with the
landlord, and consequently, his duty to pay rent
founded thereon. Id. Since there is no express
agreement to pay rent, there is no privity of contract between the landlord and the tenant with
respect to rent, and therefore, the tenant is free of
all liability for rent which accrues after an assignment of his leasehold interest.

In the event of the tenant's default in the
payment of rent, the landlord's primary remedies
are to sue for rent and/or, pursuant to a lease or
statutory provision, terminate the lease and resu-

me possession of the property. For a discussion of these and other remedies of the landlord, see "Remedies of the Landlord for Nonpayment of Rent," page 273.

III. RENT RESERVED IN THE LEASE

The rent reserved in the lease may be a specified amount, an amount based on a particular formula, an amount based upon the happening or nonhappening of some future event, or an amount determined by any combination of the foregoing. Ordinarily, the rent reserved in short term leases, particularly residential leases, will be a specified dollar amount. In commercial and long term leases, the landlord often wishes to tie the rent to the productivity of the particular parcel, and/or protect himself against decreases in the purchasing power of the dollar. The percentage lease is the device most often chosen to effect the first purpose. Stepup leases, appraisal leases, and cost of living or consumer price index leases are often employed to protect the landlord against decreases in the purchasing power of the dollar, but the devices and variables which may be used for the determination of rent are innumerable.

A. Stepup Leases

A stepup lease is one which provides for periodic increases in rent throughout the term of the lease. The stepup may be a fixed amount, a fixed percentage of the original rent charged, or a percentage of the rent being paid immediately prior to the current increase. One distinct disadvantage of a stepup lease to the tenant is that it does not take into account the possibility of the purchasing power of the dollar remaining relatively stable or increasing.

B. Consumer Price Index Leases

A cost of living index or consumer price index lease simply requires that the stipulated rent be increased in proportion to increases in the cost of living index or the consumer price index. The apparent advantage of using such variables is that, if the lease so provides, the rent may also be decreased in the event of downward fluctuations of such indexes.

C. Appraisal Leases

An appraisal lease fixes the rent at a sum equal to a fixed percentage of the valuation of the property. Such leases also require revaluation of the property at periodic intervals, usually five to ten years. In an attempt to obtain an impartial valuation, the lease normally provides that the property shall be evaluated by three appraisers, one chosen by each party and the third appraiser to be appointed by the first two. To avoid deadlock situations, the appraisal clause will normally provide that the value established by a majority of the appraisers is sufficient. In the absence of such a provision, unanimity among the three appraisers is required. In the event the appraisers cannot agree, a court, exercising its equity powers, will fix a value on the property upon application of the parties.

There are several objections to the appraisal lease. First, the value of property is affected by a number of factors which are unrelated to the purchasing power of the dollar or the continuing utility of the premises to the tenant. Thus, there is uncertainty with respect to the valuation resulting from any appraisal. Second, the valuation proceedings under appraisal leases are expensive; and third, appraisal leases discourage the tenant from making improvements to the property—any such improvements will only increase his rent.

To the extent that the appraised value of the property rises because of inflation, i.e., a decrease in the purchasing power of the dollar, the landlord is protected against such devaluation. And in fairness to the tenant, if the lease so provides, the appraisal provision can result in a decrease as well as an increase in the rent.

D. Percentage Leases

In commercial leases, particularly leases for retail purposes where location is very important, the landlord may wish to link the rent to the productivity of the location of the demised premises. This is usually accomplished by fixing the reserved rent as a percentage of gross sales, net profits, net earnings, etc. This percentage rental is normally coupled with a minimum rent of a specified dollar amount which must be paid regardless of the amount of the gross sales or net profits. Often the rent will be reserved in terms of a specified dollar amount plus a percentage of gross sales or net profits.

It is clear that in most percentage rent leases the landlord's return is directly affected by the ability and honesty of the tenant. As a consequence, by the weight of authority, the tenant impliedly covenants to occupy and use the demised premises, and to exercise due care to conduct the business in a manner which will generate profits and receipts. As a corollary to this rule, most courts hold that there is an implied covenant by the tenant not to sublease or assign the demised premises without the consent of the landlord. (See "Covenants Against Transfer of the Tenant's Interest", page 211.)

The percentage lease will usually expressly require a periodic accounting, most often an annual accounting. In the absence of such a provision, the courts generally impose a duty on the tenant to maintain accurate books and records and to permit the landlord to have reasonable access to them.

Although at first glance terms such as gross sales, gross receipts, net earnings, net income, gross income, etc., appear relatively clear, the definition of such terms is the most frequently litigated issue in cases involving percentage leases. Are federal excise taxes on liquor a part of the tenant's gross receipts? Yes, says one court. Are sales taxes a part of the tenant's gross receipts? No, says another. The list of disputes is endless. Where possible, the decisions are based upon the court's construction of the definition contained in the lease, which construction takes into consideration the circumstances of the parties, including the particular business engaged in by the tenant.

IV. AGREEMENTS TO MODIFY RENT

The general rule is that a subsequent agreement by the landlord and tenant to increase or decrease the reserved rent must be supported by new consideration in order to be enforceable. Consideration may be found in any one of a number of circumstances. For example, an agreement by the landlord which permits the tenant to remove otherwise nonremoveable fixtures and an agreement by the landlord to make repairs have been held to be sufficient consideration to support an increase in rent. Similarly, an agreement by the tenant to remain in possession when he was entitled to terminate the lease has been held to be sufficient consideration to support a rent deduction.

In the absence of supporting consideration, the courts are divided as to the validity of subsequent agreements to increase or decrease the rent reserved in the original lease. First, since there is nothing to prevent the tenant from making payments to the landlord in excess of the reserved rent, and since the rent reserved in the lease can be transferred apart from the landlord's reversion, it may be argued that one should treat an agreement to increase or decrease the rent as a gift from one party to the other, at least to the extent the lease is executed—a view unlikely to represent the true intent of the parties, but one which a few cases have nonetheless adopted. Second, where the agreement of the parties complies with the requirements of the Statute of Frauds, a few courts have held that an agreement to increase or decrease rent is tantamount to the execution of a new lease. Execution of the new lease effects a surrender of the old lease by operation of law. The third view, followed in the vast majority of decisions, is to treat an agreement to modify the rent reserved in the lease as a contract. Where the agreement is without consideration but is fully executed, most such courts hold that the agreement is valid; usually on the theory that the transaction constituted an executed gift, or that there has been a waiver of the parties' rights reserved in the rent covenant of the lease. Where the agreement remains executory, in whole or in part, the weight of authority is that the agreement is unenforceable unless supported by consideration.

V. PAYMENT OF RENT

A. Time of Payment

Virtually all courts hold that in the absence of a lease provision specifying the time of payment of the rent, the rent does not become due and payable until the end of the period covered by the rent.

First National Bank v. Omaha National Bank, 191
Neb. 249, 214 N.W.2d 483 (1974). For example, if
the landlord leases the property for a term of six
months at a gross rent of $600, the $600 rent does
not become due and payable until expiration of the
six month term. As a practical matter, a lease for
a term of years will usually provide that the contract rent is payable monthly, quarterly, or on
some other periodic basis, in advance.

An express covenant by the tenant to pay rent
in advance is enforceable, and today, virtually all
leases will contain such a provision. The usual
practice in the case of a lease for a term for years
is to specify that the contract rent is payable
periodically, and that each periodic payment is to
be paid at the beginning of the period; i.e., in
advance on the first day of the period. When the
tenant covenants to pay rent for the full term in
advance, in the absence of an agreement to the
contrary, the covenant is generally construed to
mean that the tenant agrees to make the rent
payment at the time possession is taken. Where
the lease provides for periodic payments in advance (e.g., monthly), the rent is due and payable
on the first day of the period.

An exception to the general rule exists in the
case of agricultural leases where the rent to be
paid is in the form of a share of the crops grown on
the demised premises. In such cases, in the absence of the contrary lease provision, the general
rule is that the rent becomes due and payable
when the crop is harvested.

1. Effect of Termination of the Lease—Apportionment

In the absence of covenants to the contrary, termination of the lease terminates the rights and obligations of the parties thereto, including the tenant's obligation to pay rent. If the lease is terminated between rent days, the weight of authority holds that there is no apportionment of rent for the rental period in which the termination occurs. Continental Oil Co. v. McNair Realty Co., 137 Mont. 410, 353 P.2d 100 (1960). Most such courts take the view that the landlord's acceptance of surrender between rent days constitutes a release of the tenant's liability for rent for the current period. For example, if the lease is for a term of one year with the rent payable at the end of the term and the lease is terminated during the seventh month, the landlord is not entitled to recover a proportionate part of the rent which would have been due at the end of the term. Similarly, where the tenant pays the rent for the full term in advance and the lease is prematurely terminated, the tenant is not entitled to reimbursement of a proportionate part of the rent for the unused portion of his term.

The rule of nonapportionment is followed in a number of circumstances. For example, where the tenant suffers a wrongful partial eviction at the hands of the landlord, the obligation to pay rent is completely suspended on the ground that the landlord should not be permitted to apportion his wrong by apportioning the rent. As between the

landlord and a transferee of the landlord's reversion, there is no apportionment of rent when the
transfer occurs during the rental period unless a
contrary intent appears from the language of the
instrument of transfer. The rule is also followed
in disputes between the heirs or devisees of the
landlord and his personal representative. Apportionment is denied whether the rent for the term is
paid in advance or at the end of the term.

There are several exceptions to the rule of
nonapportionment. For example, where a tenant
has paid the rent in advance and the landlord
subsequently wrongfully evicts the tenant, there is
authority for the view that the tenant may recover
that proportion of the prepaid rent which is allocable to the period he is wrongfully denied possession. There is also substantial authority for the
view that the landlord and tenant are entitled to
apportionment when the lease is terminated because of the substantial or total destruction of the
leased premises, and neither party was at fault
with regard to the destruction.

A minority of courts has adopted the view that
when the lease is terminated during a rental period, the parties are entitled to an apportionment of
the rent. The justification for the rule is that it
avoids a windfall to the landlord when the rent
was paid in advance, and avoids a windfall to the
tenant when the rent is payable at the end of the
term. The rent is allocable in the same proportion
that the tenant's time of possession during the
rental period bears to the total rental period. The

minority rule appears to be the better view, and at least eighteen states have statutes, of varying scope, which provide for apportionment of rent.

2. *Waiver of the Right to Prompt Payment*

The landlord's right to prompt payment of the rent may be expressly waived, or may be waived by conduct on the part of the landlord which leads the tenant to believe that a later payment date is acceptable. For example, where the rent is due and payable on the first day of each month and the tenant has habitually paid his rent on the tenth day of the month without objection by the landlord, the landlord has impliedly waived his right to require prompt payment. However, if after the establishment of such a regular course of dealing, the landlord notifies the tenant that in the future strict compliance with the payment date specified in the lease will be required, the tenant's failure thereafter to pay the rent on the first day of the month will constitute a default under the terms of the lease. This is consistent with the general rule that waiver of one or several breaches of covenant does not preclude express reassertion of one's rights in the future after giving reasonable notice. Also, a "no waiver" clause in the lease is normally construed to preserve the landlord's right to prompt payment of the rent.

B. Place and Manner of Payment

The lease will usually contain a provision which specifies the place at which the rent is to be paid. In the absence of such a provision, the general rule is that the rent is to be paid at the leased property. Further, the landlord is ordinarily required to go onto the premises and demand payment before he is entitled to terminate the lease for nonpayment of rent. In contrast, a few courts hold that in the absence of an express agreement, the tenant is obligated to seek out the landlord and pay him the rent due.

Rent is usually payable in money. However, the landlord may agree to accept personal property or services in return for the tenant's use and occupancy of the demised premises. Generally, the rent is not considered to be paid until the chattels, services or money contracted for are received by the landlord. Where the rent is to be paid in money, depositing the rent in the mail in a stamped, properly addressed envelope does not constitute payment unless payment by mail is specifically authorized in the lease agreement. Risk of the payment being lost in the mail usually falls on the tenant. However, most courts hold that a brief delay in the receipt of payment caused by delayed postal transmission does not justify termination of the lease for nonpayment of rent.

C. Agreements to Pay Rent After Termination of the Lease

Under the majority view, the parties to a lease may validly agree that in the event of a premature termination of the lease, not arising from the fault of the landlord, the tenant will remain liable on his covenant to pay "rent" for the remainder of the term. The parties may also enter into similar agreements imposing on the tenant the duty to compensate the landlord for the non-performance of other obligations under the lease not due to be performed by the tenant until after the premature termination of the lease (e.g., a covenant to make future improvements). While generally upheld, such agreements are not favored by the courts and are strictly construed against the landlord.

Where covenants to pay future "rent" are enforced, the payments made by the tenant are usually considered to be damages since there can be no rent in the absence of a landlord-tenant relationship. Characterization as rent or damages usually has little practical impact. However, the distinction between rent and damages does operate to deprive the landlord of certain remedies, such as distress for rent and the landlord's lien, which are available only so long as the landlord-tenant relationship exists. In the absence of a contrary agreement, the tenant's liability is single and entire, and therefore, damages are determined only at the end of the term of the original lease.

Since a covenant to pay future "rent" is penal in nature, most courts hold that in the event the landlord relets the premises, his recovery against the tenant is limited to the difference between the rent received under the new lease and the rent reserved under the original lease. Further, under the better view, the landlord has an obligation to exercise due diligence to find another tenant to mitigate the original tenant's damages. (See "The Landlord's Affirmative Duty to Mitigate", page 49.)

VI. ASSIGNMENT OF THE LANDLORD'S RIGHT TO RENT

The landlord's right to unaccrued rent is severable from the reversion and freely alienable. The severance is usually accomplished by an express assignment of rent by the landlord to another (often confusingly referred to as an "assignment of the lease"), or by the landlord conveying his reversion with an express reservation of future rent. Although a few cases have held that the landlord's assignment of unaccrued rent is an assignment of a chose in action, the weight of authority is that unaccrued rent is to be treated as real property— an incorporeal hereditament. In these latter jurisdictions, recordation of the assignment may be necessary under the jurisdictions' recording statutes to protect the assignee's interest against the rights of subsequent bona fide purchasers of the reversion who take without notice of the prior assignment of rent.

In the absence of an express reservation to the contrary, a transfer of the landlord's reversion carries with it, as an incident thereto, all unaccrued rent. The right to accrued rents, a chose in action disconnected from the reversion, remains with the landlord after the transfer of his rever-

sion. The landlord's right to accrued rent is generally freely alienable.

VII. REMEDIES OF THE LANDLORD FOR NONPAYMENT OF RENT

In the absence of a lease or statutory provision
to the contrary, the general rule is that the tenant's breach of the covenant to pay rent does not
entitle the landlord to terminate the lease. However, it is a common practice for the landlord to
reserve a right of entry (power of termination)
which can be exercised upon breach of any of the
lease covenants by the tenant. Further, at least
thirty-nine states have statutes which permit a
summary action for possession by the landlord in
the event of the tenant's failure to pay rent.
These statutes apply even where the lease does not
contain a right of entry clause. Of the remaining
eleven states, three have statutes which provide for
summary possession for nonpayment of rent in the
absence of a forfeiture clause in a limited number
of circumstances, and the remaining eight require
forfeiture under a lease provision before the summary process statute can be utilized. It would
appear that only in these latter states is a right of
entry clause in the lease necessary in all cases for
the protection of the landlord's reversionary interest.

The landlord's primary common law remedy
for the tenant's nonpayment of rent is an action
for rent. The landlord is also entitled to distrain

(seize) all personal property (whether belonging to the tenant or innocent third parties) located on the demised premises as security for the payment of accrued but unpaid rent. (See "Distress for Rent", page 284.) In addition, many states have statutes which impress a lien on the personal property of the tenant in favor of the landlord to secure the payment of rent. (See "Statutory Liens", page 281.)

The landlord and tenant may agree to narrow or expand the landlord's remedies for the tenant's failure to pay rent. In addition to reserving a right of entry (power of termination), there are several other frequently used lease provisions which serve to secure the payment of rent. It is common for the landlord to require that a security deposit be made by the tenant to assure his performance of the lease covenants, including the covenant to pay rent. The landlord is entitled to apply the deposited monies against any unpaid rent. (See "Security Deposits," page 275.) A lease may also contain a provision allowing the acceleration of the payment of future rent in the event of default in the payment of accrued rent by the tenant. Under such acceleration clauses all unaccrued rent immediately becomes due and payable upon default by the tenant, and the landlord is entitled to bring an action to recover such sum. (See "Rent Acceleration Clauses", page 48.) Finally, the tenant may by express agreement give the landlord a lien against the personal property of the tenant located on the demised premises as security for the payment of rent. (See "Contractual Liens", page 279.)

VIII. SECURITY DEPOSITS

It is very common for a lease to require that the tenant deposit a certain sum of money to assure the payment of rent and the tenant's full performance of other covenants in the lease. The deposit may be in any amount to which the parties agree, although in residential leases the security deposit is usually an amount equal to one month's rent. Statutes in some states limit the amount the landlord can require as a security deposit in residential leases. The money so deposited constitutes a fund out of which the landlord may compensate himself for the tenant's breach of covenants covered by the security. At the end of the term the tenant is entitled to a timely return of the security deposit subject to the valid claims of the landlord against such fund.

Often there is a question as to the true purpose of the tenant's deposit of money with the landlord; for example, is the deposit for security, or to fund an agreement specifying liquidated damages in the event of default by the tenant. The purpose depends upon the intent of the parties; in cases of ambiguity, the lease provision will usually be construed against the landlord.

Where the sum deposited with the landlord is truly a security deposit, premature termination of the lease caused by the tenant's breach of covenant entitles the landlord to only so much of the security deposit as is necessary to compensate him for accrued but unpaid rent and damage to the demised premises for which the tenant is responsible. Any deposit in excess of the foregoing sum must be returned to the tenant. Heyman v. Linwood Park, Inc., 41 N.J.Super 437, 125 A.2d 345 (1956).

Landlords have developed several ploys to avoid repayment of security deposits. First, the deposit may be characterized as consideration for granting the lease. Where there is no lease provision requiring that the deposit be returned to the tenant, most courts have acquiesced in the characterization and permitted the landlord to retain the deposit upon termination of the lease. Wilson v. Savon Stations, Inc., 15 Ariz.App. 136, 486 P.2d 816 (1971). If the lease requires return of the deposit at the end of the term, most courts will treat the deposit as a security deposit entitling the tenant to an accounting of its disposition from the landlord. Second, the deposit may be characterized as an advance payment of rent. Where this characterization is upheld by the court, the landlord is entitled to retain the deposit in the event of a premature termination of the lease on the theory that rent is nonapportionable. Lochner v. Martin, 218 Md. 519, 147 A.2d 749 (1959). Finally, the deposit may be characterized as liquidated damages in the event of termination of the lease because of default by the tenant. A few courts have upheld such provisions where the sum was a reasonable amount, and approximated the probable damages the landlord would incur. In most cases, the purported liquidated damages have been treated as a penalty and therefore, unenforceable; primarily on the grounds that the damages to the landlord were readily ascertainable, or that the sum was unreasonable in light of the probable damages which would be suffered by the landlord.

Requiring the tenant to make a security deposit shifts the risk of insolvency from the landlord to the tenant. The extent of the shift in risk is dependent upon the characterization of the relationship between landlord and tenant arising out of the deposit. Most courts hold that the security deposit creates a debtor-creditor relationship. The consequence of this characterization is that the landlord may comingle the deposit with his own money, thus depriving the tenant of a preferential claim to the funds in the event of the landlord's insolvency. A few courts have held that the deposit creates a pledgor-pledgee relationship which permits the landlord to use the deposited funds while at the same time giving the tenant some protection. A third view, and the one which offers the most protection to the tenant, is to treat the security deposit as a trust fund. The deposited money is held by the landlord as trustee in trust for the tenant. Under the trust fund theory, the landlord is not entitled to comingle the deposited funds with his own, and the deposit generally will not be subject to the claims of the landlord's creditors.

The fundamental problem with security deposits is primarily a practical one. It appears that a substantial number of landlords arbitrarily retain security deposits, or falsely allege that the tenant has damaged the leased premises to justify such retention. This is particularly true with respect to residential tenancies. Although the tenant may be entitled to recover the deposit, where the landlord refuses to return the deposit the burden of instituting a suit to recover the deposit falls on the tenant and all too often the amount of the security deposit is too small to justify litigation. Under such circumstances the legal rights and remedies of the tenant become meaningless.

In recent years a number of states have enacted legislation to aid the tenant in the recovery of security deposits wrongfully withheld by the landlord. Although the statutes vary, most require (i) that the deposited funds be held by the landlord in separate escrow or trust accounts, and (ii) that the landlord specify in writing all conduct by the tenant which would justify retention of all or part of the security deposit. Most statutes also provide for criminal penalties (misdemeanor) or the payment of damages to the tenant in an amount equal to some multiple of the wrongfully withheld deposit, or both. In addition, the landlord may be required to pay interest on security deposits; and a few statutes specify the manner in which security deposits shall be handled upon the transfer of the landlord's reversion.

In the absence of statute, the authorities are divided on the question of whether the landlord's covenant to return the tenant's security deposit is one which runs to transferees of the landlord's reversion. Some courts hold that the duty to return the security deposit runs to the transferee of the reversion, while others hold that the covenant is personal and remains with the original landlord.

IX. LANDLORD'S LIEN

With the exception of the lien arising out of the landlord's seizure of the tenant's property under the exercise of the landlord's right to distrain for past due rent, under common law the landlord-tenant relationship does not give rise to a lien on the tenant's property as security for rent. (See "Distress for Rent", page 284.) However, it is not uncommon for the parties to expressly provide that the landlord shall have a lien on the personal property of the tenant located on the demised premises, and approximately one-half of the states have statutes creating statutory liens on such property in favor of the landlord.

A. Contractual Liens

An agreement by the parties that the landlord shall have a lien against the personal property of the tenant located on the leased property as security for the payment of rent is valid. Normally such liens are created by express terms in the lease, but there is authority for the view that such liens may be created by implication from the language contained in the lease.

1. *Property to Which the Lien Attaches*

The property to which the lien attaches is determined by the express terms of the lease. Where the lease provides that the landlord shall have a lien on all the personal property of the tenant, the provision is usually construed to mean that the lien attaches to the property owned by the tenant at the time that the lease was executed. The lien is also limited to the personal property of the tenant which is brought upon and used on the demised premises. The parties may also agree that the lien will attach to after-acquired property of the tenant. However, in the absence of an express intent that after-acquired property be included, the lien will not attach to personal property acquired by the tenant after the lease is executed.

Some leases purport to give the landlord a lien on personal property of the tenant which is by statute ordinarily exempt from execution. The decisions are divided on the validity of the landlord's lien with respect to such exempt property. Some courts hold that a voluntary waiver by the tenant of his right to such exemption is valid and enforceable. Other courts hold that such waivers are invalid as contrary to the public policy established by the exemption statute.

2. *Priority of the Landlord's Lien*

An agreement by the parties that the landlord shall have a lien on the personal property of the tenant creates a chattel mortgage. The chattel mortgage is a "security interest" under Article 9 of the Uniform Commercial Code; and filing of a financing statement is ordinarily required in order to perfect the mortgagee's security interest as against subsequent claims against the property. Filing the financing statement has the effect of giving constructive notice to the world of the landlord's interest in the tenant's chattels. In the absence of such filing, the landlord's rights are not enforceable against subsequent bona fide purchasers or creditors of the tenant who acquire the liened property.

3. *Effect of Transfer of the Reversion*

In the absence of an express agreement to the contrary, the general rule is that an assignment of the debt carries with it the mortgage given to secure the debt as an incident thereto. Thus, an assignee of the rent, either separately or as an incident to the transfer of the reversion, is entitled to enforce the landlord's lien created in the lease.

B. Statutory Liens

Just over half of the states have statutes which impress a lien on the chattels of the tenant located on the leased property in favor of the landlord to secure the payment of rent. These statutes are in derogation of common law and are generally strictly construed. Usually, the statutory landlord's lien only secures claims for rent, although, in a few jurisdictions the coverage is expanded to cover other claims by the landlord against the tenant arising out of the landlord-tenant relationship.

1. *Property to Which the Lien Attaches*

The property to which the statutory lien attaches is defined by the terms of the statute. In general, it may be said that the lien attaches to all chattels belonging to the tenant which are on, upon, or in the leased property during the term of the lease. In the absence of a contrary statutory provision, the lien attaches to property which is ordinarily exempt from execution. There is also substantial authority for the view that the lien attaches to the after-acquired property of the tenant as well as the property owned by the tenant at the time the lease was executed. The statutory lien does not attach to choses in action, nor does the lien attach to the property of third parties which happens to be on the premises.

2. *Priority of the Landlord's Lien*

Regardless of when or whether the rent is due, the landlord's statutory lien attaches to the tenant's chattels at the commencement of the lease or, in jurisdictions which impose the lien on after-acquired property, when the chattels are first purchased and brought onto the demised premises. The landlord's security interest is superior to all claims against the tenant's property arising after the date that the landlord's lien attaches. Removal of the chattel from the premises does not extinguish the lien.

Generally, the subsequent sale of the liened property by the tenant to a third party does not extinguish the landlord's lien. To this general rule there are two major exceptions. First, the landlord's statutory lien is not effective against a subsequent bona fide purchaser for value who takes without actual or constructive notice of the landlord's lien and who has taken possession of the chattel; (e.g., cases where the chattel is sold after removal from the leased premises). There are a few decisions to the contrary, however. Second, where the liened chattels are goods sold by the tenant in the ordinary course of his trade or business, and they are so sold, the purchaser takes free of the landlord's statutory lien.

Section 9–104(b) of the Uniform Commercial Code provides that Article 9 of the Code does not apply to a landlord's lien.

3. *Enforcement of the Lien*

In a few states the landlord is entitled to use self-help in enforcing his statutory lien. However, in most states the lien is enforced by a judicial foreclosure proceeding. Many statutes also permit enforcement of the statutory lien by attachment. However, certain prejudgment attachments may be unconstitutional. Under Sniadach v. Family Finance Corp., 395 U.S. 337, 89 S.Ct. 1820, 23 L.Ed.2d

349 (1969); Fuentes v. Shevin, 407 U.S. 67, 92 S.Ct. 1983, 32 L.Ed.2d 556 (1972), and their progeny, it has become clear that landlord lien statutes which authorize prejudgment seizure of the chattels of the tenant without notice to the tenant and without affording him an opportunity to be heard prior to seizure may violate the tenant's constitutional right to procedural due process, and are therefore invalid.

X. DISTRESS FOR RENT

Distress for rent is the common law right of the landlord to go onto the demised premises and seize any personal property found thereon as security for the payment of rent which is in arrears. The landlord's right of distraint arises at the commencement of the lease as an incident to the landlord-tenant relationship. In general, the landlord may only exercise his right of distraint for rent which is in arrears, and the amount of which is certain or readily ascertainable. There is authority for the view that overdue rents include rents which have become due pursuant to a valid acceleration clause in the lease and remain unpaid. Ordinarily, the landlord is not entitled to distrain the personal property of the tenant to enforce other claims of the landlord against the tenant, (e.g., damages for the tenant's failure to perform a covenant to repair).

Originally, the landlord's right of distraint was limited to seizure of the chattels located on the demised premises, and the retention of possession of such chattels as security for the payment of rent. A lien as to such chattels arose in favor of the landlord at the time of seizure. In England in 1690, a statute was passed which permitted the landlord to sell the distrained chattels and to apply the proceeds of sale to the payment of the past due rent. Thus, distress for rent evolved from a method of securing the payment of rent to one of collecting rent. The power of sale as an incident to the right to distraint has been adopted by most jurisdictions in the United States.

Self-help by the landlord, of which distress for rent is one form, is generally disfavored in the United States. As a result, the landlord's right of distress for rent has been held to be excluded from the common law adopted in a number of jurisdictions. In other jurisdictions, the right of distraint has been abolished by statute. However, most jurisdictions recognize the landlord's right of distress for rent. Many of these latter jurisdictions statutorily regulate distraint proceedings, usually by vesting the physical exercise of the right in a public official, (e.g., the local sheriff).

The common law rule is that the seizure of the tenant's chattels by the landlord must occur during the term. The right of distraint ceases with the termination of the lease and any seizure thereafter by the landlord will subject him to liability for damages.

A. Property Subject to Distraint

With certain exceptions, discussed hereinafter, the general rule is that the landlord is entitled to seize any personal property found on the demised premises. This includes all chattels of the tenant and chattels located on the demised premises but owned by third parties.

Ordinarily, the landlord's right of distraint applies only to chattels located on the demised premises at the time of levy. The landlord is usually not entitled to follow chattels of the tenant removed by the tenant prior to the landlord's physical entry onto the demised premises to exercise his right of distraint. Many jurisdictions have enacted statutes which permit the landlord to follow property removed from the premises by the tenant in limited circumstances, usually cases of fraudulent removal. Such statutes generally do not apply to goods acquired by a purchaser for value prior to the commencement of a distress proceeding. Of course, goods owned by a third party located on the demised premises may be removed by the third party at any time prior to actual distraint.

In the absence of statutes to the contrary, the general rule is that the personal property of the tenant which is subject to a chattel mortgage and personal property sold to the tenant under a conditional sale are also subject to the landlord's right of distraint.

1. *Chattels of the Tenant Exempt from Distraint*

There are many exceptions to the rule that the landlord is entitled to distrain the personal property of the tenant for the nonpayment of rent. The rule generally does not apply to accounts receivable and other choses in action of the tenant. Where the personal property of the tenant is deemed to be in the custody of the law, the landlord may not exercise his right of distraint with respect to such property. For example, where the tenant has been adjudicated a bankrupt, or a trustee has been appointed under state insolvency laws, or a sheriff has levied execution against the chattels of a tenant, the landlord has no right to distrain for rent.

Personal property which is in actual use by the tenant is exempt from distraint on the ground that to take such property would constitute a breach of peace. Tenant fixtures which cannot be removed without injury to the freehold are also exempt from distraint. Finally, where the other chattels of the tenant are sufficient to cover the unpaid rent, the tools and instruments of the tenant's trade or profession are generally held to be exempt from distraint. The desire to foster trade and commerce is the reason usually given by the courts in support of this marshalling rule.

2. *Chattels of Third Parties*

In addition to the chattels of the tenant, the general rule is that the landlord's right of distrai includes the right to seize the property of third parties located on the demised premises. Under such circumstances the tenant becomes liable to the third party for the value of the goods distrained. Further, where the third party pays the rent in order to recover his chattels from the landlord, the third party may bring an action against the tenant to recover the rent so paid. The right of the landlord to distrain the chattels of third parties has been abolished by statute in a number of jurisdictions.

Chattels which have been delivered to the tenant in the normal course of his business for the purpose of being repaired, stored or sold (e.g., goods sold on commission where the tenant has no ownership interest) are not subject to the landlord's right of distraint. The purpose of these exceptions is to foster trade and commerce by minimizing the risk of third parties dealing with tenant businessmen; and it may generally be said that distraint of the chattels of a third party will not be permitted where such distraint will have an adverse effect on trade or commerce.

B. Effect of Assignment

The right to distrain for rent in arrears arises from the tenurial relationship created by the conveyance of a leasehold estate. In the absence of this tenurial relationship there can be no right of distraint. Thus, where a person has been granted only the right to receive rent, often referred to as dry rent or rent seck, he is not entitled to distrain the property of the tenant for nonpayment of rent. For example, simple assignment of rent without more does not give the assignee the right of distraint. However, the right to receive unaccrued rents ordinarily passes with the reversion as an incident thereto; therefore, a transferee of the landlord's reversion is entitled to seize the chattels of the tenant to enforce the collection of rent which becomes past due after the transfer.

The right of a tenant who transfers his interest to distrain the chattels of his transferee for past due rent depends upon the characterization of the transfer as a sublease or an assignment. Where the tenant assigns his leasehold interest, no tenurial relationship exists between the tenant and his assignee and therefore, the tenant has no right to distrain for rent. On the other hand, a sublease creates a landlord-tenant relationship between the original tenant and the chattels of the subtenant in the event of nonpayment of the rent reserved under the sublease. In the event of a default in the payment of the rent reserved under the main lease, the landlord is entitled to distrain the chattels of the tenant and the subtenant located on the demised premises.

C. Waiver

The right to distrain for rent may be expressly or impliedly waived by the landlord. Express waiver is usually in the form of a lease provision in which the landlord agrees not to distrain the chattels of the tenant or third parties. Since the right of distraint cannot be exercised after the termination of the lease, the right is impliedly waived by any termination of the lease which occurs prior to a seizure of a tenant's property. In general, any act by the parties which suspends or discharges the tenant's liability for rent (e.g., an extension of time for payment) will suspend or extinguish the landlord's right to distrain for such rent.

D. Statutory Modifications

A number of states have, by statute, abolished the common law right of distress for rent. On the other hand, a substantial number of states statutorily recognize the landlord's right of distress for rent while regulating the exercise of such right. The principal change effected by such regulation is to require that the seizure be accomplished by a public official. These distraint statutes have been the subject of an increasing number of constitutional attacks, and following the lead of Sniadach v. Family Finance Corp., 395 U.S. 337, 89 S.Ct. 1820, 23 L.Ed.2d 349 (1969), and Fuentes v. Shevin, 407 U.S. 67, 92 S.Ct. 1983, 32 L.Ed.2d 556 (1972), the most recent cases have held unconstitutional distraint statutes which permit seizure of the tenant's property without notice and a prior hearing.

XI. ESTOPPEL TO DENY THE LANDLORD'S TITLE

In an action for rent or possession by the landlord, it is not uncommon for the tenant to defend on the ground that title to the property is not in the landlord. In such cases, the general rule, with numerous exceptions, is that the tenant is estopped to deny the title of his landlord. The doctrine relates to the landlord's title at the time the lease was executed and therefore, the tenant is not precluded from showing that the landlord's title has been conveyed to a third party or to the tenant, or that the landlord's reversionary interest has come to an end. Although the courts often speak in terms of estoppel, the true reason for the rule is found in the patent unfairness of allowing the tenant to enjoy the possession and use of the premises and subsequently avoid his duty to pay rent by establishing defects in the title of the landlord.

Where a third party holding paramount title to the demised premises demands payment of rent or possession of the premises from the tenant, there is a split of authority as to whether the tenant, without more, may attorn to the holder of the paramount title. Some courts hold that the attornment is proper, and that the tenant may plead the superior title of the third party as a defense in an action for rent or possession brought by the original landlord. Other courts hold that the tenant must wait to be sued by the party alleging paramount title and then notify the original landlord of the suit. Absent such conduct, the tenant remains liable under the original lease. A number of states have adopted this latter view by statutes providing that the tenant's attornment to a third party is void unless directed by a court decree.

CHAPTER IX

INSURANCE AND TAXES

I. INSURANCE

Both the landlord and the tenant have an insurable interest in the demised premises, and each is entitled to insure his own interest as he sees fit. However, in the absence of a lease provision to the contrary, the landlord is not under a duty to the tenant to insure the premises against fire, or loss by other casualty, nor is the tenant under a duty to the landlord to insure against such losses for the benefit of the landlord. It may be remembered that by the weight of authority, destruction of the leased premises does not terminate the lease, and the tenant's duty to pay rent continues unabated although the primary subject matter of the lease (the building) is no longer in existence. Further, where the landlord has insured the destroyed premises, the tenant cannot compel the landlord to use the proceeds to restore the premises. A similar rule exists where the premises are insured by the tenant.

It is not unusual, particularly in long term commercial leases, for the parties to agree that the tenant shall insure the premises against loss from fire or other casualty. There is authority for the view that a covenant to obtain insurance, or to insure the premises, does not impose a duty on the tenant to renew the insurance for the duration of the term. Thus, a covenant to insure should expressly set forth that the tenant's duty is to insure, and keep insured, the premises demised under the lease.

Where the tenant covenants to insure the premises and fails to do so, the landlord may purchase the required insurance and recover the amount of the premium from the tenant. Where the tenant fails to insure and the premises are destroyed by one of the hazards the tenant was to insure against, the tenant will be liable for the actual damages to the demised premises which would have been covered by the insurance had the tenant not breached his covenant to insure.

The lease provisions will normally specify the amount for which the leased property is to be insured. In the absence of such an agreement, insurance in the amount of the full value of the leased property is required. It is also customary for the covenant to insure to specify the disposition of the insurance proceeds. A bare covenant to insure for the benefit of the landlord imposes no obligation on the landlord to use the insurance proceeds to rebuild the demised premises. The insurance proceeds are the personal property of the landlord to do with as he sees fit.

A covenant to insure may or may not run with the land. Where the lease provides that the insurance proceeds must be used to repair or rebuild the demised premises, then the purpose of the covenant is the preservation of the estate, thus it touches and concerns the land, and will be construed as a covenant running with the land which is binding on the transferees of the covenantor and convenantee. If there is no obligation to use the insurance proceeds for the restoration of the building, the covenant to insure is held to be personal and does not run with the land.

It may be argued that an agreement to insure is nothing more than an agreement to pay money which directly affects the amount of net rent reserved in the lease. Where the insurance premiums are designated as part of the rent, there is authority for the view that a covenant to insure is nothing more than a covenant to pay rent, and as such, is a covenant which runs with the land.

II. TAXES

As a general rule, the tenant is under no duty to pay taxes or special assessments on the leased premises. To this general rule there are several exceptions. First, where the landlord is a governmental body, educational, religious or eleemosynary organization exempt from the taxes and assessments assessed, there is authority for the view that the exemption will not extend to the tenant's leasehold estate, and such estate will be subject to the tax or assessment. Second, where the lease is one which is perpetually renewable, or is one for an extremely long term (e.g., ninety-nine years), the tenant is the virtual owner of the land. Under such circumstances, as between the tenant and the landlord, the tenant is generally held to be liable for the taxes and assessments.

Often a tenant will make improvements to the leased premises which result in an increased assessed value on the property for tax purposes. In the absence of a lease provision to the contrary, the courts impose the burden of the increase in real estate taxes attributable to the improvements in accordance with the presumed intent of the parties. Ownership of the improvement and receipt of benefit from the improvement are two major factors in determining the intent of the parties. If the tenant is entitled to remove such improvements at the end of the term, the general rule is that the increase in taxes attributable to the improvements must be paid by the tenant. The same rule applies where the landlord has agreed to purchase the improvements at the end of the term. If the improvements are to remain the property of the landlord at the end of the term and were not constructed for the sole benefit of the tenant, the increase in taxes attributable to the improvements is ordinarily imposed upon the landlord.

The collection of taxes may be enforced by the sale of the entire estate, including the tenant's leasehold interest. Thus, where the landlord defaults in his obligation to pay taxes and assessments on the leased premises, the tenant is entitled to make such payments to protect his leasehold interest. After making such payments, the tenant is entitled to bring suit against the landlord to recover the monies paid or, alternatively, the tenant may deduct the amounts paid from the rents reserved under the lease.

A. Covenants by the Tenant

Lease provisions allocating the parties' obligations to pay taxes and assessments on the leased property are valid. Such covenants are quite common in commercial leases. Where the tenant covenants to pay taxes, the scope of his duty is defined by the language in the lease. If the provision is ambiguous, the tenant's liability will depend upon the court's construction of the provision and the surrounding circumstances. Ordinarily, the tenant's covenant to pay taxes includes taxes arising under statutes enacted subsequent to commencement of the lease term.

1. Scope of the Covenant

Taxes can be distinguished from assessments in that taxes are levies made to generate the monies necessary to support ordinary governmental operations, while assessments are used to generate funds to pay for improvements which increase the value of the assessed property (e.g., assessments for a street paving project). The consequence of this distinction is that ordinarily where a tenant covenants to pay taxes he is under no obligation to pay special assessments. However, where the tenant agrees to pay "all taxes and assessments", his covenant will usually be viewed as imposing liability on him for general real estate taxes and special assessments levied against the demised premises.

In the absence of an express intent to the contrary, where the tenant leases only part of the taxed estate, the tenant's covenant to pay taxes only requires that the tenant pay his proportionate share of the taxes assessed against the total estate.

2. Remedies of the Landlord

In most jurisdictions real estate taxes are assessed on one date, but do not become due and payable until a later date. The tenant's obligation to pay taxes is determined by the time of assessment, rather than the time the taxes become due and payable. Upon default in payment by the tenant, the landlord is entitled to pay the taxes and bring an action against the tenant to recover the amounts paid. There is also authority for the view that the landlord may bring an action against the tenant for nonpayment without himself first paying the taxes. In addition, the tenant's breach of covenant to pay taxes will normally give the landlord the right to terminate the lease under a right of entry (power to termination) reserved in the lease. Where the demised premises are sold for taxes as a result of the tenant's breach of covenant to pay taxes, the damages recoverable by the landlord are limited to the taxes which the tenant agreed to pay. The landlord is not entitled to recover from the tenant the value of the property lost through the tax sale. The reason is that the landlord is entitled to the proceeds of the tax sale in excess of the overdue taxes; and, in theory, this sum should equal the value of the land less the overdue taxes and therefore, the harm to the landlord is limited to the sum of the overdue taxes.

B. Covenants by the Landlord

1. *Scope of the Covenant*

A covenant by the landlord to pay taxes on the leased premises would appear to be no more than a statement of his usual obligation. Such covenants have usually not been construed to expand the obligations of the landlord. Thus, tax increases attributable to improvements made by the tenant which will remain the property of the tenant at the end of the term must be paid by the tenant in spite of the landlord's express covenant to pay taxes. A contrary result follows where the improvements are not made for the sole benefit of the tenant and will remain the property of the landlord at the end of the term.

2. *Remedies of the Tenant*

A default in the payment of the taxes by the landlord entitles the tenant to pay such taxes and bring an action for damages against the landlord or, alternatively, to deduct the amounts paid from the rents reserved in the lease. Where the default results in an interference with the tenant's possession and use of the demised premises, (e.g., dispossession as a result of the tax sale), the tenant is entitled to terminate the lease and sue for damages.

C. Transferee Liability

The payment of taxes is necessary to prevent a public sale of the land for the taxes. As a consequence, a covenant to pay taxes is usually construed as one to protect the reversion and the leasehold from such sales, and therefore, touches and concerns the respective estates of the landlord and the tenant. Thus, a covenant to pay taxes on the demised premises is a covenant which runs with the land, is binding on the transferees of the covenantor, and is enforceable by the transferees of the covenantee.

Generally, a covenant by the tenant to pay taxes on land owned by the landlord other than the demised premises is a personal covenant and does not run. However, there is authority for the view that a covenant to pay taxes on other land owned by the landlord is merely a covenant to pay money, which in effect, is a covenant to pay rent. In such jurisdictions the burden of this "rent-tax" covenant runs with the land and will be binding on the assignees of the tenant-covenantor.

*

INDEX

References are to Pages

ABANDONMENT, 46
Anticipatory repudiation, 47
Landlord's options, 47
Mitigation, 47
Recovery of future rent, 47, 48
Reletting for the benefit of the tenant, 50
Rent acceleration clauses, 48
Termination of the lease, 51

ASSIGNMENT
See Transfers By Tenant

CHATTEL REAL
Lease classified as, 1

CONCURRENT LEASES, 223

CONDITION, CHANGE IN LEASED PROPERTY, 181
Acts of God, 182
Acts of strangers, 182
Alterations by tenant, 184
Fixtures, 198
Ordinary wear and tear, 184
Waste, 87, 187
    See also Waste

COVENANTS
Against transfer,
    By landlord, 222
    By tenant, 211

COVENANTS—Continued
Independence of, 9
Not to compete, 240
Power to demise, 30
Quiet enjoyment, 25, 75

COVENANTS RUNNING WITH THE LAND
    In general, 229
Covenants not to compete, 240
    By landlord, 243
    By tenant, 242
Duration, 239
Intent that covenant run, 231
    Things *in esse*, 231
Partial transfers, 237
Privity of estate, 234
Touch and concern, 232
Transfer of covenantee's entire estate, 235
Transfer of covenantor's entire estate, 235
    Reassignment, 236
Waiver, 239
Writing, 230

DAMAGES FOR BREACH
Covenant to insure, 293
Interference by third parties, 75
Landlords covenant to repair, 164
Landlord's duty to put tenant in possession, 65
Power to demise, 30
Quiet enjoyment, 25, 75
Tenants covenant to repair, 158

DEFENSES OF THE LANDLORD TO TORT LIABILITY
Assumption of risk,
    Express, 96, 149
    Implied, 96, 153, 155
Contributory negligence, 96, 153, 157
To implied warranty of habitability, 140

DESTRUCTION OF THE PREMISES, 43, 160

**DISTINGUISHED FROM LICENSES, EASEMENTS AND PROF-
ITS,** 6

DISTRESS FOR RENT
In general, 284
Property subject to distraint, 286
    Chattels of third parties, 287
    Exempt property of the tenant, 287
Statutory modifications, 290
Transfer of interest, effect of, 288
Waiver, 289

DUMPOR'S CASE, RULE IN, 217

EMINENT DOMAIN
Entire leasehold, 79
    Measure of damages, 80
Partial taking, 81
    Measure of damages, 81
    Rent abatement, 82

ESTOPPEL TO DENY THE LANDLORD'S TITLE, 290

EVICTION
Actual eviction, 25
    Partial, 25
Constructive eviction, 26
Under paramount title, 29

EXCULPATORY CLAUSES, 149

EXTENSIONS
See Renewals

FITNESS, 67
Building under construction, 69
Change in condition prior to possession, 68
Furnished house exception, 72
Latent defects, 70
Public use exception, 68

FIXTURES
Agricultural, 202
Defined, 198
Domestic, 202
Limitation on right to remove, 203
Trade, 200

HISTORICAL BACKGROUND, 1

HOLDING OVER
Nature of the tenancy created, 61
Options of the landlord, 63
Tenant's interest, 18, 58
Termination of the prior tenancy, 59

ILLEGAL USE
Housing code violations, 38
Illegal and immoral purposes, 32, 75
Landlord's right to recover possession, 37
  Residential leases, 38
Landlord's right to rent, residential lease, 41
Multiple uses, one use prohibited, 37
Supervening illegality, 42
Uses requiring permits or licenses, 33
Uses violating building and zoning laws, 33

IMPLIED WARRANTY OF HABITABILITY, 73, 108
Breach of warranty, 121
Development, 108
  Caveat emptor, 108
  Factors influencing courts, 109
  Implied incorporation of housing codes, 113
Furnished house, 72
Landlord's defenses, 141
Landlord's notice of defect, 123
Procedure for raising, 115
Remedies of tenant, 126
  Damages, 140
  Rent abatement and withholding, 131
    Measure of abatement, 131
    Protective order, 137

IMPLIED WARRANTY OF HABITABILITY—Continued
        Rent withholding statutes, 136
        Turnover orders, 138
Repair and deduct, 128
Scope of warranty, 116
    Leases to which warranty applies, 117
    Standard of habitability, 118
        Breach of warranty, 121
        Matters covered, 121
        Specific performance, 130
        Termination and rescission, 127
Tort liability, 142
Waiver, 141

INJURIES OCCURRING OUTSIDE THE LEASED PROPERTY
    In general, 172
Conditions antedating transfer, 175
    Effect of sublease, 177
    Tenant's covenant to correct condition, 176
Dangerous activities commencing after transfer, 181
Landlord's covenant to repair, 177
Landlord's statutory duty to repair, 179
"Natural condition" exception, 173

INSURANCE
Damages, 293
Duty to insure, 292
Use of proceeds, 293

LANDLORD'S LIEN, 279
Contractual liens, 279
    Priority of lien, 281
    Property covered by lien, 280
    Transfer of reversion, effect of, 281
Statutory liens, 281
    Enforcement of lien, 283
    Priority of lien, 282
    Property covered by lien, 282

LATENT DEFECTS, 70

LEASE IN REVERSION, 223

NATURE OF LEASE, CONTRACT OR CONVEYANCE, 8

NATURE OF RELATIONSHIP, 4

NEGLIGENT REPAIRS, 168
Independent contractor, 171
Knowledge of tenant, 170
Massachusetts Rule, 169
Transfer of parties' interest, 172

OPTION TO PURCHASE, 250
Duration, 253
    Separate agreement, 254
Effect of exercise, 255
Right of first refusal distinguished, 252

PERIODIC TENANCY
Creation, 13
    Void lease, 14
Distinguished from the term for years, 17
Duration, 15
Termination, 15

POSSESSION
Duty of tenant to occupy, 82
Interference,
    By landlord, 75
    By third parties, 75
        Another tenant, 76
        Criminal acts, 77
Landlord's duty to deliver, 64
    American Rule, 64
    English Rule, 65

RECORDING ACTS, EFFECT OF, 8

RENEWALS
Construction and operation, 248
Extensions distinguished, 246

RENT
Acceleration of rent, 48
Agreement to pay post-termination rent, 270
Agreements to modify rent, 264
Amount,
    Implied, 258
    Reserved in lease, 260
Appraisal leases, 261
Assignment of right to, 272
Consumer Price Index Leases, 261
Defined, 257
Distress, see Distress for Rent
Duty to pay, 258
Percentage leases, 262
Place and manner of payment, 269
Remedies of landlord for nonpayment, 273
Security for, see Distress for Rent; Landlord's Lien; Security Deposits
Stepup leases, 260
Time of payment, 265
    Effect of termination, apportionment, 267
    Waiver of right to prompt payment, 269

REPAIRS
Common Law Rules, 84, 85
    Exceptions, 86
Defenses of landlord to tort liability, 149, 153
Duty of landlord,
        In general, 84, 85
    Areas retained under his exclusive control, 94
    Common areas, 88
    Express covenants, 158, 162
        Destruction of premises, 160
        Notice of defect, 167
        Remedies of tenant, 164
        Tort liability of landlord, 165
    Fitness for use, see Fitness
    Implied warranty, see Implied Warranty of Habitability
    Repairs required by government regulations, 96
    Statutory obligations, 99
        Civil sanctions, 101

References are to Pages

REPAIRS—Continued
>   Criminal sanctions, 100
>   Tort liability, 103
Duty of tenant,
>   Express covenants, 158
>   Destruction of premises, 160
>   Waste, 87, 187
Negligent repairs, 168
Personal injury and property damage, 84, 85, 165

RETALIATORY EVICTION, 39, 144
Burden of proof, 147
Conduct of landlord and tenant, 146
Remedies, 149

SECURITY DEPOSITS, 275

SPECIAL LIMITATIONS ON TERM
Defined, 20
Distinguished from condition subsequent, right of entry, 20

STATUTE OF FRAUDS, 5
Oral lease, 5
Writing, requirements of, 5

SUBLEASE
See Transfers by Tenant

SURRENDER, 45

TAXES
Allocation,
>   In general, 294
>   Improvements by tenant, 295
Covenant by landlord, to pay,
>   Remedies of tenant, 298
>   Scope of covenant, 298
Covenant by tenant to pay, 296
>   Remedies of landlord, 297
>   Scope of covenant, 296
Transferee liability, 299

TENANCY AT SUFFERANCE
Creation, 18
Duration, 19
Termination, 19

TENANCY AT WILL
Creation, 17
Duration, 18
Termination, 18

TERM FOR YEARS
Creation, 12
Distinguished from the periodic tenancy, 17
Duration, 12
Termination, 13

TERMINATION
Breach of condition by tenant, 21
    At common law, 21
    Equitable relief, 24
    Power of termination, right of entry, 22
    Restatement view, 22
    Statutory modification, 21
    Waiver, 23
Destruction of the premises, 43
Expiration of landlord's estate, 52
Frustration of purpose, 32
Illegal use, 32
Power to demise, breach of covenant of, 30
Quiet enjoyment, breach of covenant of,
    Actual eviction, 25
    Constructive eviction, 26
    Eviction by paramount title, 29
Recovery of possession by landlord,
    Self-help, 53
        Lease provisions, 55
        Wrongful reentry by landlord, 56
    Summary process statutes, 56
Special limitations on term, 20
    Distinguished from conditions subsequent, right of entry, 20

TERMINATION—Continued
Termination of landlord's supporting estate, 30

TRANSFERS BY LANDLORD, 221
Concurrent leases, 223
Covenants against transfer, 222
Effect of, 222, 228
Lease in reversion, 223
Mortgage of the reversion, 224

TRANSFERS BY TENANT, 207
Assignment and sublease distinguished, 208
    Partial assignments, 210
Covenants against transfer, 211
    Breach of covenant, 213
        Cotenants, partners, etc., 214
        Involuntary assignments, 216
        Leasehold mortgages, 215
        Reassignment to original tenant, 214
    Landlord's consent unreasonably withheld, 218
    Remedies of landlord, 221
    Rule in Dumpor's Case, 217
    Waiver, 220
Effect of, 208, 225, 227
Percentage leases, 208
Statute of Frauds, 207

**TRANSFERS BY TENANT OR LANDLORD, EFFECT OF—COVE-
    NANTS RUNNING WITH THE LAND**
Assignment by tenant, 225
    Reassignment by assignee, effect of, 227
Covenants running with the land, see Covenants Running
    with the Land
Sublease by tenant, 227
Transfer of reversion, 228

USE OF PREMISES
Duty of tenant to occupy premises, 82
Permitted uses, 184

References are to Pages

WASTE
   In general, 87, 187
Assignment or sublease, effect of, 194
Conduct of tenant, 189
   Cutting timber, 189
   Removing minerals, 191
Covenant to repair, effect of, 193
Equitable, 192
Permissive, 192
Remedies of landlord, 195
Statute of Limitations, 195

†